THE
INFORMATION
REVOLUTION

The Not-For-Dummies Guide to the History, Technology, and Use of the World Wide Web

J. R. Okin

Ironbound Press
Winter Harbor, Maine

First Ironbound Press edition, 2005

Ironbound Press books may be purchased for educational, business, or sales promotional use. For information, please write: Special Markets Department, Ironbound Press, P.O. Box 250, Winter Harbor, ME 04693-0250

Cover image, *The Blue Marble: Land Surface, Shallow Water, and Shaded Topography*, courtesy of NASA's Visible Earth, located at: http://visibleearth.nasa.gov/

Ironbound Press Web Site: http://www.IronboundPress.com
Ironbound Press email inquiries: info@IronboundPress.com

Printed and bound in the United States of America.
Printed on acid-free paper.

Library of Congress Control Number: 2005925936

ISBN 0-9763857-4-0 (cloth)
ISBN 0-9763857-3-2 (paper)

10 8 6 4 2 ✳ 1 3 5 7 9

Other books available from Ironbound Press by J. R. Okin:

- The Internet Revolution: The Not-For-Dummies Guide to the History, Technology, and Use of the Internet

- The Technology Revolution: The Not-For-Dummies Guide to the Impact, Perils, and Promise of the Internet

Foreword

Never doubt that a small group of thoughtful, committed citizens can change the world. Indeed, it is the only thing that ever has.

Margaret Mead
Cultural Anthropologist (1901-1978)

This popular quotation from Margaret Mead speaks directly to the invention of the World Wide Web. It speaks equally well to the grassroots effort that was responsible for developing and popularizing the Web. Most significantly, perhaps, Mead's words speak to the promise of the Web and to the promise of the Internet as well.

The Web — like the Internet — is a tool that empowers individuals. The clearest evidence of this can be found in how its composition has been shaped (and continues to be shaped) by the contribution of individuals. Moreover, thanks to the generosity of its inventor and many others, the Web's future — whatever it may entail — will be determined by those of us who use the Web, who add to and enrich its *information space*, and who expand its capabilities and test its limits — including those of us who want to change the world.

The Web's ability to empower individuals along with its ability to adapt and grow as new information, products, and services become part of its information space are responsible for the Web inciting a revolution, as this book explains. Think of the Internet as inciting a revolution in communication. By interconnecting computers, the Internet transformed the ways in which people are interconnected. Think of the Web as inciting a revolution in information. By interconnecting information on the computers of the Internet, the Web transformed the ways in which people locate, use, and share information.

The World Wide Web is many things to many people. It is much more than a new type of marketplace for the buying, selling, and trading of merchandise and services. One of the principal (but less apparent) reasons for the Web's popularity, and which helps to explain why it is so many things to so many people, is that the composition of the Web — like that of the Internet — is extraordinarily egalitarian. No one individual, organization, or government owns or operates the Web. Just as significantly, the Web does not differentiate or discriminate among the sites that use its technology to manage and share information or the information contained on those sites. No one individual or organization can argue that they have a larger or more prominent location on the Web because the Web does not include any type of hierarchy that makes such distinctions possible.

The egalitarian composition of the Web derives in part from the Web's very humble beginnings. The Web was not created by an entrepreneur in the business world seeking to make his or her fortune. Nor was the Web created by a corporation that was trying to realize a new paperless environment for publishing newspapers, magazines, and books or to build a faster, cheaper, more direct way to buy and sell products. Instead, the Web was created by a scientist by the name of Tim Berners-Lee. He dreamed of changing — in a deceptively simple but powerful manner — the way in which information is managed and shared; he pursued that dream; and he realized it. Moreover, he gave his hard work away, which, as you will soon understand, helped to cultivate a grassroots involvement with the Web early in its development that continues today to influence the course, composition, and popularity of the Web.

The underlying egalitarian composition of the Web is not apparent to most individuals who use the Web today. However, this was not the case during the first several years of the Web's existence, in the early to mid 1990s, when the Web functioned exclusively as an online distributed library of personal, professional, academic, and business-related information. Commercialization of the Web had not yet occurred. Even one of today's most commercial enterprises on the Web, Yahoo!, had an entirely different presence on the Web during those early years. Yahoo!'s original name, "Jerry's Guide to the World Wide Web," conveys some sense of how much things have changed for both Yahoo! and the Web, as does the fact that Yahoo! was entirely free of advertisements and corporate sponsorships during that time.

What is a surprise to most people who now routinely use the Web to buy products, get directions, read the news, check their bank accounts or stock portfolios, or perform any number of other commonplace, fast, and simple tasks involving the retrieval of information is that the Web was engineered and built to do more than provide online on-demand information access. From its inception, the Web was envisioned as a comprehensive system for managing and sharing information. In other words, the Web was created as much for the purpose of organizing and publishing one's own information as for the purpose of accessing the information of others.

With commercialization, however, came numerous changes to the Web: small, moderate, and large in scope; good, bad, and ugly in effect. Commercialization quickly obscured both the Web's humble beginnings and the egalitarian and empowering functionality of its technology. The effects of commercialization, however, while rampant, did not diminish the system that Tim Berners-Lee created. The same system that enables IBM, Microsoft, and other large corporations to create Web sites to sell their products and services also enables individuals and small organizations to create Web sites to organize virtual communities of like-minded people, trade goods and information directly with one another, publish poems, short stories, novels, films, and music, or promote their own business ventures. One goal of writing this book was to help others recognize and appreciate how the Web empowers individuals and why the egalitarian composition of the Web is so important and revolutionary.

Although it may seem otherwise, corporations are responsible for only a small fraction of the Web's overall composition. Moreover, their presence on the Web — no matter how highly acclaimed, engaging, popular, or useful — is far removed from the motivation behind the Web's creation, the reasons for the Web's remarkable appeal to such a large and diverse audience, and the characteristics of the Web that are responsible for an information revolution. It only seems, therefore, that corporations rule the Web; nothing could be farther from the truth. Just beyond the e-commerce portal sites and storefronts and the mass-media newspapers and magazines exists a corporate-free and commerce-free Web of amazing richness and diversity that millions of people have already discovered and that more people are discovering every day.

The technology of the Web that turned individuals into information creators and distributors and into self-publishers has had a subtle but profound effect on the control and distribution of information. Large corporations, government agencies, and other well-funded organizations had the means and opportunity to share and distribute information long before the Internet and the Web came into existence. Prior to the advent of the Web, however, individuals and small organizations were exceedingly limited in their options to publish and in their ability to reach an audience beyond that of the local community. The Web didn't just give individuals a voice, it changed the very definition of publishing, no less so than Gutenberg's invention of moveable type in the 15th century that revolutionized the printing and distribution of information and that gave birth to the publishing industry.

The Web has removed many of the barriers that restricted not only who could publish but what could be published. As a result, the Web has vastly increased the quantity and variety of information sources that are available to us; it has simplified our access to information; and it has removed virtually all time constraints on delivering information to us. In bringing about these changes, the Web has decidedly and permanently weakened the hegemony (i.e., the dominant and controlling influence) wielded by traditional publishers, media corporations, and our governments. The impact of all of these changes is only just beginning to be felt.

As I wrote in the foreword to *The Internet Revolution*, my experiences with the Internet (and the Web) — as an ordinary user, as a systems engineer and developer, and as a dot com manager — and my fascination with the impact of the Internet and its technology inspired me to write a book about the Internet. My goal was to combine the story of the Internet's creation and development with an explanation of its technology that anyone could understand and an exploration of the Internet's impact on our lives, jobs, and community and social structures. The story of the Internet cannot be told without also including the story of the World Wide Web. After two years of research and writing, I created a book that presented all of these subjects and that was divided into three nearly equal parts.

I decided to publish each of the three parts as a separate book. This volume, which focuses on the history and technology of the Web, is the second in the series. The first book, which focuses on the history and technology of the Internet, is entitled *The Internet Revolution*. The third book, which focuses on the impact of the

Internet's and the Web's technology, is entitled *The Technology Revolution.*

In this book I have tried to present a comprehensive guide to the World Wide Web. I describe how the Internet was navigated and how information was managed before the arrival of the Web. I present the history of the Web's creation, evolution, ownership, and management. I explain how the Web works, why its technology spread so rapidly, and how the Web's arrival impacted the Internet. I describe the diverse ways in which the Web is being used by organizations and by individuals, as an information resource and as a multimedia platform for the sharing and distribution of all types of content. I also examine how the Web's technology has been co-opted in creative but questionable ways to track information about our movements and behavior on the Internet. Finally, I explain how the Web is changing — and why it must change — in order for it to survive.

I believe that each of the three books in the series can be read and understood (and, hopefully, enjoyed) independently of the other two. Together, the three books present a broad and thorough depiction of the revolution of our times, that began as a remarkable technological innovation but became — because of us — a force that has changed and is changing the way we work, play, ask questions, find answers, buy and sell products, communicate, and interact with others.

J. R. Okin
May, 2005

Acknowledgments

Writing is a solitary and sometimes lonely pursuit. But producing a book is a collective effort that owes its completion to many different types of contributions from a large number of individuals.

To my family, who, over the last three years, expressed support, urged me on, sheepishly asked how I was doing, and eventually were kind enough to stop inquiring about the book, I convey my thanks (for all of the above). More specifically, to my father, to Peter, Lisa, Daniel, and Stephen, to Rick, Thea, Sara, Emily, and Megan, thank you all for your patience and for the gentle nudges conveyed in words said, and left unsaid, to finish up the book and move on. I must convey a special thanks to Toni DeAngelis, whose nudges resemble kicks and whose words of encouragement often come in the form of marching orders, but whose caring and love are nonetheless transparent and are always overwhelming.

To my 'extended' family in Maine, I owe a separate measure of thanks. The questions, kind words, and encouragement I received from Mary and Greg Domareki, their children, Sarah, Catherine, John, Greg, Luke, and Bridget, Sarah's husband, Mike Kazmierczak, and their son, Michael, and Greg's wife, Erin, and the rest of their large and loving family helped me in no uncertain terms to stay the course and find my way to the completion of this project.

To my friends, who answered questions, provided solicited (and unsolicited) advice, checked in on me, and reminded me again and again that there was an audience for the book, I am forever grateful. I owe thanks to Carol Schur, who was kind enough to read an early draft of the book and provide valuable feedback, to Ann Hagerman, who was always generous with her suggestions and opinions, to Barry Orr, who called and emailed and was never in short supply of humor or kind words, to Helene Armitage, who offered support, suggestions, and encouragement when I first started out, and, off an on, throughout the course of the project, and to Ellen Dreyer, who provided much needed information about the inner workings of the world of publishing along with some gentle words of encouragement.

To my editor and good friend, Bob Lippman, who never tired in his efforts to correct my mistakes, to question my arguments and conclusions, and to identify material that needed further explanation or that demanded simplification, I am in your debt. I could not have asked for a more skillful or thorough editing of the book; and, thanks to you, I now have a new appreciation for the meaning of the phrase, brutal honesty. I am grateful that you found the time to take on this project and I very much appreciate your commitment to seeing the work through to its conclusion. Whatever value or use this book may find, it was greatly enhanced by the time, effort, and skill you put into editing its contents.

Finally, to Mary Domareki, who kept me from giving up, who held my hand, who cajoled me, and who never wavered in believing in me, words are inadequate to express how I feel. I will have to work hard to find a way to repay you. But I will find a way.

Contents

0 The Pre-Web Internet and Information Management

Waiting for the Web's Arrival   17

The History of Hypertext   24

Information Management and the Internet   45

1 The Web is Born

A Working Definition of the Web   57

Tim Berners-Lee and a Short History of the Web   59

Web History Details   68

The Web is Formed   79

The Web is Discovered   93

The Web Spins Threads of Control   100

2 The Mechanics of the Web

The Mechanics of the Web   107

The Building Blocks of the Web   108

The Applications of the Web   124

3 The Information Web

The Information Web   143

Finding Information   145

Contents

Storing and Representing Information   161

Automating the Discovery and Protection of

    Information   173

4 The Multimedia Web

The Multimedia Web   181

Publications   184

Audio   189

Video   195

Multimedia Built for the Web: Applets, Flash, and

    3D   203

5 The Business Web

The Business Web   209

Web Business Successes   216

Web Business Failures   231

Businesses that Build and Support the Web   236

6 The People Web

The People Web   243

There Is No Place Like Home: Web Home Pages   245

In Search of Publicity: Public People on the Web   248

In Search of Work: Web Job Hunting   250

In Search of Love: Web Dating   252

Contents

In Search of Family: Web Genealogy   256

The Quest for Self Expression: Blogs and Blogging   259

7 The Shadow Web

The Shadow Web   263

Web Banners: Advertisements that Track Our
Movements   267

Web Logs: Files that Record Our Movements   273

Web Bugs: Code that Captures Our Actions   277

Affiliate Management: Organizations that Live Off
Our Movements   282

Data Mining: Operations that Turn Our Data into
Gold   288

8 The Semantic Web

The Semantic Web   291

Representing Information: Metadata, RDF, and
XML   297

Discovering Information: Navigating the Semantic
Web   309

Trusting Information: The Web of Trust   312

The Big (Semantic Web) Picture   314

Contents

A Milestones, Netiquette, and Jargon

World Wide Web Milestones   317

Netiquette   321

Common Internet Age Jargon   325

B Notes

Notes   335

I Index

Index   337

The Pre-Web Internet and Information Management

Waiting for the Web's Arrival

It was not long ago, on an Internet that did not yet include the World Wide Web, that finding files and resources or even locating a site on the Internet was considered a challenge. One could not hop quickly and effortlessly from one Internet site to another with the click of a mouse button or view the Internet and interact with it using a colorful, icon-rich graphical interface. Instead, everyone worked hard to gather and maintain his or her own list of Internet sites, kept notes on each site's resources and how to access them, and consulted with friends and colleagues to learn about additional Internet resources. Overall, one's interaction with the Internet was very narrow in focus and primitive in operation, particularly by today's standards. But the Web changed all this, decidedly and permanently.

What most people will never be able to fully appreciate, given how relatively few people traveled the Internet before the Web's arrival in the early 1990s, is the magnitude of the change effected on the Internet by the introduction of information management systems in general and the Web in particular. Early information management systems — Archie, Gopher, WAIS, and the Web most of all — transformed the Internet from a vast, little known repository of independent and isolated information resources into an integrated, searchable, and navigable information space. This transformation was equivalent to taking piles and piles of books, periodicals, photos, illustrations, and other documents — enough to fill any number of football stadiums — and installing that information in a library.

Information items (or objects) that had been accessible across the Internet but that were for the most part hidden, undiscovered, unadvertised, or unrecognizable were found by these information management systems; they were then categorized, labeled, and tagged with a unique address so that they could be easily and quickly located and retrieved. Each system created its own searchable catalog or index, making it possible to browse its collection of information resources and quickly locate specific items. Each system also provided additional tools to further assist individuals in locating the information they needed. In other words, information management systems brought order and organization to an Internet that was as difficult to use and disorganized as it was distributed and decentralized.

The information space created by these information management systems has come to hold a seemingly endless number of resources and a wealth of information the likes and extent of which the world has literally never before known. Computers and networking fundamentally changed the way information could be stored, reused, and shared. The Internet and information management systems made that information findable, accessible, and searchable. The sheer volume and breadth of information now available over the Internet demonstrates that the Internet revolution is in large part an information revolution. Information management systems — especially the World Wide Web — precipitated and fueled this information revolution when they transformed the Internet into an information space.

Before the Web's arrival, the Internet was difficult for experienced computer people to use and nearly impossible for everyone else. If you did not know what you were looking for, precisely where it was to be found, and how to access it, you were out of luck. If you needed help, it was out there, somewhere. But it, too, was not all that easy to find or, for that matter, to follow. Imagine that you had heard of a new Internet site that contained weather forecasts organized by region and city, but you had not been told the site's address. No search engine existed to help you find the site. Moreover, if you did manage to locate the site, there was no browser to help you examine and navigate the site's contents. The information was there, contained in thousands of text files describing the weather conditions for each region and city and thousands of graphics files storing the associated weather satellite images. But it was up to you to discover the information you wanted, retrieve it, and determine how you were going to work with it.

The tools that existed to travel the Internet and retrieve information consisted of basic commands like TELNET or RLOGIN to access a remote site and FTP to transfer files. It required time, persistence, and a fair amount of experience in the use of these commands to achieve the desired result; and since every Internet site was different, coming up with a method for locating, accessing, and using information from one site did not necessarily simplify matters when it came time to perform the same basic operations on another site. The entire process was manual, time-consuming, and technically challenging. There was little hope that this Internet — no matter the volume or diversity of information it contained — would ever gain widespread popularity or become a household word.

But the Web turned this situation around in two critically important ways. First, it gave information providers the tools they needed to make their content findable and accessible. The Web enabled them to organize and manage their information resources, to present their information in a simple, architecture-independent, non-proprietary format, to make their resources more readily known and available to others, and to control access to them from across the Internet. Second, it enabled information providers to interconnect information in a new and powerful way through something called hyperlinks. A hyperlink is an electronic cross-reference that functions like a traditional cross-reference — a notation in one place that directs the reader to related, often more detailed information in another place. More than that, however, a hyperlink also functions to physically interconnect information — a reader clicks on a hyperlink notation and is taken to the referenced information, or destination. Through hyperlinks, information providers became able to interconnect their information with information and resources on other Internet sites, as well as to interconnect information between their own documents and other information objects on their own site. As will become clearer in the following chapters, it is this interconnection of information through hyperlinks and the resulting formation of an ever-growing web of criss-crossing information threads that is responsible for the Web's name. Even more importantly, this interconnection of information has had the largest and most lasting impact on our use of the Internet.

In addition to enhancing the organization, integration, and accessibility of information on the Internet, the Web also addressed the limitations and frustrations faced by individuals in search of information. It accomplished this through the creation of a new type of simple, fast, easy-to-use computer application called a Web browser. A browser made it possible for anyone to navigate the Internet's information resources. It kept the details of how and where information was stored hidden from the user; and it transparently handled the complex and tedious process of copying information files and determining how to interpret and display them. Browsers made locating and retrieving information as easy as clicking on a highlighted word or typing in a simple address. In effect, browsers and the Web brought the Internet and its ever-increasing store of information to the individual, greatly reducing the effort and skill necessary to discover what the Internet had to offer and how to put those resources to use.

You may not think of the Web as an information management system. You see its product, or effect, in the form of Internet destinations where you can check the local weather forecast, track and trade stocks, look up what's playing at the neighborhood movie theater, or perhaps find your soul mate. You use it as a tool that helps you pay bills or balance your checkbook, maintain and share your calendar, keep informed about current events that are related to your particular interests, or do research for a school project or for writing a book. But the Web serves these functions, and many others, by operating as a relatively simple, but powerful and distributed information management system. It succeeds so well at this task that many people mistakenly equate the Web with the Internet, confusing the Web — a service that provides access to the vast amount of information available across the Internet — with the large, complex infrastructure of host computers, routers, wires, transmission devices, and protocols for managing the safe, fast, and efficient transmission of data that is the Internet.

The Web's beginnings were strikingly different than those of the Internet. As explained in *The Internet Revolution*, the inspiration for the creation and development of the Internet came from the military and its need for a decentralized and redundant communications network. The demand for more economical and egalitarian use of expensive and remotely located computer resources also contributed significantly to the Internet's design and development. Additionally, the contributions of individual Internet users had an early and lasting impact on the Internet's form and function. The unanticipated introduction and immediate popularity of such services as email, chat, and newsgroups are examples of just such contributions. The Web itself is another example.

The birth and early development of the Web, however, were the result of a far more localized, focused, and controlled effort. Its creation can be attributed to a single person, Tim Berners-Lee, and to a single location, CERN, the European Particle Physics Laboratory in Geneva, Switzerland. Berners-Lee was undoubtedly in the right place at the right time. He worked in an environment filled with the latest computer and networking technology at a time when the Internet and networking standards had spread internationally and commercialization of the Internet was on the horizon. An inventive, smart, and determined individual, Berners-Lee faced the task of organizing and improving access to a large, disparate body of information at CERN. But instead of developing a specific solution that would only meet the information requirements at CERN, he engineered a distributed, all-purpose information management system that could accommodate virtually any type of information, one that we now happily and universally refer to as the Web.

Many people believe that the Web is something utterly new and unique. In some respects, this is true. Certain pieces of the Web's technology, along with its influence on the evolution of the Internet, its impact on business, and its revolutionary effect on the distribution and interconnection of information, are without precedent and represent distinct and singular achievements. But the motivation behind the Web's creation was neither new nor unique. Moreover, some of the core concepts and much of the engineering that contributed to the Web's construction and that were critical to its success, such as hyperlinks, had existed in one form or another for many years, as is described below. Berners-Lee's inspiration for the Web dates back considerably further than the ideas and technology on which he built the Web — to a popular, household book from Victorian England. The following chapter on the history of the Web's creation and development describes all of these influences at length.

When Berners-Lee set out to build his information management system in the late 1980s he identified three relatively recent influences on computer systems as driving forces behind the future use of computers and the management of information. He incorporated all three into his design of the Web. The first influence was the Internet and its open, non-proprietary, distributed architecture. Berners-Lee, like many others at the time, saw in the Internet an infrastructure lacking in resources or, at the very least, lacking the ability to advertise and offer its resources. The Web would fix this problem by exploiting the Internet's interoperability in the creation of its document management service. In the process, the Web's service would become something that Internet site owners could use to make their resources more readily known and accessible. Moreover, Berners-Lee leveraged some of the existing Internet services that had become popular for document management, like FTP and newsgroups. Through the Web he made these services easier to use and expanded on how they could be used. The Internet provided Berners-Lee with the infrastructure that the Web needed for it to implement a simple, very fast mechanism to interconnect documents across a network. His vision for the Web was large and inclusive, very like the vision for the Internet shared and pursued by the engineers at ARPA. Like the Internet, therefore, he designed the Web as a large-scale distributed system, one that took full advantage of the growing popularity of the Internet and, in particular, the standardization of its protocols and their guiding principle of interoperability.

The second influence on Berners-Lee's design of the Web was the growing migration to personal computers. From its inception, the Web was viewed by Berners-Lee as a two-way information platform. He wanted the Web to be used by individuals as a tool for managing and sharing their own information as much as a tool for accessing the documents of others. This design element relied on the relatively new paradigm of computer use provided by workstations and personal computers. The paradigm was built on the notion of independent computers customized for the use of an individual. Only a few years earlier this type of personalized computer use would have been inconceivable. Computers were still predominantly large, expensive, remote devices, few in number and accessed through dumb, character-based terminals (a dumb terminal simply consists of a keyboard and a display) that were distributed through offices and common rooms for shared computer access. The introduction and proliferation of personal computers was changing how and why computers were being used. Berners-Lee recognized this change in his design of the Web. Through the Web he promised to make each individual a publisher, by enabling individuals to share documents across the Internet; and he intended to turn each computer into its own platform for distributing information, by enabling even the smallest computer to make its files and resources accessible across the Internet. Although the Web was in no way restricted in its use to personal computers, its success (like that of the Internet) relied on the growing popularity of personal computers in the business world and at home.

The third influence that contributed to the design and success of the Web was a somewhat loosely defined system for storing and accessing information called hypertext. While the Internet would make Berners-Lee's information management system *world wide*, and personal computers would make it accessible to many individuals, it was hypertext that would be most responsible for making it into a *web*. Hypertext had existed for over twenty years by the time Berners-Lee started to conceive of the Web in the late 1980s, but it had only been available for a couple of years in any type of commercial product. Even after twenty years of development, which included the creation of some very advanced prototypes and academic systems, very few people knew about hypertext, and fewer still understood its potential to change the way people interacted with information. But Berners-Lee spotted the potential of hypertext, and he incorporated it as a key component in the design of his information management system. Hypertext became responsible for interconnecting the Web's documents, much as TCP/IP and packet switching (which are described at length in *The Internet Revolution*) became responsible for interconnecting the Internet's computers.

The remainder of this chapter presents an overview of the history, engineering, and philosophy behind hypertext, including descriptions of a few of the earliest hypertext systems. It also describes several of the most popular and effective information management systems that existed on the Internet before and during the arrival of the Web. The assorted strengths and weaknesses of these information management systems influenced the design and development of the Web. They also serve to illustrate the burgeoning interest in and rising need for information management systems on the Internet, at a time when the Internet's size and scope was continuing to grow and just as its resources were proving ever harder to locate and use.

The History of Hypertext

The Internet provided the underlying infrastructure, or platform, on which the Web was built and through which it would function. It provided the means to identify the location of a Web server and to allow a Web server and Web client (e.g., browser) to exchange information. These basic operations shared the same essential form and function as those provided for other, earlier services, such as FTP (for file transfer), TELNET (for remote login), email, and chat. The similarities between the Web and these other Internet services, however, ended exactly where hypertext began. Hypertext provided the threads that bound the Web together. It interconnected information much as the Internet interconnected computers: quickly, efficiently, seamlessly, and effortlessly. It was hypertext that enabled an individual to traverse the Web, jumping from document to document, from page to page, and very often from Internet site to Internet site, with the simple click of a button. This easy and rapid movement between information, files, and locations represented a fundamental and dramatic change in both an individual's behavior on and interaction with the Internet.

First and foremost, hypertext introduced an entirely new facility for organizing and interconnecting information. Its purpose was simple: to enable authors — as well as readers — to associate and link one piece of information (i.e., a reference) with another piece of information (i.e., a destination). The reference not only established a connection between the two pieces of information, like a traditional cross-reference, but it also functionally interconnected the information in the form of a bridge that was capable of taking the reader to its linked destination.

Hypertext was designed to overcome the limitations of hierarchical and indexed information storage systems and of traditional printed documents. Such systems and printed materials relied on structured views of the information prepared by the author or publisher. They used familiar mechanisms, such as indexes, tables of contents, and page numbers, to order, organize, and identify the information they contained. The paradigm long used in these systems, as illustrated by any book or periodical published in the last few hundred years, was designed to assist individuals in interacting with information by enabling them to quickly grasp the overall structure of the material and to more easily identify and proceed to specific areas of interest. This static, predefined, and predominantly sequential presentation of information worked well for printed material that the reader could hold, highlight with markers, and bookmark with paper clips, ribbons, or scraps of paper. But when that same information was made accessible through a computer, the dynamics of this interaction changed.

First, something was lost when the reader was no longer able to physically manipulate the information, such as in placing several open books side-by-side on a desk. Second, the traditional, structured paradigm for guiding the reader through the information no longer seemed sufficient without the physical counterpart that allowed the reader to page through, randomly open, or scan the printed material. Third, the unfamiliar online presentation of the information called out for fresh and inventive ways to present and organize the information and to assist the reader in his or her interaction with it.

Hypertext was an information management system that was designed specifically for the needs of this new, computer-based approach to information access. It abandoned the highly structured arrangement of printed material that relied on the rigid, hierarchical, sequential order of chapters, sections, subsections, pages, and paragraphs in favor of a radical approach that replaced order and formal structure with a more adaptable and customizable matrix of associations that was capable of interconnecting any piece of information in one document with any other piece of information in the same document or some other document. This matrix of associations was something original and very different, something as bold, far-reaching, and powerful as the

Internet itself, and something that most people initially dismissed as confusing and unworkable.

Before hypertext, the process of taking any type of printed document, such as a book, and creating a digital representation of it for display on a computer was an act of mimicry. What was displayed on the screen matched what was printed, page for page and paragraph for paragraph. For some, the ability to produce documents for display on a computer heralded the demise of traditional publishing and the promise of a paperless world. These individuals focused on the newfound freedom to access a bookcase of manuals from a wafer-thin CDROM and to view a century-old archived document without needing to travel a thousand miles to the library where it was stored. Others, however, focused less on the information content (and the process of duplicating in a digital form what existed on paper) and more on the technology and what this innovative and unprecedented way of interacting with information might bring to the process of reading and the acquisition of knowledge.

While the content of an online book might exactly match its printed counterpart, this did not necessarily mean that the reader's experience with each was the same. The structure and format of the printed material (i.e., a table of contents, index, footnotes, and even pages) were specifically designed for the publication of information on paper. The unaltered, digital reproduction of this same information worked to the advantage of publishers, which viewed computers as merely one more outlet for publication; and the familiarity of the information's presentation worked to the advantage of readers by easing their transition to reading material on their computers. But duplicating a document for display on a computer could not duplicate the reader's experience with its printed counterpart. A reader could follow the given hierarchy, reading page after page, chapter after chapter; and he or she could quickly locate a specific chapter or indexed term, and go directly to that page. Nothing, however, had been added to compensate the reader for not having the paper in hand. No attempt had been made to take the next step: to use the technology and its capabilities to create a new, different, and perhaps even more rewarding experience.

When, therefore, the question was raised about how the digital representation and presentation of information might be used to refine, augment, or otherwise enhance a reader's experience, a new type of information publication system called hypertext was invented and developed as the answer. The developers of hypertext viewed the technology of computers and the digital representation of information as a means to liberate information from the confines of the printed page and, more than that, as an opportunity to reinvent the publishing industry rather than simply expand its influence. Moreover, they identified the individual reader — not some generalized group — as the audience for information published in hypertext; and they wanted to provide that reader with more options in how to read, follow, understand, or otherwise interact with the information.

The principal objective in the development of hypertext was to empower both the author and the individual reader with the means to freely interconnect information in a more organic fashion — something that resembled how we think and make associations. The developers of hypertext wanted, for instance, to mimic our capacity to connect a particular scent, like that of freshly baked oatmeal cookies, with the memory of a specific event or person. In terms of publishing information, this meant giving authors the tools to define these associations for the reader and providing the reader with the same or comparable tools to add their own linked associations. For the reader, the process and practice of using hypertext was the the closest, digital equivalent to turning down the corner of a page, inserting a paper clip or bookmark, highlighting text with a marker, and writing comments in the margin of a page.

But hypertext was more than this. It not only compensated the reader for losing the physical interaction with the information, it allowed for additional information to be communicated, collected, and retained. For example, the author enjoyed an enhanced capability to introduce anecdotal information, without necessarily disturbing the overall structure and flow of the material. The author could also choose to *chart* different paths through the information for different types of readers, helping a reader less familiar with the subject avoid detailed descriptions that might be discouraging or distracting while enabling a reader already familiar with the subject to be guided through the more advanced material.

These capabilities stood in sharp contrast to the static, imposed hierarchical presentation of printed information.

With hypertext, a book or other document was no longer a single, self-contained object arranged in sequential pages and described by a table of contents and index. Instead, hypertext documents comprised hundreds or thousands of distinct and identifiable objects, enabling readers to bookmark not just a page, but an individual illustration, paragraph, sentence, phrase, or word. Any of these individual objects could also be linked, one to the next. This linking of objects formed a matrix of associations that existed outside of the familiar linear presentation of the information. They enabled the reader to jump from place to place instead of or in addition to progressing through the information from paragraph to paragraph and page to page. Links could also be made to external objects, such as other hypertext documents or document objects (e.g., photographs, charts, or illustrations). For example, the description of a Siamese cat in one chapter of a book could contain a link to the status of cats in Egyptian culture in a later chapter; and this description could contain a link to a separate book on the history of cats. The reader was free to ignore these links, follow them one step and then return, or to continue to follow them one to the next on a unique journey of discovery.

As explained below, hypertext redefined the way a reader interacts with information. The following sections summarize the history of hypertext, from a concept waiting for the necessary technological advances through which it could be built, to a newly coined term and philosophy that began to convince people of its promise, to the first experimental tools that demonstrated its potential, to the first commercial products that brought it onto our computers at work and at home. Later chapters explain how hypertext specifically empowered the Web to interconnect information much as TCP/IP empowered the Internet to interconnect computers.

As We May Think

As We May Think is the title of an article that appeared in the July edition of the Atlantic Monthly in 1945. The ideas presented in it inspired the first creators of hypertext systems more than twenty years later. The article was written by a scientist named Vannevar Bush, the Director of the Office of Scientific Research and Development and the scientific advisor to President Roosevelt who, in 1950, became the first Director of the National Science Foundation (NSF). Bush was responsible for managing the work of six thousand prominent scientists as they applied their knowledge to wartime activities during World War II. His work included overseeing development of the first atomic bomb. With the war over, and prompted by Roosevelt to apply what was learned during wartime to the new peace, Bush asked in his article: "What are the scientists to do next?" His response to this question was to explore how science might be applied to make knowledge more accessible to more people.

During the war, scientific efforts had been focused on enhancing man's (and woman's) physical powers. This meant engineering more accurate and more destructive weapons and building devices that heightened our natural abilities to see, hear, locate, and disable an enemy. Now, with peace at hand, Bush wanted to focus on enhancing woman's (and man's) knowledge and understanding. His desire was to use science to improve the human condition. More specifically, he wanted to improve how we access information and how we acquire and maintain control over it. As explained below, he used the article to explore why this work was needed and proposed how the work might be pursued.

The war had brought the scientific community closer together. It had also accelerated the pace and expanded the scope of work that was being undertaken. One result was that there were more scientists, and more scientific research was being conducted, than ever before. Consequently, Bush was inundated with information. Books, papers, articles, and reams of data were all being produced and delivered to his office. He could not, however, keep pace with the volume of information and the speed at which it was arriving. He knew that this problem was becoming common and it was only going to get worse over time, which prompted him to consider the larger issue. He wondered how any scientist could manage to stay current with the research in his or her field of study given the ever-increasing mass of data being produced, without making fundamental changes to how information was shared and accessed:

> The summation of human experience is being expanded at a prodigious rate, and the means we use for threading through the consequent maze to the momentarily important item is the same as was used in the days of square-rigged ships.[1]

Recent scientific discoveries were leading scientists and the pursuit of science in new directions. Bush was surrounded by many of these new discoveries and his position made him uniquely aware of both the potential for change that could come from these technological innovations and the knowledge that was being gained and shared in the process of this work. He was also aware that the storage and presentation of all this information had not changed. It was precisely the same as it had been a hundred years earlier: the same basic types of books, periodicals, tables of contents, and indexes were still in use. He concluded that, while the amount of data was steadily increasing, no concurrent innovations had been made with respect to distributing, accessing, and making use of the data. This led him to consider how technology might be used to address this growing, but largely overlooked problem.

Bush recognized the widespread impact of recent advances in technology. The rapidly expanding use of radio tubes, for example, was for him a simple example of how "cheap complex devices of great reliability"[2] were transforming the world. He decided to consider how these advances in technology might be applied to accessing and controlling information. Keeping true to his nature as a scientist, Bush succinctly described the main problem with contemporary information storage and access and then proceeded to propose a solution. A good forty-five years before the advent of the Web, Bush not only recognized and understood the principal problem the Web would later solve, but he even effectively described how hypertext systems and the Web would be engineered to implement the solution:

When data of any sort are placed in storage, they are filed alphabetically or numerically, and information is found (when it is) by tracing it down from subclass to subclass. It can be in only one place, unless duplicates are used; one has to have rules as to which path will locate it, and the rules are cumbersome. Having found one item, moreover, one has to emerge from the system and re-enter on a new path.

The human mind does not work that way. It operates by association. With one item in its grasp, it snaps instantly to the next that is suggested by the association of thoughts, in accordance with some intricate web of trails carried by the cells of the brain. It has other characteristics, of course; trails that are not frequently followed are prone to fade, items are not fully permanent, memory is transitory. Yet the speed of action, the intricacy of trails, the detail of mental pictures, is awe-inspiring beyond all else in nature.[3]

Bush contrasts the limiting, hierarchical approach to information storage and access, in which information is categorized and organized into lists (e.g., tables of contents and indexes) that require the reader to repeatedly enter and exit the information (e.g., starting on one path begun by looking up an index entry and then returning to the index to start on another) with the more fluid and interconnected cognitive associations of the human mind. While lacking the technology to implement his ideas, Bush nevertheless excelled at defining the problem and even proposed a methodology that would provide a solution. Storing, cataloging, and indexing information was only part of accessing and controlling knowledge. The missing element was a means to form and follow natural associations to interconnect the data, links that joined any one piece of information with any other and, when taken together, formed an "intricate web of trails" resembling our own cognitive functions. This became the guiding principle behind the development of both hypertext and the Web. Even today, as commercialization pushes the Web ever farther from its scientific and academic roots, this unconstrained and customizable linking of data remains the defining element of the Web.

Bush also describes a device that he calls a *memex*. Its description sounds strikingly like our personal computers, and its use sounds much like our use of computers in conjunction with the Web. It houses vast amounts of data that can be accessed quickly and easily and acts largely as a supplement to one's memory. The device includes tools for bookmarking information sources and for creating personal documents that contain a combination of text, images, and annotations. In essence, he envisions a world in which technology has made information freely available and where we have the means and the power to chart and recall our path through this store of information, all the while building a personal library customized to our individual needs and interests. The Web was built on these very principles, described by Vannevar Bush more than half a century ago. He would surely recognize the Web, and our interaction with it, as a realization of his memex device.

While Vannevar Bush captured the essential nature of the Web with his description of linking and multi-threading information by means of natural associations, it took another twenty years before a technology was developed that offered some promise that such a system could actually be built. In 1945, Bush's best hope for advancing his ideas on improved information access and integration was through the relatively recent technology of microfilm. In 1965, the growing prominence of the computer created new and better possibilities. As presented in the next section, it was then that the term hypertext was coined and that the first computer-based document production system incorporating associative links was built, bringing Bush's memex one step closer to being realized and, ultimately, bringing all of us one step closer to the World Wide Web.

Ted Nelson and Xanadu

Ted Nelson coined the term hypertext in a paper he presented at the national conference of the Association for Computer Machinery (ACM), which took place in Pittsburgh in 1965. He used the term to describe a type of *non-linear* writing — writing that branches into many directions — that allowed for the unlimited interconnecting of information. Nelson believed that hypertext would empower readers to choose their own paths through information, rather than being explicitly guided through information by the singular, sequential view — the traditional beginning, middle, and end — prescribed by an author or publisher.

Nelson viewed hypertext documents as containers of independent information objects, and each object held one or more links to other objects. Since the objects existed in a non-linear matrix instead of a linear hierarchy, no two readers would necessarily progress through the information in the same way, and one reader might easily follow a different path and encounter different information each time he or she began to read. Years before the creation of the very first computer network, and decades before the widespread use of the personal computer and the arrival of the Web, Nelson envisioned that hypertext would create new types of documents and transform how people read and how works were written and published. He also coined the associated term *hypermedia*, which applied the concept of non-linear documents and information interconnections to non-textual elements, such as images, audio, and video components, that could be included in these associated links.

Nelson later defined an idealized version of a hypertext publishing environment called Xanadu, named after the land described in the dream-inspired Coleridge poem, "Kubla Khan." Several attempts were made to build the software and create a Xanadu system, but none ever succeeded. If anything, his plans were probably too ambitious, too all-encompassing. In brief, the plans for Xanadu define a document universe contained in a network of computer servers distributed throughout the world. It allows for all published material to be interconnected at the smallest object level — a paragraph — and incorporates a copyright system to compensate authors for use of their material. No information would ever be deleted. (This feature would have prevented the problem with dead links — links that no longer connect to any information — often encountered on the Web that result when information is deleted, moved, or otherwise made inaccessible.) Xanadu is rich in ideas and many have compared it to the Web. But such a comparison is hardly fair. While both incorporate hypertext as a central feature, that's largely where their similarity begins and ends.

The Hypertext Editing System

One of the first working hypertext systems was called the Hypertext Editing System (HES). HES was developed in 1967 at Brown University, where Andries van Dam collaborated with his college friend, Ted Nelson, using funding supplied by IBM. The project began primarily as an attempt to transform some of Nelson's hypertext concepts into a working system. But they ended up curtailing that effort and instead focused primarily on document printing and formatting.[4]

HES closely resembled a first-generation word processing system more than any type of hypertext document system. Many of its features could be considered prototypes of the features commonly found in today's desktop publishing applications. HES did, however, include hypertext links and it retained a list of links visited that made it possible to use a *back button* feature to return easily to a previous document or reference. While HES showed great promise, was well received by those who saw it demonstrated, and was adapted for use at several universities, it lost its funding and its development stopped soon afterward.

HES was a document production and information management system way ahead of its time. Demonstrations of HES to large IBM customers, such as The New York Times and Time/Life, showed how far removed a computer-based document editing and production system was from the existing production environments and their dependence on pens, paper, and typewriters. Most writers and editors who saw the demonstration were overwhelmed by the seeming complexity of doing such work on a computer monitor. Although Nelson and van Dam did not know it at the time, IBM did find one customer for HES when it sold the system to the Houston Manned Spacecraft Center. HES was used by NASA to produce documentation for the Apollo space program.

The On Line System

In 1968, a far more advanced hypertext document system called NLS, or oN Line System, was demonstrated by its creator, Doug Engelbart, at the Fall Joint Computer Conference. Engelbart, like many others, was inspired by Bush's vision of memex. He was keenly interested in adapting computers to how humans behaved and worked, which led him to explore how to employ computers to increase productivity and expand human capabilities. His work was along the same lines as J. C. R. Licklider's time-sharing computer model (described in *The Internet Revolution*) and the interactive computer use described in Licklider's seminal paper, "Man Computer Symbiosis." As explained below, Licklider and ARPA provided the funding that Engelbart needed in order to develop NLS.

Engelbart was already working at the Stanford Research Institute (SRI), where the second node of the ARPANET would eventually be installed, when Licklider became head of the IPTO in 1962 and began to fund assorted research projects. Engelbart managed a project called Augment and had put together a large team consisting of forty-five programmers and engineers. The group developed productivity tools designed to reverse the existing computer/human relationship and enable users to augment their native intelligence and knowledge through computer access. The development of NLS as a system to cross-reference and share research papers became part of this project in 1963, with Licklider providing funding for the work. Engelbart had been inspired to create NLS by Bush's nearly twenty-year-old vision of a more effective way to store and interconnect information.

While NLS was an experimental system, it was a highly successful proof-of-concept: a working prototype of the first fully functional, multi-user hypertext system, and the model for many subsequent hypertext products. NLS grew over time to include more than 100,000 document objects (also known as nodes). It stored plans, specifications, all types of documentation and reports, and a wide variety of other types of information. With it, people could easily share and annotate documents and use hyperlinks to jump from place to place within a document or between documents. To complement and facilitate its use, Engelbart developed two devices that enabled faster interaction with the computer than that provided by a standard keyboard. One was a mini five-key keyboard called a chord key set; the other was a pointing device that manipulated a cursor on the screen and was called a mouse.

NLS was very well received when Engelbart demonstrated the system in front of several thousand people in 1968. But, like his mouse, which amazingly took twenty years before it became a standardized and commonplace computer component, his hypertext system was too far ahead of the times, and funding slowly dried up. Many of the common hypertext elements found on the Web today were part of NLS. But NLS also included other, more advanced features, such as being able to define a document to present multiple views (i.e., differing content) depending on the type of user accessing it or some selected preference of the user.

Two elementary, but revolutionary features of NLS established a completely original way to view documentation and, therefore, information. One feature was responsible for storing documents, and pieces of documents, as independent objects; as objects, they could be referenced and accessed separately (i.e., a single paragraph of a research paper or a single section of a large book could be identified and navigated to directly), providing a new context for that information that might or might not include its encompassing material. The other feature was responsible for freeing document objects to be accessed and used by applications other than the application that created the information. Document objects not only existed independent of any encompassing information, but they could also be accessed from different vantage points and for different purposes. This feature greatly enhanced the capability of reusing information. For example, a single description of how a function key worked might be included in a user's guide, pop up in an application's context-sensitive help, and appear in a quick reference card or a glossary. The specific description, or information object, would exist in one place; each application that wanted to include it only needed to reference that single location.

The File Retrieval and Editing System

Inspired by Engelbart's NLS demonstration, van Dam continued his hypertext work at Brown and developed the File Retrieval and Editing System (FRESS). In FRESS, van Dam combined some of the best hypertext and multi-user features of NLS with the document-processing features of HES. One of his key objectives was to develop some measure of device independence (i.e., enabling FRESS to work on and with different types of computer equipment). After all, how could one create a large-scale document-sharing environment if the system were limited in its operation to a narrow range of hardware? He was thinking, like the ARPANET and Internet engineers, about the basic and essential interoperability of computers. For FRESS to succeed, it had to run on, or be accessible from, many existing and dissimilar computer platforms. This requirement was no different than that of the ARPANET, which required only minimal changes to the host computers for them to connect to the network and share information. Accordingly, van Dam and his team developed the concept of virtual input and output devices. These virtual devices consisted of software-based computer terminals and printers that functioned to absorb hardware incompatibilities. They were similar in concept to the network virtual terminal (NVT) component developed for the ARPANET's TELNET protocol.

Among other unique features, FRESS included bi-directional links, which meant that the destination for a link would also point back to the originating reference. FRESS also allowed a user to create his or her own customized path through a document by labeling links with keywords, and it included what may have been the first undo function, which allowed a user to reverse one or more recent changes to the document.[5] With FRESS, students in a class could easily annotate documents by inserting links and their own notes; and they could choose to view the entries made by other classmates, or by their professor, or none at all. (Such innovative and powerful features have yet to be realized on the Web.) FRESS was in active use for two decades, which is a strong indication of how well it was received by those who had the opportunity to use it.

An experiment that van Dam conducted with FRESS in the mid 1970s illustrates how hypertext could be used as a teaching aid, and how valuable it could be once people became accustomed to the concept and practice of interconnecting and sharing knowledge. He explains:

> For this English poetry course we used a very large hypertext with well over a thousand links. Three times a week students had to sign up for an hour each on our one and only Imlac graphics workstation and do their reading and their commenting on-line, following trails, making trails. We used a kind of progressive disclosure: the first time through they saw the poem they were supposed to critique and analyze, with no references. The second time they saw it with a few links to other poems on the same subject or by the same poet. There would also be some word glosses, some professional analyses, but still not very much context. And they would be reviewing what other students had written on the first pass, and the teacher's and TAs' comments as well, and then they would form a new opinion of what they had read. And then they would do that a third time, when they had yet more access to what people had written communally and what had previously been put in the database. It was very interesting. People loved it, despite the fact the system went down a lot, that it was hard to get at it, that you had to schedule time. And this 'communal text,' as it was called by the poetry people who wrote about it later, became very rich in additional annotations. Electronic graffiti, as I thought of them.[6]

The experiment foreshadowed in miniature how hypertext would come to be used as a teaching aid in educational institutions and elsewhere some twenty years later. However, it is still more the exception than the rule that hypertext is being used in as inventive and powerful a way as in van Dam's experiment from three decades ago.

The Aspen Movie Map and Movie Manual

In 1978, what was very likely the first hypermedia system was demonstrated. The development effort had been led by Andrew Lippman, a member of the MIT Architecture Machine Group. The system simulated an excursion through the city of Aspen, Colorado. A database of images of the city was built when four cameras mounted on top of a truck, each camera capturing 90 degrees of the view, took photos of Aspen at 3 meter intervals. The images were interconnected, or linked, based on their immediate proximity to each other (i.e., each image was linked to the immediately adjoining images to the north, south, east, and west). The resulting archive of linked photographs was then imported into the hypermedia system they called the Aspen Movie Map. The links between the images, branching in one or more directions at every intersection, allowed for any number of different journeys through the city to be explored.

Once a user selected a route through the city from a listing of predefined journeys, the system would display the images that corresponded to that journey in quick succession, producing the effect of a motion picture. The links between the photographs established the necessary continuity, as each image called the next image along the route to be displayed in sequence. The system was initially designed to display as many as 30 images a second. But this rate of display was quickly lowered to 10 images a second, reducing the simulated speed from roughly 200 miles per hour to 68 miles per hour. The system also allowed a user to enter some buildings in the city and take a tour of their interiors. The same multi-camera, linked photography approach was used to create the database for these walking virtual tours. The system also included a street map of the city that could be used to jump directly from one location to another. Today this type of hypertext object is called an imagemap. An imagemap is a graphical object, such as a drawing or a photograph, that is divided into segments, and each segment contains an individual link to additional information.

A later system, called the Movie Manual, applied the same concept of a user-selectable virtual tour to car maintenance and repair. In this system, car images included links to more detailed images and information. By pointing to a specific car part, the user could retrieve information about that part in the form of text, audio, and video. It's not difficult to see the potential of such an interconnected, easy-to-access information system. The Movie Manual clearly illustrated how the new information access paradigm of hypertext systems allowed information objects to be linked according to an adaptable matrix of associations. In this instance, that matrix was used to interconnect information in a way that matched how the parts of car were interconnected, thereby extending the value of the information by closely integrating the information's form and accessibility with the specific subject matter it presented. In other words, hypertext enabled form to follow function.

Both of these hypermedia systems, like the hypertext systems of FRESS and NLS, were excellent proof-of-concept examples of a new way to store, organize, and present information. They demonstrated what the technology could do, even though they failed to become commercial products. Many of the far-reaching objectives of these systems have yet to be realized either in whole or in part as commercial products. But, by the mid 1980s, the business world was starting to take notice of hypertext, and things were about to change.

Commercial Hypertext Products

In 1985, a computer workstation from Symbolics included a hypertext system called the Symbolics Document Examiner in conjunction with the 8,000 page manual that came with the workstation. The hypertext manual was contained in 10,000 nodes and included some 23,000 links. Given the size of the manual and the expectation that the reader would be unfamiliar with hypertext, the system was designed to be as intuitive and as simple to use as possible. The vast size of the manual made the expensive development of the hypertext system, and the additional cost of producing both an online and printed manual, feasible. The hypertext manual promised, if favorably received, to facilitate more frequent documentation updates, lower production costs, and perhaps one day eliminate the expense of printing the manual.

Unlike the hypertext systems described above, the Symbolics Document Examiner was not a research project and it was not designed to advance the capabilities of hypertext. Its purpose was narrow in scope and practical. It was focused on the production of one very large document; and its goal was to convince the audience of that document that the hypertext version of the manual could be accessed easier, faster, and with greater convenience than its printed counterpart. The guiding principle behind the construction of the hypertext manual was to create a node for each individual, coherent piece of information contained in the manual. To make the transition easier for the reader, the familiar book metaphor was retained by dividing the material into chapters and sub-sections. Users could move quickly through the book using the defined hypertext links; and they could create links of their own by bookmarking places in the text. A survey of users showed that most preferred the hypertext manual to the printed version.

Other early hypertext products focused not on distributing individual documents but on providing an application for businesses and individuals to use in creating their own hypertext documents. Xerox, for example, created a hypertext document system called NoteCards, which it released in 1985. At the same time, Brown University released its Intermedia product for the Macintosh A/UX system. And, in 1987, Apple Computer introduced HyperCard, a free hypertext application that was distributed with all Macintosh machines. For a short time, HyperCard was the most widely used hypertext application.

By the late 1980s, the philosophy and engineering behind hypertext were finally dovetailing with the existing computer technology; and what these and other early, commercial hypertext products demonstrated was that there was a small, but eager and growing audience for such products. Most people when shown the benefits of hypertext soon realized how and why hypertext documents were superior to other forms of online documents and to printed versions of the same information. But learning how to use a hypertext system often required specialized training; this was particularly true for the writers, editors, and production staff responsible for creating hypertext documents. It took time and patience to become familiar with how one of these systems worked; they also required a period of adjustment simply to become comfortable with the practice of jumping from link to link as opposed to reading page after page. Moreover, many people were understandably resistant to the notion of replacing printed material with information accessible through their computer. As the following section explains, even with commercial products being produced, many fundamental problems remained unresolved or were being overlooked, and they stood in the way of hypertext attaining widespread use or making any kind of significant impact on how information was stored and accessed.

The Future of Hypertext

With hypertext, as with the Web when it was first introduced, you either "got it," or you scratched your head and wondered what all the fuss was about. In the late 1960s, and for the following two decades, work on hypertext structured document systems continued in relatively small, isolated groups. Slowly, but surely, more and more people recognized the potential benefits of interconnecting data, as envisioned by Bush in 1945, and the hypertext movement began to gain momentum; and, finally, commercial applications started to appear, as described above. At the same time, computer hardware was adapting towards individual and private computer access, leading in the 1980s first to the introduction and then to the growing popularity of the personal computer and its scientific counterpart, the more powerful, individual workstation. These advances in hardware, and the resulting surge in individual computer use, complemented nicely the principal tenets of hypertext. For the first time, individuals now had access to the necessary hardware and the software with which to build their own library of interconnected information. But hypertext was still far from becoming the next revolutionary technology. It was not yet ready to transform the way people worked, learned, or stored information.

Meanwhile, in 1987, the first World Wide Hypertext conference was held in Chapel Hill, North Carolina. Andries van Dam, who gave the keynote speech, ended his talk by describing what he believed were the key deficiencies and technical obstacles holding back the great hypertext revolution in which his audience so fervently believed. These problems are described below. (Some of these problems would shortly be solved by Tim Berners-Lee's creation of the World Wide Web.)

According to van Dam, a fundamental problem hindering the further development and acceptance of hypertext was standards or, more exactly, the lack of standards for hypertext. Hypertext development was being conducted in a vacuum. Everyone was inventing and reinventing their own methodology for creating a hypertext system, and no one was thinking about interconnecting the hypertext documents in one system with those stored in any other hypertext system. There was no compatibility; and no one was thinking about or discussing the issues of compatibility and interoperability. What made this especially strange was the fact that hypertext was by its very nature a system that demanded interoperability. The more interoperability, the better for everyone. Therefore, the pursuit of hypertext standards was in everyone's best interests.

Another key problem that was being overlooked related to the size of hypertext document systems and how they would function over time as they grew larger and larger. Ted Nelson had conceived of a global hypertext system encompassing all available information. But no one was yet thinking about the technical challenges of a large system that would be growing exponentially. Everyone working on the development of hypertext systems understood that, the larger the system and the more documents and links it contained, the more valuable such a system would be. But no work was being done to confront the technical challenges that such a system would present. For instance, who would manage the system? How would hypertext links remain current? Would there be a global database of links, or some sort of distributed system? How would incompatibilities be handled?

van Dam remarked that document versions and change control also had to be implemented well in any hypertext system, if there was going to be any real hope of replacing printed documents. Multiple versions of an article could easily be spread out across a desk for comparison and analysis. How would a person track and display changes between versions of a document in a hypertext system?

Navigation through hypertext information needed significant improvement, van Dam told his audience, if large-scale use of hypertext systems was ever to be attained. Better, more intuitive tools were needed to guide users through hyperspace. Given that hypertext created a new paradigm for an individual's interaction with information, the design of navigation tools would prove critical to the ease or difficulty — and the resulting success or failure — of its use. If the system didn't make it easy to chart a path through a document or a collection of documents and also make it easy to recall that path later on, no one would choose to chart a path in the first place. Moreover, if navigation tools limited a reader to following prepared links as some had done, thereby denying the reader the ability to add links and annotations and create their own associations and trails, a fundamental component of hypertext was being abandoned. van Dam asserted that new constructs were needed to implement the new paradigm. New types of navigation tools were needed to bring those new constructs to the user and to make them easy enough to be used so that they would be used.

Another area that van Dam viewed as not being addressed was the design of hypertext documents. A new way to represent information demanded new ways to design and display that information. Recycling typographic controls used by the print media was not going to be sufficient. Additionally, hypertext needed to accommodate all types of displays, from laptops, to large screens, to white boards. This meant that document design had to be adaptable so that its display and use could be maximized for the equipment being used.

Andries van Dam's final comments concerned intellectual property rights and author compensation. Hypertext and online document access bypassed the existing safeguards against copyright infringement. Ted Nelson had devoted thought to this issue some twenty years earlier, arriving at a novel approach using micropayments that would go directly to authors. This issue remains largely unresolved today, although there has been discussion of using some sort of micropayment scheme for the Web. But it would now be difficult to impose any such structure on the Web, given the limited way in which hypertext has been implemented, as will become clearer in later chapters.

The next chapter describes how Berners-Lee managed to build on the hypertext efforts described above by creatively adapting the technology to suit the purposes of the Web. His novel approach to hypertext was so radical that at first it was dismissed by most members of the hypertext community. But it was difficult to argue with a system that worked and that very quickly acquired immense popularity. The Web was not, however, the first or only information management system on the Internet. Several popular and highly effective systems, which are described in the following section, arrived just before or at the same time as the Web; and each went a long way towards making the experience of traveling the Internet more rewarding and enjoyable.

Information Management and the Internet

During its more than three decades of use, the Internet has changed considerably with respect to how it is accessed and used, who is using it and for what purposes, the number and variety of services it offers, and even what it looks like to most people. What has not changed is that most Internet operations consist of sharing information and information resources. The first Web site, which came online in 1990, was no exception; its purpose was to assist with information management and sharing. But many people were hard at work creating information management systems before the Web's arrival. Even more people are pursuing this type of work today, developing systems for information management on the Internet that will offer alternatives to the Web, or replace it entirely.

As Internet access grew in the 1980s, more and more resources became available across the Internet. Connecting to the Internet had become easier, and standardized protocols, such as FTP and TELNET (for copying files and logging into remote computers, respectively), were freely available and could be used to turn any computer into an Internet-accessible repository of documents. What had not become any easier, however, was the ability to locate resources on the Internet. It was a challenge to find a specific document, and there was no facility to browse or search through the Internet resources that were available or to otherwise gain an appreciation for the volume and diversity of information that people had decided to make public and share. The process of trying to locate information on the Internet before the arrival of information management systems was like trying to find your way around a library in the dark. You knew there were shelves filled with books and magazines, librarians, and perhaps even elevators and vending machines. But you were limited to what you stumbled across or what someone had explicitly told you how to find and use.

If you were on the Internet prior to 1993, the year the first graphical, multi-platform Web browser (called Mosaic) was introduced, it was probably because you were in academia (and were associated with the computer science department), or because you were working at a research facility in a private company or in a government agency. Instead of a browser, a command prompt, which often took the form of a blinking cursor in a bare window, was your point of access, or doorway, to the Internet. It waited for you to enter a command — TELNET or FTP or MAIL, for instance — to start up an Internet service and then visit a remote site or transfer a file. You had to go out in search of the Internet and all that it contained, and every Internet site was an island unto itself, adding to the effort required to discover what it contained and how it was organized.

While some people found these conditions to be an endless source of frustration, others saw in them an opportunity. The Internet was waiting for something or someone to come along and establish some measure of order or organization. The sections below describe several of the most popular information management systems created to help people find, organize, search through, and advertise information on the Internet. Some of these systems represent the work of individuals, as is true of the Web. These individuals routinely used the Internet and first created tools for their own use to help them locate resources and retrieve files, but later made these tools available for others to use. Other systems were the product of more formal development efforts, work done in the hope of creating commercial products and services for an Internet on the verge or commercialization and privatization. Before the Web arrived and reduced the use of and interest in these early systems, they were responsible for convincing novice as well as long-time Internet users that information management was going to have a considerable impact on the Internet's future. On a more practical level, they made using the Internet a much more enjoyable and productive experience for many people, and they allowed people to better appreciate the unlimited, empowering potential of the Internet.

Finding Files with Archie

Archie was a client-server application that greatly simplified the process of browsing and locating the freely shared Internet files that were made available on anonymous FTP file servers. (A client-server application is one designed to run over a network in which one computer, known as the client, makes requests for information and/or resources from another computer, known as the server.) Sites that contained these repositories of free files were scattered across the Internet. They typically contained such files as computer programs, updates to computer programs or operating systems, games, documentation, graphics, and photos. The original software for the World Wide Web, for example, was made available through an anonymous FTP site; anyone interested in learning about or setting up a Web server was free to (and encouraged to) visit the site and copy the files for their own use. Most people learned of a site's existence through word of mouth, an email message, or a newsgroup. To find out what files were on any particular site was a manual and tedious process; one had to visit the site and issue commands to move from directory to directory and list each directory's contents.

Archie was created to automate the process of visiting each FTP site and listing its contents. It could be programmed to routinely connect to any number of FTP sites; it would produce a listing of their contents and then create a concatenated, searchable listing of the files on the local computer of all the sites it had visited. Someone looking for a particular file or interested in browsing what was available on any of the FTP sites visited by Archie could then consult this one local file listing instead of visiting each site and searching through any number of directories.

Archie was created in 1989 by Alan Emtage, Peter Deutsch, and others at McGill University in Montreal, Canada. It was developed from a simpler tool written by Emtage in response to the frustration he felt at having to spend endless hours visiting and searching FTP sites for software that could be used at the university. The tool he created was a collection of scripts (i.e., small programs) that ran by themselves at appointed times, connected to specific FTP sites, listed the contents of those sites, and returned the lists of files to his local account at McGill. The scripts saved him considerable time and freed him from the laborious, mechanical process of connecting to and searching each of the FTP sites.

The benefits of Emtage's simple tool were quickly acknowledged by Deutsch, and they decided to develop it into something that people other than themselves could use. Since what they were doing amounted to creating a master index, or archive, of FTP sites, they chose to call their creation Archie (the word archive without the 'v'). Many people would later assume that they had named it after the popular comic book character of the same name. This led to competing tools that were seemingly named after other characters from the same comic book (see below). It also led to questions about copyright infringements.

Archie consisted of two basic components. One part was the original Emtage tool that brought back the lists of files from the FTP servers on the Internet. The other part was a simple service called an Archie server that ran on an Internet site (the first site was located at McGill) and enabled anyone to read and search through the collected archives. TELNET could be used to connect to an Archie server. Or one of several freely available Archie client programs could be used for this purpose; they provided additional features to simplify the process of accessing and using an Archie server. Once connected, the user could search for filenames using partial or full name matching, display a list of the FTP servers that had been archived, and display a list of other Archie servers. The results of a search included a list of filenames that matched the search criteria that had been entered and the names of the associated FTP servers where the files could be found. A user could even choose to have the search results mailed back to them rather than wait for them to be displayed.

Archie's scope, unfortunately, was limited. Moreover, it was a tool that only a system administrator or some other computer-savvy person could appreciate and readily use. It did not (and could not), for instance, attach any meaning to the filenames retrieved from the FTP servers. A user was at the mercy of the naming conventions used by the people who created each of the FTP sites; there were no formal standards or guidelines for naming files. Therefore, a user might not find files they were looking for if the files were not named as expected; and if multiple files from multiple FTP sites were returned in the results of a search, no additional information was available to help distinguish one from the next or to make clear which version a file might be or which computer system it was written for.

Despite its limitations, Archie was an immediate success, so much so that it was not long before the Archie server at McGill was consuming most of the bandwidth connecting eastern Canada to the rest of the Internet. The simple service that Archie offered filled a gaping void in the Internet, which was made abundantly clear by its immediate popularity. It was a simple, but effective system for helping to manage and make known much of the information that was quickly accumulating on the Internet. Even with its (now) apparent deficiencies, Archie was an early and significant step towards transforming the Internet into the information space made possible by the Web. Organization was sorely lacking in the ever-expanding realm of the Internet. Every reasonable effort made to find or superimpose some order helped people locate and make better use of the Internet's resources.

Locating Resources with Gopher (and Veronica and Jughead)

In 1991, the first friendly, menu-oriented interface for information access arrived on the Internet. It was developed at the University of Minnesota and named Gopher after the University's golden Gopher mascot. (Minnesota is known as the Gopher State, which also may have been a contributing factor in naming the application.) The name offered the added benefit of being a pun on the Gopher protocol's primary function: to retrieve, or "go for," information. Like Archie, Gopher was a client-server application that retrieved information from multiple Internet sites in order to collect that distributed information in a single, concatenated archive. Unlike Archie, the information collected was not limited to the contents of FTP sites. Moreover, Gopher was able to organize and categorize the information it collected, greatly enhancing a user's ability to search for and locate specific files. Given its ease of use, Gopher Internet sites (servers that ran the Gopher information service) proliferated quickly. Within a few years, there were more than 10,000 Gopher sites scattered all over the globe.

Gopher was the product of an effort, popular on college campuses in the late 1980s and early 1990s, to use the local computer infrastructure to create a campus-wide information system (CWIS). Ironically, the committee set up to design such a system for the University of Minnesota created a specification that the computer experts argued could not be built. Instead, a skilled and pragmatic programmer named Farhad Anklesaria created the simple, but powerful Gopher system. Since the system ignored their specification, the committee angrily rejected it. But Gopher quickly multiplied at other sites. Only after compliments on the system started flooding in to the university did Minnesota actually install its own Gopher system.

Like the Web, which at this time was in its infancy, Gopher brought something new and exciting to the Internet. Its simple, menu-driven interface, an example of which appears below, brought the user information organized by topic and arranged as if it were one large, local database of information.

```
            Internet Gopher Information Client v1.24D
                        Root Directory

     --> 1.  Welcome to the Vassar College Gopher.
         2.  Administration Services
         3.  Dean's Office
         4.  English Department
         5.  Astronomy Department
         6.  Frequently Asked Questions
         7.  Library
         8.  National Weather Service
         9.  Other Gopher Sites
         10. Phone Books

     Press ? for Help, q to Quit, u to go up a menu    Page: 1/1
```

Figure 1. Sample Gopher Screen

A user could access a Gopher site either by using TELNET (to manually connect to a site and start the service) or by starting up a local Gopher client that transparently handled accessing the server and starting the service. The user then selected a menu item from the displayed list and proceeded through subordinate menu listings (each menu item either contained submenus or a listing of resources), until he or she came upon the resource (e.g., a document file) that they wanted to retrieve. Unlike Archie, Gopher not only displayed a listing of resources, it was also capable of handling the interaction with a remote resource on behalf of the user. If the resource was a text file, for instance, it retrieved the file and then proceeded to display it. With Archie, a user had to manually FTP to the site where the file was located, retrieve the file using the appropriate FTP commands, and then open the file using whatever local application was suitable for the type of file that had been retrieved.

Every Gopher site, like Web sites today, was unique in the information its system contained. Some were entirely local, displaying information related to a single university or government agency. Others were more expansive in concept, covering large numbers of topics or providing comprehensive coverage of a single subject. Regardless, the design of the system, which was much like that of the Web, concealed both the details of the system and the location of the objects from the user. The menu listings made everything appear local, but in actuality the information content accessible through Gopher was distributed; the resources that were displayed might reside anywhere on the Internet. This localized view of distributed resources constituted much of the power and beauty of Gopher.

Gopher also contained searchable indexes (called indexed directory resources) to enable a user to locate specific information more quickly and easily. If a menu item was followed by the <?> symbol, it meant that it was a collection of information designed for an indexed search. When a user selected such an item, the user was presented with a prompt to enter one or more keywords to use in executing the search. Gopher then created a customized menu listing containing the matches returned by the search.

Two search-related tools were incorporated into Gopher in order to simplify and refine access to the mass of information quickly accumulating on the Internet. Both were named after Archie's comic book friends, since their purpose was much the same as that of Emtage's tool. But instead of indexing FTP sites, as Archie did, they indexed Gopher sites.

The first was named Veronica and was created at the University of Nevada at Reno. (As a safeguard against copyright complaints, the creators of Veronica formally declared that the name was an acronym for Very Easy Rodent Oriented Net-wide Index to Computerized Archives.) Veronica built a master index of Gopher site menus by connecting to Gopher sites, traversing their menu structures, bringing this information back to the originating Gopher server, and combining all the information into one listing. This listing would then appear like any other indexed menu item on the local Gopher site, thereby enabling a user to search any number of collected Gopher sites in one, simple operation. The concept of Veronica is similar in scope and function to current Web search engines. Both visit and traverse their respective type of sites on the Internet, collect information about their resources, and build a local database from the information they obtain. Users can then browse or search through this locally collected information to find and retrieve specific files or resources.

The other tool was named Jughead. (Its formal acronym description was Jonzy's Universal Gopher Hierarchy Excavation And Display.) It was similar in concept to Veronica, but its design reflected a slightly different perspective. Unlike Veronica, Jughead limited its search to a specific set of one or more named Gopher sites. Jughead created a searchable index for a narrowly defined area, like a particular university, and displayed an indexed menu item for that smaller set of Gopher sites. As resources multiplied on the Internet and redundancies and conflicting data started to appear at different locations, Jughead provided a finer measure of control over indexing sites. It was especially useful for indexing the Gopher servers in a local environment.

For a while, Gopher and the Web competed against each other for dominance in the realm of Internet information access and management. Both were relatively simple to learn and provided easy access to the growing diversity of information housed throughout the Internet. Both could handle a wide variety of resource types, including text files, graphics files, and video files. Both could also handle the other's files: from the Web you could call up and navigate Gopher sites; and from Gopher you could find and launch HTML files. Finally, from the server's, or information provider's, perspective, both provided the software and methodology to organize, manage, and share their information with others across the Internet.

In the end, the Web showed itself to be the more versatile and more popular information management system. The introduction of the Mosaic Web browser in 1993 marked the beginning of the Web's rise to dominance. But really it was the larger vision of the Web's engineering that doomed Gopher (and many other information management systems) to a shorter than expected life. Key to the Web's engineering and to its success was its inclusion of hypertext.

Indexing and Searching Information with WAIS

Unlike Archie, Gopher, and even the Web, the Wide Area Information Service (WAIS) was from its inception an Internet business venture designed to make money. Nevertheless, both free and commercial WAIS software and services were eventually created and distributed. WAIS was one of the first advanced search facilities developed for use on the Internet. It combined the ability to locate resources and files that matched supplied search criteria (e.g., keywords or a phrase) with a function that ranked the matched items against one another to help distinguish more likely candidates from less likely ones.

Development of WAIS began in October, 1989, in a project managed by Brewster Kahle at a supercomputer company called Thinking Machines. The first version that worked over the Internet was released in April, 1991. Like Archie and Gopher, WAIS was a client-server application. WAIS servers stored databases of information that had been specially indexed through a WAIS utility. A WAIS client resided on a user's computer and provided the interface through which a user could select a database and enter search criteria. Like Gopher, WAIS enabled a user to locate resources quickly and to retrieve those resources without knowing where on the Internet they were stored. WAIS differed in how it stored information in databases and how it performed its searches.

An information provider that wanted to make its resources findable through WAIS first had to build an index of those files and directories. A special WAIS utility was used to create these indexed libraries, or databases, of information resources. The practice of building an index from source data is common with many of the search engines available on the Web today. Indexes serve to summarize information about the location and contents of files. Search facilities read these indexes and attempt to match the supplied search criteria against the information they contain. A WAIS index could be built from the contents of a single directory, or it could contain references to files located on any number of computers spread across the Internet.

A user who wanted to search the Internet using WAIS could do so through a wide variety of clients. TELNET could be used to connect directly to a WAIS server. A local, WAIS client application was another popular possibility. WAIS searches could also be performed through Gopher and the World Wide Web. Since WAIS indexed information into individual databases, a user first had to select which database or group of databases they wished to use in their search. If the client being used did not list the database the user was looking for, or the user was unsure which database to select, it was possible to conduct an initial search against an index of known databases (as opposed to their content) to return a list of databases that might offer the most matches for the file or resource being sought. A simple form allowed the user to select one or more databases and enter search criteria; this form was similar to a Web form, with boxes to check next to the database names and an open area that accepted the input of text. The results of a WAIS search consisted of a ranked listing of sources, with the most promising results displayed at the top with a ranking of 1000 and others listed below with progressively lower scores. The higher the score, the more references were found to the search criteria that had been supplied. Not surprisingly, choosing the right keywords and knowing how to enter them affected the quality of the search results, no different than using a search engine on the Web.

The resources that were located through WAIS, like those found through Gopher and the Web, might consist of practically any type of file found on the Internet: plain text files, image files stored in GIF or JPEG format, audio files, and HTML files, among others. The ranking that WAIS provided, however, greatly reduced the effort required to distinguish the most likely candidates. The specific capabilities of the user's WAIS client determined what could be done with resources returned by a WAIS search. It might or might not be possible, for example, to view the resources directly; but it was always possible to retrieve a resource and save it on the local computer for later use. Many WAIS clients allowed the user to save queries so that a particular query could be easily re-executed at a later date. It was also possible to save the names of the indexed databases returned by the initial query so that the next time they could be selected immediately.

WAIS's strength was that its search facility based its results on the contents of documents, not simply on their names or locations, as Gopher's search mechanisms did. Therefore, it provided a faster and more efficient means of locating a particular resource. By itself, WAIS was a powerful tool: it successfully bridged the gap that separated information about file names and locations from information about their content. Moreover, when combined with the Web, WAIS established the first generation of Web search engines that helped accelerate the growth and usefulness of the early Web.

The next chapters, which present the history, evolution, and technology of the Web, will explain in more detail how these early information management systems influenced the engineering of the Web and how each of them, for at least a short time, became interconnected with the Web. They will also make clear how critical hypertext was to Berners-Lee achieving his goals with the Web, and how his work, in turn, made a significant contribution to the evolution of hypertext.

The Web is Born

A Working Definition of the Web

On his World Wide Web home page, Tim Berners-Lee describes his invention of the Web as:

> an internet-based hypermedia initiative for global information sharing.[1]

This description nicely summarizes what Berners-Lee hoped to accomplish with the Web, as well as what the Web has become through its decade or so of use. It also offers a good starting point from which to build a working definition of the Web.

First, Berners-Lee classifies the Web's operation as Internet-based. In doing so, he identifies the Web as a service of the Internet: an application that runs across the Internet, relying on and functioning with lower-level Internet services (e.g., TCP/IP). We can infer from the Web being Internet-based that it was designed with interoperability in mind. If you want to create a global networked application for use by as many people and from as many locations as possible, as Berners-Lee did, you design it for the Internet; and, as is explained at length in *The Internet Revolution*, when you design anything for the Internet, interoperability is where all your efforts must begin and end. In making the Web Internet-based, Berners-Lee knew that its success or failure would be measured by how well or badly he handled the engineering of the Web's interoperability.

Second, he categorizes the Web's composition as a hypermedia initiative. This helps to define what the Web does, the type of application it is. As was presented in the previous chapter, the term hypermedia and its associated term hypertext were coined by Ted Nelson in 1965 to describe a type of non-linear writing made up of interconnected information objects. In labeling the Web a hypermedia initiative, therefore, Berners-Lee is identifying it as this type of information management system: one that allows information to be structured in a non-hierarchical, non-linear fashion and that enables information objects (e.g., an entire document, a single phrase, or an image) to be linked with other documents or objects in virtually any manner that the author, publisher, or reader desires.

Third, he defines the Web's purpose to be global information sharing. Considering the Internet's primary goals were resource sharing and networked communication, his defining the Web's goal as global information sharing is in many respects the ideal complement. Like the creators of Archie, Gopher, and WAIS, Berners-Lee was faced with an ever-growing accumulation of information that was spread out over a complex and expanding network of computers, and locating, accessing, and sharing information was becoming more and more difficult. The Web was Berners-Lee's solution to the problem of how to share and interconnect this information. By choosing to deliver his solution as a service on the Internet, he enabled the Web to take on a global presence.

From the above, we arrive at the following working definition of the Web: the Web is an Internet service that functions as a hypermedia information management system for the purpose of global information sharing. This definition, much like the working definition of the Internet presented in *The Internet Revolution*, captures the principal characteristics that identify the Web's form and function, especially with respect to its technology. What it fails to capture and convey, however, is an indication of the Web's effect; it omits any reference to the presence that the Web has acquired through its use. It cannot, therefore, answer one of the most commonly asked questions about the Web (which is also a question frequently asked about the Internet): how it manages to be everywhere and yet in no one place, and how it can function without being controlled by some government agency or organization. Berners-Lee's explanation of why this is true for the Web applies equally well to the Internet. He wrote:

> The Web was not a physical 'thing' that existed in a certain 'place'. It was a 'space' in which information could exist.[2]

Our use of the Web has turned it into an information space, much as our use of the Internet has turned it into a meeting place called cyberspace.

This chapter presents the history of the Web's creation and evolution, starting with an overview of the key events in the Web's history. It describes how the Web's technology was first built, who built it, and the factors that influenced its design. It also describes how the Web grew to popularity and became commercial, and how and why the Web acquired some measure of formal, structured management through the creation of an organization called the W3C.

Tim Berners-Lee and a Short History of the Web

Tim Berners-Lee was born in London, England in 1955, and received a degree in Physics from Oxford University. Physics represented a middle ground between his long-standing interest in electronics and computers and his interest in mathematics. His parents were mathematicians who had both worked on one of the first commercial computers, the Ferranti Mark 1, making him an early second-generation computer scientist. During the late 1970s and early 1980s he worked as a programmer. Much of his work directly or indirectly involved the presentation and organization of information; for example, he developed typesetting software and worked on a generic markup language for document files. This work helped to prepare him for his creation of the Web.

During 1980, Berners-Lee spent six months on a consulting contract at CERN, the European particle physics laboratory in Geneva, Switzerland, where he wrote programs to help control the laboratory's particle accelerators. This short, initial period of employment at CERN had two effects. It introduced him to the extraordinary variety of people and computer technologies at CERN; and it inspired him to write his first Web-like application, which he called Enquire. (A description of Enquire is presented below.)

During his short stay at CERN, Berners-Lee also wrote a hypermedia-like program that allowed equipment operators to access and control various pieces of equipment through one of the lab's computer systems. Faced with the limitations of a 64-character by 24-line computer monitor, which was only capable of displaying a very small amount of information at one time, Berners-Lee divided the overall system into independent components or modules that represented each piece of equipment and its specific controls. He then interconnected the components in a linked, hierarchical structure, not unlike what was done in the Aspen Movie Manual hypermedia system that provided information on car maintenance and repair. An operator would start with a basic schematic of the entire system and then point-and-click through progressively more detailed information until the desired component was reached. The screen would then show a detailed view of the selected component and enable the operator to work its controls.

The solution Berners-Lee provided in creating this friendly, functional interface to such a large and complex system, despite the limitations of a small screen, was as elegant as it was simple. And it offers an early glimpse into how he was thinking about the management and presentation of information. His work on creating the Web was still roughly ten years away, but this early program illustrates that he regarded the structuring and interconnection of information in the same way as the developers of hypertext systems: as a collection of objects that could be linked and organized in a manner that specifically suited the information content and its use. Even though the organization of the information in this system was hierarchical, the method of navigating through the information was something new, bold, intuitive, and foreshadowed how information would be navigated on the Web.

Four years later, Berners-Lee returned to CERN on a fellowship. Much of his time there was spent working on something called Remote Procedure Calls (RPC). RPC was a relatively new methodology that allowed programmers to distribute processing for their applications over a network of computers. Instead of relying on one large, expensive mainframe computer to execute programs and return results, programmers could employ RPC to have their programs executed on any one computer of a network of smaller, cheaper machines. But it would still appear that their programs were executing on a single machine. As such, RPC promised reduced operating costs and greater flexibility with respect to developing and running programs. A well-implemented RPC system would harness the combined power of the network — a collection of interconnected computers able to share information and access each other's resources was more powerful than the simple sum of those resources — without requiring the programmers to understand the vagaries of the network itself. Since the RPC methodology was relatively new, Berners-Lee first had to spend time and energy convincing the management at CERN that an RPC implementation would prove useful, before he could build it. After gaining management's approval, he proceeded to implement a client-server RPC system over TCP/IP. This work would prove to be invaluable when, several years later, he came to design how the Web would function over the distributed network of the Internet.

By 1989, the RPC system was fully implemented and stable and Berners-Lee had recreated his Enquire program, which allowed him to track all the people, projects, and equipment in his work. (The original Enquire program, which he had left at CERN on an 8-inch disk, had been lost.) He had also become familiar with the relatively new, large-scale documentation management system at CERN called CERNDOC, which is described below.

With more time to devote to his own interests, Berners-Lee proceeded to organize his thoughts on information management in general and Enquire and CERNDOC in particular and, in March, 1989, he delivered a formal proposal for what would become the Web. This proposal, the first of two, took the form of a memorandum to his boss, Mike Sendall. Unfortunately, no one who read the proposal knew quite what to make of it. The information management system that Berners-Lee described in his proposal was designed to overcome the deficiencies that he recognized in both his Enquire program and CERNDOC. But it did so in such a new and original way that instead of being perhaps the *next thing*, it was so far removed from any existing document management system that no one knew quite what to make of it. His boss's comment, "Vague but exciting," written onto the proposal's cover, clearly indicated his support and interest; while his comment, "And now," at the end of the proposal, had the effect of sending Berners-Lee off to rework his proposal into something more practical and more easily understood.

Between his first proposal on information management and his second, describing his WorldWideWeb hypertext project, Berners-Lee spent considerable time refining and redefining his ideas and figuring out how to implement them. During this period, early in 1990, he attended a hypertext workshop that confirmed his belief that, despite the lack of commercial hypertext products, hypertext held the key to developing an information management system for CERN. At about the same time, the first NeXT computer arrived at CERN. NeXT was the company formed by Steve Jobs after he left Apple Computer in 1985 and it had created a desktop computer that combined the power, adaptability, and open architecture of Unix with the ease of use and built-in applications of the Macintosh. NeXT included a powerful development platform called NeXTStep as well as a large object library (i.e., a collection of reusable programs and program fragments). The system was designed with application developers in mind and, accordingly, it provided a rich development environment that was meant to reduce the time and effort needed to develop and prototype programs.

Berners-Lee managed to convince his boss to order him a NeXT for use in developing his information management system. The purchase of a NeXT led to Berners-Lee's meeting Robert Cailliau, the CERN manager who would co-author Berners-Lee's second proposal for the Web. Cailliau was an ardent Macintosh user. He had also discovered the Macintosh's built-in hypertext system — one of the earliest commercial hypertext products — and had put it to use in building a HyperCard application for making presentations, storing information about the activities of his group, and managing information for his trip reports. Cailliau was already thinking along similar lines as Berners-Lee with respect to information management and hypertext when he went to see Berners-Lee and his newly acquired NeXT.

While Berners-Lee drove the development effort forward, Cailliau focused on how to describe this new type of information management system so that others could more easily grasp its significance and potential. He also brought some much needed management experience to the project that impacted both the content and form of the proposal and the way in which the project would develop. Their proposal included Berners-Lee's new name for the project, WorldWideWeb, despite some protests from Cailliau, and presented a more business-like approach than Berners-Lee's original proposal, including a list of specific goals, a timetable, and a list of the resources that would be needed to complete the project. In brief, what they were promoting in their joint proposal was a user-friendly tool that would provide a single access point to all the information stored at CERN. CERN gave them the go ahead to continue working on the project, but failed to provide the additional personnel requested in the proposal. Nevertheless, by the end of 1990, and with only a half dozen or so people truly believing in and understanding the vision behind the Web, they set out to implement their plan. This meant applying their prototype of the Web to the information stored on the various systems connected across CERN's network. It also meant documenting and refining their work on the Web and exploring how to introduce it onto the Internet.

Before 1990 ended, while waiting on the decision of CERN's management, Berners-Lee had completed his initial development of the Web. The first Web server (http://info.cern.ch) was made public on the Internet before Christmas, although no one (yet) had the means to make much use of it. A feature-rich Web browser was running on Berners-Lee's NeXT machine and on another NeXT machine that had been installed in Cailliau's office. This first Web browser and Web server were used by Berners-Lee and Cailliau for communicating with each other and for managing the project.

Berners-Lee realized early on that the success of the Web — especially on a global scale — would be dependent on the development of browsers for as many types of computers and operating systems as possible. Since CERN had made it clear that such development was outside the scope of work they were willing to fund, Berners-Lee developed a toolkit that would help simplify and hasten the creation of browsers by other developers. He then requested and received permission to release the toolkit free of charge. Less than one year later, there were several X-Window workstation browsers available, and browsers for the Microsoft PC and Macintosh platforms were in the process of being developed.

With the initial obstacles overcome, a working Web server up and running, and a toolkit available to help others build browsers, Berners-Lee and Cailliau faced a new and different sort of challenge: how to convince people at CERN to use the Web. At the very least, they needed to give people a reason to use it. But before they could set about trying to convince people to use the Web, they first had to make the Web accessible to as many people as possible; very few people used a NeXT, and they could not wait for other people to create browsers or depend on that happening if no one could access the Web in the first place. Their first task, therefore, was to create a simplified Web browser that could be accessed from any networked computer through TELNET. This line-mode browser (as opposed to a graphical browser), completed by spring 1991, allowed the user to select numbered items off a list, not unlike Gopher; and it effectively eliminated the need to create browsers for all the various computer platforms at CERN. The line-mode browser had no embellishments, no bells or whistles. But it was fast, easy to use, and accessible from anywhere. It established the necessary interoperability to allow virtually anyone to access the Web server at CERN, including those on the Internet at large.

The solution to the question of how to convince people at CERN to use the Web came from XFIND, a locally created utility that was used throughout CERN to search and access all types of information. XFIND was even connected to the CERN phone book. XFIND's weakness was that it only ran on the computer center's IBM mainframe, and a user had to log in there before they could access it. By creating a gateway between the Web and XFIND, Berners-Lee enabled the many physicists at CERN, as well as remotely located users, to access XFIND without logging in to the IBM mainframe. This was a very practical application of Berners-Lee's Web. A local, commonly used tool that could only be accessed from a single computer was suddenly made accessible from any computer that had access to the Web. This was the beginning of a powerful new paradigm: the use of the Web as a single interface among, and access point to, an endless number of localized information resources, documents, and tools. Berners-

Lee applied this paradigm to other existing information sources by building additional gateways between the Web and servers that provided information through FTP, WAIS, and Archie.

Berners-Lee spent much of 1992 spreading word of the Web by attending conferences and encouraging others to build on what he had started at CERN. At the end of 1992, of the roughly one million Internet sites that existed worldwide, perhaps fifty ran Berners-Lee's Web software that enabled a computer to function as a Web server and thereby be counted as a Web site. But 1993 was different; it marked the turning point for the Web with a sudden surge of interest in the Web. This was due in large part to the release of a graphical Web browser called Mosaic by the National Center for Supercomputing Applications (NCSA) at the University of Illinois. Over the course of 1993, Mosaic became available for the three most prevalent computer platforms: X-Windows, the Microsoft Windows PC, and the Macintosh.

During 1993 the Web went from being a new, predominantly unknown service that accounted for a negligible amount of Internet traffic to a service that appealed to both novice and experienced Internet users and that accounted for some 2.5% of all Internet traffic; and the number of Web servers increased by a factor of ten to some 500 or more. But, for Berners-Lee, the popularity and growth that Mosaic brought came at a price. A large part of his vision for the Web was already being set aside: what he had meant to be a publishing and information-sharing platform was already showing signs of being used simply as another information gathering tool. Mosaic, and most of the popular browsers that followed, contained at most half the functionality of the original Web browser on the NeXT. Completely absent from these browsers were the capabilities that allowed the user to build, organize, and publish information. Consequently, Berners-Lee's vision of a personal Web space that existed alongside the public information space of the Internet was absent from the Web that was suddenly and furiously taking shape on the Internet.

It was also in 1993 that the first World Wide Web conference took place. It was organized by Dale Dougherty of O'Reilly and Associates and held in Boston. Some twenty people attended the conference, including Berners-Lee and several people from NCSA who had been responsible for creating Mosaic. The meeting was designed to discuss the future of the Web. What Berners-Lee took away from the meeting and brought back to CERN, however, was the clear and urgent conviction that the Web required some kind of formal, controlling organization or steering committee; otherwise, the conflicting interests and goals of individuals would result in implementation incompatibilities in the Web that would make it impossible to build the global information space he so strongly desired.

Berners-Lee continued his Web work at CERN by improving the existing Web software contained in his library toolkit, named libwww, refining the specification for his HyperText Markup Language (HTML), which was already well on its way to becoming more a presentation markup language than an information markup language (i.e., a language to specify typographic elements like boldface and italics rather than one to identify and categorize the content of information), and, perhaps most importantly, mapping the quickly growing Web (i.e., documenting the location of new Web sites and categorizing their subject matter). These efforts did little, however, to stop or even slow the work of others in adapting the Web in any way they wished. He needed, therefore, to find a way to establish standards that would safeguard the fundamental interoperability of the Web. But he also needed to create a forum and a process that would allow everyone to participate in how the Web would evolve. Amazingly, at CERN, the only full-time salaried members of the staff working on the Web were Berners-Lee and Cailliau. Meanwhile, outside of CERN, new corporations were forming, and they were devoting all of their considerable resources to development of the Web. One such corporation was named Netscape. Berners-Lee's solution was the creation of a World Wide Web Consortium that would bring together the interests of commercial, educational, and governmental bodies. The only question that remained was whether this consortium would be formed at CERN or across the Atlantic, in association with Michael Dertouzos and MIT.

With consent from CERN, Berners-Lee released the Web software into the public domain in April, 1993. The release of the software was necessary for the Web to sustain its grassroots following and appeal to corporations that were concerned about future license fees or mandated changes that might disrupt their use of the Web. It allowed anyone to use and develop the Web in any way they chose, provided CERN's involvement was mentioned in the code. Several months later, in October, he took his first formal step to establishing a controlling body for the Web when he delivered a memorandum to CERN management stating his intention to form a Web consortium, the title of which read: "World Wide Web Decision Point for CERN." Meanwhile, Cailliau developed his own plan to keep control and development of the Web within Europe. He was fearful that control of the Web would end up in the U.S., since the U.S. demonstrated the largest Web use and the most interest in its development. He called his initiative Alexandria, after the great library that housed all the books of the ancient world; and he appealed to the European Union to quickly form a standards organization for the Web before the opportunity was lost.

The escalating browser wars of 1994 introduced the first incompatibilities onto the Web, as developers willfully added features to HTML that only their browser would be programmed to read and interpret. These incompatibilities made apparent to Berners-Lee and others the urgency for a controlling body, if the Web was to have a future. As 1994 progressed, so did an agreement between MIT and CERN regarding the creation of a global World Wide Web organization, called the W3O, and an associated consortium of companies, called the W3C, that would provide funding in exchange for involvement in future technology decisions related to the Web. The idea was to allow the U.S. and Europe to work together to develop the Web protocols, manage the standards process, publish code in the form of reference implementations for anyone to access, and provide help to those interested in advancing the cause of the Web. Unfortunately, due to miscommunication and some mistrust, controversy erupted over how the U.S. and European organizations would interact, which would control the finances, who would receive credit for the creation of the Web, and, in general, who would really exercise control.

During this period, Berners-Lee was approached by commercial organizations eager to employ the Web for economic gain. Remarkably, he turned these offers down and remained faithful to his vision of the Web. He pursued control of the Web through both CERN and MIT. He then waited and watched to see which would take on the responsibility for housing and funding the W3O and W3C as politics and economics entered into the fray. Ultimately,

MIT won out; and in October, 1994, Berners-Lee and his family traveled across the Atlantic to Boston, where he began the difficult task of taking control over the Web's components (e.g., HTML and HTTP) as director of the W30. Some people regarded MIT's involvement and Berners-Lee moving to the U.S. as an affront to Europe, where the Web was born. But Berners-Lee's belief in the truly global nature of the Web meant that, for him, where he and the W30 were located was not of great significance.

Berners-Lee unofficially announced the formation of the W30 and the U.S. and European relationship established between MIT and CERN at the first International World Wide Web conference held at CERN in May 1994. The response from the packed audience to this news, and to his talk on the future of the Web in general, was highly enthusiastic. Everyone there understood the need for some controlling body and many were reassured by Berners-Lee's prominent involvement. But before the dust settled on the disputes surrounding where the Web's future would be controlled and by whom, two final changes occurred. First, CERN decided to relinquish its affiliation with the Web; accordingly, early in 1995, it transferred its European authority over the Web to France's national research institute for computer science, INRIA. Second, the idea of both an organization (W30) and a consortium (W3C) generated more questions and concerns than it was worth. Both structures were quickly consolidated under the banner of the W3C.

Web History Details

This section presents additional details on some of the more crucial developments in the Web's history. It includes a description of Enquire, Berners-Lee's first Web-like program for information management, an explanation of how standardized file markup arrived at CERN and led to the creation of HTML, and descriptions of the two formal Web project proposals written at CERN.

Enquire: A Hint of What Was to Come

When Berners-Lee first worked at CERN in 1980, he was not yet aware of hypertext or of Vannevar Bush's memex device. He did, however, understand the kinds of tasks computers excelled at, and he was interested in creating a program that applied a computer's facility to store and order information in a manner that mimicked a person's facility to freely associate various pieces of information. Like Bush, he wanted to create something that would aid his own memory; working in his spare time, he built a program to store information about colleagues, the computers in the lab, and his projects. Even though his program was only for his own use and ran on a single computer, rather than on a network of computers, he was already envisioning a global implementation that would link people, computers, and information.

Berners-Lee named the program Enquire, taking the name from a 19th century English almanac that he recalled from his childhood entitled "Enquire Within Upon Everything." The almanac was a compendium of information covering a wide range of subjects, including common rules of etiquette, cures for common ailments, and details on how to bury a relative. It even included aphorisms, like "Take care of the pence and the pounds will take care of themselves." In essence, it was an all-purpose source of information that could be consulted when one couldn't recall something or when one wanted to learn something new. It's easy to think of it as a 19th-century version of the Web, containing a wealth and diversity of information unrivaled by other contemporary information sources.

Enquire was a simple but powerful program. You started it by entering the program's name at a command-line prompt. This brought up the first or main page, which resembled, in purpose at least, a home page on a Web site.

```
Documentation of the RPC project                        (concept)


    Most of the documentation is available on VMS, with the two
    principle manuals being stored in the CERNDOC system.

     1) includes: The VAX/NOTES conference VXCERN::RPC
     2) includes: Test and Example suite
     3) includes: RPC BUG LISTS
     4) includes: RPC System: Implementation Guide
        Information for maintenance, porting, etc.
     5) includes: Suggested Development Strategy for RPC Applications
     6) includes: "Notes on RPC", Draft 1, 20 feb 86
     7) includes: "Notes on Proposed RPC Development" 18 Feb 86
     8) includes: RPC User Manual
        How to build and run a distributed system.
     9) includes: Draft Specifications and Implementation Notes
    10) includes: The RPC HELP facility
    11) describes: THE REMOTE PROCEDURE CALL PROJECT in DD/OC



Help  Display  Select  Back  Quit Mark  Goto_mark  Link  Add  Edit
```

Figure 1. Enquire Screen Page

Each page, or node, included a list of associated or linked pages at its bottom in the form of a numbered list. When you entered the number of the link item you wanted to pursue, Enquire displayed that page. You might, for instance, start by selecting a project description, and from there bring up information on the project's manager, and from there call up information on another project being managed by this same person. In this way, you charted your own course through the information, unrestricted by any imposed hierarchy. This was not hypertext, but it certainly sounds just like it.

Equally important, Enquire was an interactive program: in addition to finding information, it allowed you to add information pages and define how this new information was associated with existing information, thereby continuously adding to the store of data and to its interconnectedness. Even more to the point, you could not add a page without first linking it to an existing page. Everything had to be connected to at least one other point of reference. Ten years before the advent of the World Wide Web, here was a scaled-down information management system that clearly functioned as an interconnected web of information.

Enquire also stored information that defined and described the links between the pages. Whenever he added a link, Berners-Lee had to further qualify that link by specifying how the two pages were related. For instance, if a page described a programmer and it contained a link to a page describing a specific program, he then had to describe whether this person used the program, was its author, or had some other relationship to it, in order to document the nature of the link between the two pages. Moreover, this link then worked both ways: if Berners-Lee's home page included a link to his program, Enquire, the page on Enquire would then also include a link back to its author. Think how much richer the Web would be if it included such bi-directional links.

Enquire included two different types of links in order to account for the difference between building links in one's own set of documents and linking to someone else's documents. Links between pages in a single source were considered *internal* links. An internal link was bi-directional and would appear on the pages on either side of the link. Links to outside sources, whether another local file or someone else's file, were considered *external* links. An external link only functioned in one direction; otherwise, a single page with multiple links referencing it might be overrun with reverse links, and it would be necessary to store the link information in two places rather than one, which would quickly cause link information to become difficult, if not impossible, to manage.

The original Enquire program, which was created in 1980, was written in Pascal and ran on the none-too-common Norsk Data SINTRAN-III operating system. As mentioned earlier, it was left at CERN on an 8-inch floppy disk and was lost. When Berners-Lee returned to CERN and rewrote Enquire, this time for a DEC VAX minicomputer, he did so hastily and only managed to include functionality for internal links. He realized in using this more limited version of Enquire that his program failed to address a rudimentary but critical requirement for it to have any kind of future: Enquire was not engineered with the capacity to scale. It had no means to adapt or distribute its management as the system grew and more people started to use it; the larger it became, the less efficiently it would run. It could not, therefore, be used to implement a large and distributed information management system. He realized that his solution — his engineering for what would become the Web — was elsewhere.

CERNDOC and SGML: The Importance of Standardized Markup

Throughout the 1970s and 1980s, the work conducted at CERN was continually growing in both scope and scale; and the documentation related to CERN projects was being produced at an ever-increasing rate. What made matters worse was that scientists as well as support staff were routinely coming and going to and from the laboratory from countries all over the world, and they had little or no means at CERN to store and track the documentation they were producing or permanently record the raw data associated with their research. Information was being lost; or, at the very least, it could not be easily found and used by others.

The CERNDOC project, begun in 1984 (the year Berners-Lee returned to CERN), was designed to solve this problem. CERNDOC was a document filing and retrieval system that ran on the laboratory's central IBM mainframe. The vision behind CERNDOC was all-encompassing. It was designed to house tens of thousands of documents, allow for keyword searching through this database, display documents for review on a screen, and allow documents to be printed.

CERNDOC was developed just prior to the document production revolution begun by the brand new, WYSIWYG (What You See Is What You Get) electronic publishing tools, which were first available on Apple's Macintosh PC. It was engineered with simple, character-based terminals in mind and displayed text in a typewriter-like typeface; no graphics capabilities or typesetting embellishments were included. It was meant to collect, organize, and provide simplified access to documentation that was otherwise largely inaccessible. As such, it represented a sizable improvement to the everyday CERN working environment and it promised to become an important resource both to those at CERN and to scientists located elsewhere. It also demonstrated the importance placed on information management by CERN, since the project represented a considerable investment in time and resources in terms of its development and its ongoing maintenance.

For Berners-Lee, CERNDOC provided an example of a large-scale document management system that succeeded at storing and supplying much needed online access to information and that could be used to compare and contrast his own evolving ideas about information management and access. The structure of CERNDOC was purely hierarchical. Documents were categorized and organized according to traditional and familiar criteria, such as author and subject matter. The result was a tree-like structure containing branches and sub-branches that a user could traverse up and down in search of a particular document or in browsing a particular category. What was missing, from Berners-Lee's point of view, was a means to interconnect information across this rigid, imposed structure. The hierarchical structure of CERNDOC stood in sharp contrast to the fluid interconnectedness of Enquire and the free-forming, non-linear associations touted by the hypertext community. Additionally, hierarchical structures required some sort of centralized control and management; and a centralized document management system would not scale. Berners-Lee recognized that any type of hierarchical structure could never accommodate the anticipated growth and distributed content of his vision for the Web. He was thinking in global terms even when trying to tackle the immediate information management needs at CERN.

One element of CERNDOC that did appeal to Berners-Lee was the language used to encode all the documents in the system: the Standard Generalized Markup Language (SGML). SGML offered the means to represent or codify any element in a document so that it could later be identified and handled in any number of ways. For instance, in a word processor you might choose to put a book title in italics. In doing so, you are visually identifying a segment of text apart from the surrounding text and programmatically identifying a piece of information and differentiating it from the information surrounding it. This action of italicizing text, however, is a weak and limited form of identification and differentiation. Since the action is tied to a typographic feature, it is a function of presentation more than anything else. A title marked up as italics cannot be distinguished programmatically from a new technical term also marked up as italics. The word processor identifies these different elements, or information objects, the same way and treats them the same way in displaying them on a screen or printing them on a page. Lost in the process is why these elements were identified and marked up from the surrounding text in the first place (i.e., that one is a title and another is a new term that is being introduced).

SGML was created with the express purpose of identifying and differentiating all elements of a document through a highly customizable markup language. (Incidentally, SGML was one of the few common components in existing hypertext systems.) With SGML, for example, you can identify the title of a document as a title element and a new term as a terminology element, and still enable both to print as italicized text. Once a document is marked up with SGML, all sorts of new and powerful possibilities present themselves. For example, you could create different typesetting templates that would enable a single document to print in distinctly different formats; in one, you might print title elements in italics, while in another, you might use boldface. Unlike word processors, SGML separates information content from information presentation. More importantly, SGML clearly distinguishes one document element from another and serves to retain information about each document element that can be used for other purposes. By identifying all new terminology elements with SGML, for example, you now have the option to use a tool to locate all of those elements in a document, or across several documents, to create an index or appendix of new technology terms. Similarly, by identifying title elements, you now have the option to easily extract all the titles referenced in one or more documents to create a bibliography, conduct title searches, or create hyperlinks from each title to the location of the associated document.

The CERNDOC project showed that CERN management was keenly interested in implementing a large-scale, multi-purpose information management system that would benefit the local scientists and staff and the scientific community at large. By the late 1980s, CERNDOC housed a large and diverse database of documentation stored in SGML. Berners-Lee artfully used both conditions to his advantage. By pointing out the limitations of CERNDOC, he could more easily convince others of the viability of his own proposed approach to information management. By using SGML as a guide in developing his own, more simplified document markup language for the Web, HTML, he could be confident that it would easily fit into the existing document creation environment; and through HTML, he would be able to introduce hypertext to the community at CERN.

Information Management: A Proposal

Berners-Lee's March, 1989 proposal sought to convince CERN management that a distributed, hypertext-based information management system would meet CERN's document management needs and provide CERN with a better and more comprehensive solution than was possible with CERNDOC. On the cover of the proposal was the following illustration.

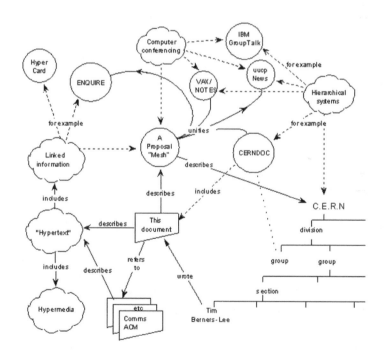

Figure 2. Proposal 1 Cover Diagram

This illustration presents a graphical view of the information sources and systems at CERN and how the Web (referred to as "Mesh" near the center of the illustration) would unify CERN's information by interconnecting them all. Today, someone familiar with the Web and with hypertext information systems should be able to examine this illustration and grasp its meaning. At the time, however, it presented such a radical departure in both how information was represented and how it was organized or structured that no one who received the proposal would have known what to make of it; Berners-Lee's thinking on the subject was something new and they had no frame of reference.

In 1989, information was typically arranged in some type of hierarchical structure, as the remnant of CERN's organizational chart in the illustration's bottom-right corner shows. Neat and orderly flowcharts were used to represent how information was organized and related. Most people recognized how to follow these hierarchical representations, with their boxes, connecting straight lines, and increasing level of detail. The circles, clouds, and cutoff rectangles, and the dotted, solid, and curving lines of Berners-Lee's cover illustration were as far removed from the flowcharts of the time as the system it depicted was from the existing methodology for information storage, retrieval, and connectedness.

In his proposal, Berners-Lee describes a non-hierarchical information management system that he represents as a collection of circles and arrows. The circles represent nodes, or pages of information about objects (e.g., people, projects, and hardware) and the arrows represent the relationships between objects (e.g., Fred is the boss of Ben or Mary manages project A). He then proceeds to contrast this organic web of notes, which attempts to model the real world, with the artificial, limited, and imposed hierarchy of tree-based systems like CERNDOC, the VMS help system, and newsgroups on the Internet.

He continues in the proposal to describe his experience with Enquire to present an explanation of hypertext. Then he lists the core requirements for the system he wants to build and briefly explains the reason for each:

- **Network accessibility**: the system would be distributed and operate over the network (as opposed to being centralized and running on one computer, like CERNDOC) to better accommodate the distributed computing environment at CERN and to simplify access.

- **Platform independence**: the system would be engineered with few if any hardware dependencies (like the Internet's protocols) to facilitate its implementation on CERN's wide assortment of hardware platforms.

- **Decentralized control**: the system would be managed in a distributed fashion and not require any type of centralized control (like the Internet), since only some type of decentralized management would allow the system to continue to function efficiently as it grew.

- **Widespread data access**: the system would be sufficiently modular and generalized to allow it to interconnect with existing data and information management systems (e.g., CERNDOC and XFIND).

- **Privacy**: the system would include features for users to make information available to others and to control access to that information.

All of these core requirements were fulfilled by the Web. The proposal also presents Berners-Lee's expectations regarding what the system could achieve. He discusses, for example, the benefits of conducting data analysis by mining the information accessible through the system, something that has recently become a considerable (and questionable) practice on the Web. He notes that the possibilities introduced by this type of large-scale data analysis include more easily locating missing information or anomalies and being able to take differing perspectives on information sources and acquire new insights or arrive at new conclusions. But, as is discussed later in the book, this practice of data mining, as it has come to be called, also has the potential for abuse. Berners-Lee briefly mentions the issues of copyright infringement and data security that are introduced onto a computer network that employs this type of information-sharing system. These were already known issues in the hypertext community. But he dismisses such concerns as secondary to the importance of information sharing in the CERN environment and states that features could be added at a later date to address these issues. Secondary or not, these very issues remain at or near the top of most lists that detail problems with today's Web.

The remainder of the proposal presents a highly generalized view of what such a system would look like at CERN and how it would be used. No details are provided on how development work would be conducted or about what could be expected in terms of deliverables; nor is a proposed schedule included. His boss's comments that the proposal was vague, but exciting nicely summarizes the only reasonable conclusion that one could draw from reading this first formal proposal for developing the Web. The proposal bears witness to Berners-Lee's vision and presents the foundation upon which the Web was subsequently built. Given all the information that was absent from the proposal, however, it does not describe a project that could be funded by any management team at the time (or now, for that matter).

WorldWideWeb: Proposal for a Hypertext Project

Berners-Lee's second proposal, co-authored by Robert Cailliau and distributed in November, 1990, was everything the first proposal was not. First, it focuses on an emerging technology, hypertext, as the foundation supporting the project. Second, it describes a specific systems architecture, complete with browser and server, and explains in detail how this architecture will function. Third, it provides project management information that describes the equipment and personnel needed to develop the system, along with goals and a general timetable for each phase of the project.

While the first proposal was written by a visionary and reads more like an essay extolling the benefits of hypertext information systems over existing hierarchical information management systems, the second proposal was written by an experienced project manager, is deliberately matter-of-fact and businesslike in its tone, and purposely downplays how radically different it is in concept from the other systems used at CERN. Even though the title of the second proposal suggests otherwise, there is clearly less of the Web in this proposal than there is in the first. For one thing, this proposal is concerned solely with implementing a system at CERN and contains no generalities about an implementation of the system on a larger scale.

This was the proposal CERN management needed to see in order to evaluate the work for possible funding. It enabled the managers to understand what work was going to be done and the potential benefits of that work for their environment. While they did not fund the project to the extent requested — and there's very little likelihood they (or anyone else) recognized the widespread potential benefits of such a hypertext system — they provided sufficient funding for Berners-Lee and Cailliau to design and build what would come to be known as the World Wide Web and that would, in a few short years, transform the Internet and pave the way for a revolution in how we access and publish information.

The Web is Formed

As soon as Berners-Lee received his NeXT computer, he began work on building his hypertext information management system. This was in September, 1990, shortly before Robert Cailliau got involved and began work on the second proposal. The development environment delivered with the NeXT was richer and more advanced than those included with other contemporary workstations, and Berners-Lee's project afforded a perfect opportunity to see what the machine could do. First, though, he needed a name for the project. He rejected Mesh (which appeared on the cover of his first proposal, from the previous year), MOI (for Mine of Information), and TIM (The Information Mine). When he settled on World Wide Web (which was first written without the spaces, as shown in the title of the second proposal) as a name that best conveyed the type of structure formed by the associated links of the hypertext-based system and signified its global design, it didn't take long for friends to complain that the name was too long. Some even complained that its acronym, WWW, had far too many syllables, making it difficult to use in conversation. Today, many people who work in the Web business world and who must commonly say the Web's acronym, such as when spelling the name of a Web server or the location of a Web page, avoid the excessive number of syllables by using the shortened expression: DubDubDub.

Engineering the Web: How to Begin

Berners-Lee originally hoped to buy one of the existing hypertext systems available in 1990 rather than build a hypertext system from scratch. But he immediately ran into several large obstacles. One was that people at the various hypertext technology companies found it difficult to understand the large-scale vision of the Web. Even though commercial products, like Guide from Owl Ltd., already included tools that looked and worked strikingly like Berners-Lee's Web browser concept (though they lacked an Internet component), no one was capable of grasping or believing in the global networked construct being proposed by Berners-Lee. The people building commercial hypertext applications were having enough difficulty trying to convince companies with conservative needs and interests in the power and benefits of hypertext. The idea that hypertext could be used across the Internet and on such a large scale was too far removed from the specific operating conditions and overall objectives that such companies had developed as part of their business models.

The second obstacle involved how existing hypertext technology made texts available for viewing and how they stored link information. Consider a product like Dynatext, developed by a company called Electronic Book Technology that had been started by hypertext guru Andy van Dam. With Dynatext, you created and edited documents in one form and then used a separate process to build the documents into electronic books for the purpose of creating optimized file versions for viewing. This practice of creating one type of file for composing and editing documents and another type for distributing the documents in their final form was common in the hypertext systems of the time. This was due to the fact that the coding of hypertext files was complex and the link information — the code that described each hypertext link and defined its destination — typically had to be updated whenever changes to the documents were made. The simplicity of something like HTML, the coding language Berners-Lee created for the Web's hypertext documents, stood in sharp contrast to the complexity of these other systems. Moreover, the same HTML file was used for performing edits and for displaying the document; no conversion or optimization process was necessary. The differences between the simplicity of Berners-Lee's HTML files and the complexity of the hypertext files from other systems were too great for any type of compromise to be reached. Yet again, the approach taken by Berners-Lee was so far removed from that taken by the hypertext community that none of the commercial hypertext developers believed his system could succeed.

Berners-Lee also needed a system that would scale, which meant that it needed to be decentralized. Otherwise, the Web could never become global. Here was yet another obstacle that prevented him from buying an existing hypertext system for use with the Web. All of the existing systems relied on some type of centralized database to store and maintain link information. This type of centralized control insured that link information remained up-to-date and consistent as changes were made to the system's hypertext documents. But such a system would be impossible to manage for anything other than a single or small computing environment. The only solution was for him to build a hypertext system himself.

NeXT is First

Berners-Lee began writing code in earnest for his World Wide Web project at CERN in October, 1990. He regarded the advanced features and sophisticated programming environment packaged with his NeXT computer as a considerable asset in building the software modules that would constitute the Web. They reduced the time and effort needed to write code and develop prototypes, which is precisely what they were designed to do. He would, however, come to regard the NeXT as a "cautionary tale."[3] The NeXT was a product as different from other workstations and personal computers as his proposed Web was from other hypertext and information management technologies. Its unique and progressive features — the selling points that were meant to generate large sales — were often cited as the reasons why the

NeXT failed to win over the market it was designed to dazzle and convert. It was, if anything, too different from the tools and environment commonly used for developing programs. It demanded dramatic changes in the way people worked in order for its new and powerful features to be taken advantage of. Berners-Lee realized that the Web would make similar demands. For the Web to succeed, people would need to adapt to the unfamiliar, non-hierarchical paradigm for structuring information that set the Web apart from other information management systems.

Like other Internet services, such as FTP and TELNET, the Web was designed as a client-server application. The client component was a Web browser application, which was the piece of the Web that Berners-Lee first began to build with his NeXT; it would allow a user to find and view hypertext documents as well as to create and edit such documents. The server component was a Web server application, which was built next; it would allow people to make documents and other information resources available over the Internet and to control access to those documents and resources. But before either the Web browser or server would be of any use, he first needed to write the code for the three core elements that make up the Web's technology:

- The HyperText Transfer Protocol (HTTP)

- The Universal Resource Identifier (URI)

- The HyperText Markup Language (HTML)

These three elements define how a Web client and a Web server communicate over the network (HTTP), how the address for a Web resource (e.g., a Web page) must be written (URI), and what form a Web document must take for it to be viewed by a Web client (HTML). Understanding what these three elements do and how they interrelate is essential to comprehending how the Web works. The following chapter provides a straightforward but detailed explanation of what they are and how they work. For now, the following descriptions should suffice.

HTML is a simple language definition for text files that describes the parts that make up a conforming HTML file (i.e., how the overall file must be structured with respect to a beginning, middle, and end) and the code that can be used to identify specific features of a document (e.g., its title, a paragraph, a list, and a hyperlink). In other words, just like other language definitions, HTML establishes the rules or syntax that must be followed to create a document that will be recognized and interpreted by a program that reads HTML, and it defines the code or vocabulary that can be included in an HTML file that will determine how the file is interpreted and displayed. The rules define how to mix control information or code, known as markup, with a document's text, images, and other data. The specific markup is used to identify the title of the document, its headings, paragraphs, boldface text, bullet list items, and so on. A Web client, such as the browser Berners-Lee created on his NeXT, was programmed with the complete specification that defines HTML and it used this information to read an HTML file, interpret its markup, and then display the file.

The URI (later renamed the Uniform Resource Locator or URL) defines the syntax for addressing resources on the Internet. An HTML file is one type of resource. But an Internet resource can be any type of object, including a graphics or audio file, an FTP or Gopher site, or an email address. This addressing scheme, which was not unlike that used for letters sent through the postal service, consists of several parts that, when taken together, uniquely identify the location of a resource. A common URI is the Web address of an HTML document, for example:

```
http://www.lobsters.org/recipes/lobsterroll.html
```

A URI can be entered into a browser in order to access the named resource. It can also be specified as a hypertext link in an HTML file; the link is clicked on to access the resource at the address specified by the URI. The URI shown above has three parts. The first part, http, identifies the protocol that the browser must use in order to retrieve the resource. The second part, www.lobsters.org, identifies the machine where the resource can be found. The third part, recipes/lobsterroll.html, identifies the location of the resource on that machine.

HTTP is the protocol that delivers Web files across the Internet. Like FTP, it functions in a client-server model and controls both the communication process, or handshaking, between the client and server and the exchange of data. The browser functions as an HTTP client and follows the rules of the protocol to reach across the Internet and request permission to retrieve a file or access a resource at the specified location. It then waits on the HTTP server's response as the server checks for permission to access the location and then checks to see if the file or resource exists and is available. The server responds either with an error message or with the data from the requested file or resource.

Key to the success of HTTP, and hence of the Web itself, was that HTTP be defined as simply as possible, so that it would retrieve HTML pages — the most common Web resource — extremely quickly. Berners-Lee kept the client-server conversation to a bare minimum, so that he could achieve his goal of retrieving a page in roughly one-tenth of a second. The speed with which hypertext pages were displayed across the Web convinced many people that the Web was not only viable; it was the future.

By December, 1990, Berners-Lee had completed his WorldWideWeb graphical browser/editor on his NeXT. He had also written the server software for HTTP, thereby creating the very first Web server. At this point, both his Web browser and his server resided solely on his NeXT computer. He then created an alias (i.e., info.cern.ch) for his machine. The alias functioned as an abstraction; it could remain the same even if the machine it was associated with changed. This would allow him to create addresses (i.e., URIs) for documents and resources using the alias as the machine name, but these addresses would not be forever tied to this one machine. (The Web may only have consisted of one machine, but he was always thinking of the future.) He then used his Web server to collect, manage, and make available all the documentation and program code he had written on and for the Web.

When Cailliau's NeXT arrived, the number of Web surfers suddenly doubled, from one to two. Berners-Lee and Cailliau could now at last demonstrate the Web and use it as it was designed to be used: to share information for the further development of their project. They didn't yet have formal funding from CERN. Nevertheless, by Christmas of 1990, the Web was live on the Internet. Their problem now was that the very machine that allowed Berners-Lee to develop the Web code so quickly was the most limiting platform from which the Web could grow (which is why the NeXT was considered a cautionary tale).

The Web that Was Lost

Before we move on from the Web's birth on the NeXT platform, it's intriguing to consider what the Web might have become had the NeXT computer been the rule rather than the exception. The first Web browser was written on a NeXT and the computer's more advanced architecture enabled Berners-Lee not only to develop code faster and more efficiently, but also to build a more powerful and sophisticated browser than would have been possible on a different type of computer. But the browser he built on the NeXT could only operate on that one computer platform. Subsequent browsers, including most if not all of those used widely today, did not include all of the features and functionality of that original NeXT Web browser. Consequently, part of the original Web was lost. This loss amounts to more than some missing bells and whistles. It includes a missing portion of the Web, a type of personal Web for individuals, and several important features that contributed to the new paradigm for information management made possible by hypertext.

Berners-Lee considered his Web to be more than a means to manage and provide access to information. It was also meant to be a tool that allowed an individual to publish his or her own information, to annotate information for future reference, and to create a personal Web that would coexist with the global World Wide Web. His NeXT Web browser was as much a Web builder as a browser. It did not, for example, have or need a function for bookmarking locations. That's because it functioned more like his Enquire program: an individual's home page and personal library of documents and resources resided on that individual's local computer; and links to the public Web were part of those pages and documents. This is considerably different than an individual's typical home page today that consists of some location on a remote machine that displays news, weather, and other commonly served information. Berners-Lee's original Web was as much a private information management system as a public one. It allowed for everyone's Web to be unique; and each individual would choose whether or not to share part or all of their Web with others.

Another distinctive and lost feature of the NeXT browser was that it opened a new window with each link, rather than continually reusing a single window. This meant that graphical elements were not displayed together with their associated text. Instead, they too came up in a separate window. One reason for this approach was that it worked better for scientists, who were expected to be the first audience for the Web. Scientists could more easily refer to associated items, like graphs and photos, when they were displayed separately; they could scroll through one text while other texts and their linked, associated items also remained in front of them.

The NeXT browser/editor also supported and illustrated the belief that new ways to access and view information called for new paradigms to present that information. Unfortunately (for some), the browsers that won market share did so by reaching out to the familiar, and Web pages soon became little more than magazine-like layouts with embedded links. What was sacrificed in the process was an information-rich Web that focused more on content than on format. This issue is discussed at length in a later chapter, when we look at one possible future for the Web: the Semantic Web.

What was lost with the NeXT browser was arguably what needed to be lost in order for the widespread use that Berners-Lee envisioned to occur. Browsers needed to be simple, intuitive, and fast. They needed to hide the technology of the Web in order for the Web to grow. For the Web to find any users, however, it first had to grow beyond the NeXT.

Building the Web: Where to Begin

The principal issues that Berners-Lee and Cailliau faced at the start of 1991 were:

- How do you get people on the Web without first creating a browser for all the various computer platforms currently in use?

- How do you create a Web of resources to induce people to use the Web without a large community of Web users to create and make available these resources?

■ Should they narrow their focus and adapt the Web specifically for use at CERN in the hopes of garnering support and funding, or continue to think in more general and global terms?

They addressed the browser issue by asking a CERN intern, Nicola Pellow, to develop a line-mode, non-graphical browser. This type of simplified browser would work on almost any type of terminal. Equally important, it would provide access to the Web via a TELNET window since it could be run from a Web server; other browsers had to be installed on and run from an individual's client computer. The following shows how CERN's home page on the Web appeared through this browser:

```
CERN Information                                    Welcome to CERN

CERN is the European Particle Physics Laboratory in Geneva, Switzerland.
Select by number information here, or elsewhere (Return for more).

Help[1]                  On this program, or the World-Wide Web project[2].

Phone Book[3]            People, phone numbers, accounts and email addresses.
                         See also the analytical Yellow Pages[4], or the same
                         index in French: Pages Jaunes[5].

CC Documentation[6]      Index of computer centre documentation, newsletters,
                         news, help files, etc...

News[7]                  A complete list of all public CERN news groups, such
                         as news from the CERN User's Office[8], CERN computer
                         center news[9], student news[10]. See also Private
                         groups[11] and Internet news[12].

From other sites:-
1-24, <RETURN> for more, Quit, or Help:
```

Figure 3. CERN Line Mode Browser Page

In appearance Pellow's line-mode browser looked very like Berners-Lee's Enquire screen. Its design was purposefully simple. It was meant to be easy to use, with choices made simply by selecting a number; and it required no special equipment (not even a mouse) or training. The browser's effect was immediate; it made the Web accessible to anyone on the Internet. This was a critical achievement in their efforts to get the Web noticed and develop a grassroots interest in the Web's future.

Berners-Lee addressed the issue of a lack of resources on the Web by enabling the Web to access and display other types of Internet resources through a Web browser, not just HTML files. The first resources he added were Internet news articles and newsgroups. These were two early types of community forums on the Internet that allowed people to share information by holding discussions on specific topics and asking and answering questions. The information in these articles and newsgroups had been growing rapidly through the 1980s and into the 1990s, as had the number of people accessing and adding to this accumulating store of information. People used these resources either through a local program configured to access Internet sites that provided these information services, such as rn (read news) or nn (no news), or through TELNET. Now they could use a Web browser to use these Internet resources, too. In one simple step, Berners-Lee enhanced and simplified access to these community forums and the large and diverse store of information they contained while promoting and justifying greater use of the Web.

Additionally, Berners-Lee made it possible to access Gopher and WAIS sites through the Web by further adapting the URI and its operation within a Web browser. The information services of Gopher and WAIS were quickly gaining in popularity; and, as more and more of these sites became available on the Internet, they threatened to overshadow his own work. But his design for the Web was meant to be all-encompassing and he very clearly demonstrated the larger scope of the Web by incorporating access to these other Internet-based information management systems into the Web. In doing so, he quickly and cleverly changed the Web forever: far from lacking resources, it now provided access to more Internet-based information than any other single application.

Berners-Lee needed to attract interest in the Web and demonstrate its usefulness to the CERN community, just as he had already done through the efforts described above with respect to the larger Internet community. Accordingly, he decided to apply the same overall approach to making existing Internet resources available through the Web to the local CERN resources. His first target was the CERN phone book, something that virtually everyone at CERN needed to access from time to time. The phone book was stored in a database on an old mainframe computer, and its administrator had to provide access to it from a wide variety of equipment. This resulted in a great deal of maintenance work, as well as a lot of ad hoc programming to accommodate all the various computer platforms at CERN. A single interface provided by the Web would greatly diminish the time and effort needed to administer access to the phone book. It was not difficult, therefore, for Berners-Lee to convince the administrator of the phone book, Bernd Pollermann, to help him with the programming that would be required to make CERN's phone book accessible through the Web.

Pollermann's job was to create the phone book server, while Berners-Lee took on the task of installing a browser on everyone's machine. The server needed to perform two basic functions. First, it had to interpret the information provided by a user (e.g., a last name to be used in a search of the phone book), pass this information on to the existing mainframe-based database, and collect the resulting information delivered by the database. Second, it had to convert this resulting information into a compliant HTML file so that it could be interpreted and displayed by a Web browser. The server ended up being half Berners-Lee's HTTP Web server (written in C) and half Pollermann's interface to the mainframe's data (written in REXX). The successful completion of this server meant that the CERN phone book, its search engine, as well as other catalogs of information that were stored in the same database, were made accessible through the Web. To make this newly created resource known to as many people as possible at CERN, Pellow's line-mode browser was ported to and installed on as many different platforms as possible, including everything from mainframes to PCs using DOS. Since the browser was simple to use and provided access to information that people at CERN needed all the time, it was readily accepted and used.

Berners-Lee's and Pollermann's work on the CERN phone book quickly and quietly succeeded in getting the Web dispersed throughout CERN. The next step was to get people to understand that this was really just the beginning. Berners-Lee wanted to get the people at CERN to view information, like the CERN phone book, as he saw it: not as a collection of highly specific and unique information objects, but as generalized information objects that, at least on one level, were all equivalent. To him, information existed as abstract objects; and these abstract objects were waiting to be interconnected. His goal was simple, but large: "one information space."[4]

The Web Begins to Spread

The Web first arrived in the U.S. in May, 1991. Not surprisingly, it was through the physics community that the Web first crossed the Atlantic; it was also due to a shared enthusiasm for the NeXT computer platform. Paul Kunz from the Stanford Linear Accelerator Center (SLAC) in Palo Alto had read about the Web on one of the newsgroups that he followed; he had also spoken with Berners-Lee about the Web over the phone. Neither introduction to the Web had caused Kunz to pause and consider how he might apply the Web to the information resources in his own environment at Stanford. But when Kunz visited CERN and watched a demonstration of the Web given by Berners-Lee on his NeXT, the Web caught his attention and started him thinking.

Kunz already had a NeXT back in California, which greatly simplified the process of setting up Kunz's computer for use with the Web. He and Berners-Lee had no difficulty transferring the necessary programs over the Internet to his machine; they then tested the installation. From CERN, Kunz and Berners-Lee accessed Kunz's NeXT computer in California, started up the newly installed Web browser, and used it remotely to view Web pages back at CERN. Even with this doubling in the distance traveled by the data (the Web browser in California had to copy the Web page contents from CERN to California and the displayed page then had to travel back to CERN for them to see it), Kunz was amazed at the speed with which the Web copied and interpreted the information contained on the Web pages.

As soon as Kunz returned to California, he met with SLAC's librarian, Louise Addis, showed her the Web, and instructed her to begin work on creating a Web server with an interface to their large, online catalog of documents. This work was similar to that done by Berners-Lee and Pollermann with XFIND and the phone book at CERN. The SLAC library housed a collection of scientific preprints (i.e., advanced copies of published scientific papers) dating back to 1962; and a database at SLAC called the Standard Public Information Retrieval System (SPIRES) that contained online versions of these preprints had over time become a widely used resource in the community of particle physicists. Kunz and Addis recognized that the Web was the solution they needed to simplify access to SPIRES from across the Internet. On December 12, 1991, http://slacvm.slac.stanford.edu went live on the Internet and became the very first Web site in the U.S.

The eagerness with which the Web was accepted at SLAC prompted Berners-Lee and Cailliau to push more strongly for expanded resources at CERN. It also inspired them to promote their work beyond the world of physicists to the general programming community. The success that the Web achieved with the database of documents at SLAC, just like the successful application of the Web to XFIND and the phone book at CERN, demonstrated the greatest strength of the Web and, potentially, its greatest appeal: simplified and unified information access to any type of information and in connection with any type of existing information management system.

Berners-Lee started posting notices about the Web on several newsgroups, including the one for hypertext enthusiasts, alt.hypertext. These notices included information about the Web's design, goals, and software. People began downloading the software and many who managed to create their own Web sites started emailing comments, suggestions, problems, bugs, and requests for enhancements back to Berners-Lee. He, in turn, posted their Web site addresses on the info.cern.ch site and recognized that their contributions would help ensure the future success of the Web. Eventually, the growing number of newsgroup postings related to the Web required the creation of its own newsgroup called comp.infosystems.www. The sharing of information through the newsgroup postings and the direct exchanges of information between the early Web site creators and Berners-Lee mark the beginning of the grassroots involvement and growth of the Web that continues to this day.

Hypertext '91 Conference

The hypertext conference, Hypertext '91, took place at the very end of 1991 at a hotel in San Antonio, Texas. Berners-Lee and Cailliau attended the conference and what happened there clearly illustrates how far apart the Internet, hypertext, and the Web were at this time. They had hastily submitted a paper for the conference, but it was rejected. It was considered incomplete in that it failed to include sufficient references to current work being explored in the hypertext community and it promoted concepts that were contrary to some of the guiding principles of hypertext architecture at that time. They were, however, allowed to set up a demonstration.

Setting up their demonstration of the Web was fraught with difficulties. First, no Internet connections were available at the conference. The hypertext community saw absolutely no relationship between its future and that of the quickly growing and nearly commercial Internet, so the organizers of the conference had not requested that any Internet connections be made available. To get Internet access, they first had to convince the hotel manager to run a phone line into the conference room. They then had to convince people at the local university to allow them to access their Internet service. They also had to convert their Swiss modem to work on the lower U.S. voltage and through a different type of plug. This required taking the modem apart and soldering the line wires directly to the modem. In the end, it all worked, and they were able to show the NeXT graphical browser as well as the simpler line-mode browser.

At the time, members of the hypertext community modeled their systems as large, complex, all-inclusive solutions to the business of information management and presentation. These systems provided the means to create, edit, share, and publish hypertext documents; and there was nothing small or simple about them. Additionally, they were expensive to purchase, difficult to integrate into an existing computer environment, and required specialized training before they could be used. Therefore, the people who were demonstrating these systems at the conference, as well as most of the other attendees, were unimpressed by the demonstration of the World Wide Web. To them its simplicity meant that it was limited; and it lacked the refinements and power of their hypertext implementations. Many did not even consider the Web a true hypertext system at all. But while few people recognized the power and potential in the Web's simple design in 1991, every demonstrator at the very same conference only two years later included some connection to the Web as part of their hypertext product.

The Web is Discovered

It was apparent to Berners-Lee and Cailliau in 1992 that, for the Web to gain widespread acceptance, it would be necessary to build graphical browsers for the most popular computer platforms. This meant creating browsers that would run on Microsoft Windows PCs, Apple Macintosh computers, and X-Windows workstations running the Unix or SunOS operating system. They didn't have the time or the resources to develop these browsers. Fortunately for them, people outside of CERN took up the work of creating these browsers in pursuit of their own interests and objectives.

The Web Browsers

University students were largely responsible for creating most of the early graphical Web browsers. A very advanced browser was released in May, 1992 by Pei Wei, a student at the University of California at Berkeley. He called his browser ViolaWWW and it was written in his own interpretive computer language called Viola. ViolaWWW was essentially a Java-like enabled browser (i.e., a browser capable of running small, independent programs) years before the Java programming language was introduced by Sun. It displayed graphics along with text, handled animations, and could download and run embedded applications very like today's Java applets. It was, however, very difficult to install and only worked on workstations running the Unix operating system.

Cailliau was a longtime Macintosh user, so he set out to write a browser for it. The project he began was later finished by Nicola Pellow, and by the end of 1992 there was an incomplete but functional browser named Samba for the Macintosh.

An X-Windows browser for Unix systems, called MidasWWW, was also created in 1992. It was written by Tony Johnson at SLAC and was specifically geared to an audience of physicists. MidasWWW was the first browser to incorporate the use of plug-ins. Plug-ins are independent applications that display one or more specific file types; they are launched by the browser on the user's computer when the user selects a type of file associated with one of these applications. Johnson created this functionality in MidasWWW out of the need to handle the display of PostScript files. The database at SLAC stored its document preprints as PostScript files, a file format designed not for display, like HTML files, but for printing. The plug-in functionality allowed him to associate a program that could interpret and display PostScript files (in Johnson's case, this was a freeware program called Ghostscript) with the filename extensions, .ps and .eps, used in naming PostScript files. When a user clicked on a hyperlink that identified a PostScript file, MidasWWW would automatically launch Ghostscript to display the file on the user's computer. The same approach could be used for other types of files and other applications. As such, plug-ins provided a simple, modular approach that greatly increased the value of a browser as a unifying application capable of accessing and displaying virtually any type of file. Unfortunately, Berners-Lee failed to convince Johnson to consider developing his browser for a larger audience just as he had failed to convince Wei to do the same with his ViolaWWW browser. For both Johnson and Wei, their browsers fulfilled their respective needs, and that was sufficient.

1993 brought several substantial innovations in the development of browsers. Dave Raggett at Hewlett-Packard in Bristol, England, devoted his spare time to creating a browser called Arena. Raggett was interested in displaying magazine-like Web pages with graphics, tables, and text all intermixed. The features and functionality of Arena, therefore, focused on the presentation of information, as did many of the popular browsers that shortly followed.

In sharp contrast to Arena was a non-graphical browser that ran on basic character-mode terminals, also known as dumb terminals. It was, in essence, a full-screen version of Pellow's line-mode browser. It allowed a user to scroll up and down through a document, as opposed to paging through a document in one direction. It also included the capability of using a keyboard's arrow keys to move a cursor through the text; and in this manner a user could navigate to a hyperlink and then press the Return key to select it. This browser, called Lynx, was developed at the University of Kansas as part of a campus-wide information system. It began life as an independently developed hypertext system that used Gopher as its main protocol and included its own hypertext language. But a student named Lou Montulli modified Lynx for use with the Web, and it was released as a Web browser. Lynx was successfully ported to many platforms and continues to be used today.

Recognizing early on how useful the Web would become to the legal community, a co-founder of the Legal Information Institute at Cornell University, Tom Bruce, created a Web browser called Cello for the Windows PC. Bruce's interest was in providing law findings and other legal information online. A test version of Cello was made available in March, 1993, and the final version was released that summer. Cello was the first browser available for the Windows PC market and was designed to view hypertext documents that contained embedded graphics, audio, and video files.

The first browser to gain widespread use appeared in 1993; it was named Mosaic. An X-Windows version was released first, followed by a version for the Macintosh and another for the Windows PC; this made Mosaic the first multi-platform browser. Mosaic was created at the National Center for Supercomputing Applications (NCSA) at the University of Illinois at Urbana-Champaign by a staff member named Eric Bina and a student named Marc Andreessen.

The Mosaic browser supported audio and video files, forms, bookmarks, history files, and more. More important than its features, perhaps, was the fact that Mosaic was very easy to download and install, which is probably the principal reason it quickly became the most popular non-commercial Web browser. Also important to its appeal, and new, was the keen interest taken by Andreessen and others in continuously fixing bugs and making enhancements as feedback poured in from users. The popularity of Mosaic demonstrated the rapidly increasing interest in the Web and gave rise to much speculation concerning the commercial possibilities of both the Web and Web browsers. Not surprisingly, many of the people behind Mosaic later worked together to create the first commercial Web browser, Netscape's Navigator, as discussed below.

The Internet in a Box

In 1994, the first shrink-wrapped Internet product came on the market. It was produced by a company called O'Reilly, an early and avid supporter of both the Internet and the Web. O'Reilly was principally a publisher of computer-related books, and it used its expertise with the quickly evolving technology of computers and networking to explore how the Internet and the Web could be used for electronic publishing. In 1992, O'Reilly published the first book to bring the Internet to the general public. It was called "The Whole Internet User's Guide and Catalog" and it included a separate, albeit short, chapter on the Web.

In 1993, O'Reilly launched the Global Network Navigator (GNN), which was described as an online interactive guide to the Internet. GNN was a very early general information site; it contained news stories, a quarterly magazine, an art gallery, advertising, and an online version of "The Whole Internet" book. Initially, subscription was free; but soon after it was launched it became a pay service. It was, in general, designed to compete with America Online (AOL), but it offered more far-ranging and sophisticated services for Internet users than those provided by AOL.

Success with GNN prompted O'Reilly to create an Internet in a Box product. Even though people could freely download the software they needed to access the Internet and to browse the Web, the download process was not simple and much of the required software configuration (e.g., entering the IP address for a DNS server or the half dozen pieces of information relating to an email account) was beyond what most individuals were willing to attempt on their own. O'Reilly's product was designed to eliminate the need to download software and minimize the amount of information an individual needed to understand and type in before they could get started. It provided two ways to connect to the Internet, a subscription to GNN, software that included the Mosaic browser, email, a USENET news reader, and more. It also included three books on how to make use of the Internet's resources.

For the very first time there was an off-the-shelf product that could bring the Internet into people's homes. The Web was key to making this happen, if only because of its ability to put a friendly and familiar face on the growing number of information sources spread out across the Internet. The Web was also key to making this product, and many others to follow, a success.

Dinosaurs Demonstrate the Web

While 1993 brought a number of new and innovative Web sites online, one site in particular, created by a commercial art student named Kevin Hughes at Honolulu Community College in Hawaii, impressed many people by its ability to both educate and entertain. It also clearly demonstrated the vast potential of the Web, which most people had yet to comprehend.

Hughes decided to take on the task of creating a campus-wide information system after downloading a copy of Mosaic and exploring what others had done on the Web by visiting the sites listed on Berners-Lee's CERN Web server. Unimpressed by the generally dry and static sites he visited, he decided to do something new and different. While wandering the campus with a camera in the process of making a virtual tour, he came across an exhibit about dinosaurs. It was then that he decided to make an online version of the exhibit for access via the Web.

As he toured the exhibit with Rick Ziegler, a history professor from the college, Hughes took photos and then recorded Ziegler as he described each item. After digitizing the photos and recordings into files, he created a collection of Web pages and organized them with navigation buttons for stepping forward and backward through the tour. The Web pages combined the photos with descriptive text in a magazine-style layout; one could click on a photo for a larger image of that dinosaur or click on an icon of a speaker to hear Ziegler's narration. The site also included a movie.

This kind of multimedia Web presentation was new and striking. More than any site that had been created, it persuasively conveyed the broad and powerful potential of the Web to integrate different types of information content and, in the process, create something larger than the simple sum of its parts. It also foreshadowed what was to come. The site was used as an example by Berners-Lee, Cailliau, and others to convince many people of the Web's limitless potential.

Netscape Shows the Web to the World

Jim Clark, the founder of Silicon Graphics, Inc. (SGI), which produced workstations optimized for the generation of 3-D graphics, co-founded with Marc Andreessen in 1994 the first large-scale commercial enterprise that would change the Web, and the Internet, forever. Originally, their company was named the Mosaic Communications Corp.; but a few months later, in April, 1994, due to legal issues with NCSA over the use of the name Mosaic, they renamed the company Netscape.

With many of the original team members who developed NCSA Mosaic, and with Lou Montulli, who had created the Web version of Lynx, Netscape launched a development effort to create a commercial version of the Mosaic Web browser. They released a test version of their commercial browser in October, 1994. The first formal version, named Navigator 1.0, was released two months later on December 15. They nicknamed their browser Mozilla, a play on Godzilla and Mosaic, thus making clear their intention to devour the browser market that Mosaic had so clearly established.

Versions of Netscape were released for Unix workstations, the Macintosh, and the Windows PC. The code they created was written from scratch, so that there would be no copyright infringement with respect to Mosaic; and they prided themselves on creating browsers that were faster than Mosaic. They released their product not as other commercial software was then released, in a shrink-wrapped covered box, but over the Internet itself, free for the taking from anywhere in the world. In doing so, they set a precedent that many would soon follow. People wondered how they were going to make money by giving away their product. But the money would come later. Meanwhile, Navigator was being downloaded faster than they could count.

The overwhelming, apparently overnight success of Netscape made headlines. Accordingly, it also brought far more attention to the Web, to the Internet, and (potentially) to a new way of making money. In a few short months, most people browsing the Web were doing so with Netscape's Navigator. More importantly, there were suddenly a lot more people on the Web and, therefore, on the Internet. When Navigator was launched, the Web was in fifth place measured by the amount of traffic each service generated across the Internet. Four months later, in April, 1995, the Web reached first place, displacing FTP, and it constituted more than 20% of all Internet traffic.

While 1995 brought the Web to the attention of the world, it was the business world in particular that was suddenly scrutinizing the Web and, more generally, the Internet as a platform for new business ventures. Jim Clark knew that Netscape would soon be facing serious competition from many well-financed rivals, not least of which would be Microsoft. So he took the company public on August 9th, 1995, a short sixteen months after it had been formed. After one day of trading, and with no profits on the books, Netscape produced the largest initial public offering (IPO) ever and was suddenly worth $4.4 billion.

Microsoft Bows to the Web

In April, 1994, just as Jim Clark was renaming his company Netscape and work had begun in earnest on establishing a commercial side to the Web, Bill Gates suddenly reversed his company's position on the Internet and on the Web, which had largely amounted to ignoring their existence, and decided that Microsoft's next operating system, Windows 95, would come packaged with software for accessing the Internet. He also spent $2 million to get quickly into the browser market by licensing code from a small company called Spyglass, a spin-off from NCSA. Later that year, at the Comdex computer trade show, Gates announced that the Microsoft Network (MSN) would be created and that software to access MSN would be built into Windows 95.

In one bold move, Gates decided to take Microsoft into competition not only with existing online services like America Online and Compuserve, but with the nascent Web browser market dominated by Netscape. Gates had tried, but failed, to buy his way into Netscape and license the browser for inclusion with Windows 95. However, two weeks after Netscape's IPO in August 1995, Windows 95 started to ship, and with it was the first version of Microsoft's Internet Explorer browser, based on the Mosaic code from Spyglass. The product was weak; it was slow and lacked features common in other browsers. Because of the way it was packaged, however, it was only a matter of time before it would eclipse Netscape and become the most commonly used browser, which it did four years later in 1999.

Meanwhile, earlier in 1995, Compaq had become the first computer hardware manufacturer to include a browser with its product when its PCs began shipping with Netscape Navigator. The browser market and the Web had quickly become a commercial playing field. No one knew what to expect, but everyone realized that things were only just getting started.

Before 1995 drew to a close, Gates set the tone for what was to come. He gave a speech to the press in December that focused on Microsoft's Internet strategy. His message was that Microsoft would, going forward, "embrace and extend" the Internet. To the business community this meant one thing: fierce competition from a monopolistic company with enough resources to overwhelm the competition. To the largely grassroots Internet community with its commitment to and dependence on open standards, his message meant something else: Microsoft would introduce its own features and standards and try, through its dominance of the market, to make them de facto standards. For both communities, however, these were fighting words.

The Web Spins Threads of Control

The Web is by definition decentralized, like the Internet. Decentralization was key to allowing the Web, and the Internet, to scale (i.e., to continue to function efficiently as its size and usage increased). It was also hoped that decentralization would allow users of the Web to create and publish information just as easily as they could browse information provided by others. To some extent, this hope was realized. But how do you achieve decentralization *and* allow unlimited access to the code that defines and implements the functionality of the Web *and* expect to maintain the kind of interoperability that enables the Web to function in so many places and on so many devices? In other words, who defines what is, and what is not, the Web?

In the beginning, there was Berners-Lee, his vision, his Enquire prototype, and a quest to produce something like Vannevar Bush's memex device. Then came the first code and the creation of HTML, HTTP, and the URI/URL. The Web was born. Berners-Lee and CERN then proceeded to make everything known about the workings of the Web freely available. How else could the Web become the global entity Berners-Lee sought? In doing so, however, he also gave away any absolute control over the Web's future.

For the first couple of years, while the Web developed at CERN and while it was still easy for Berners-Lee to exercise control because so few people even knew of the Web's existence, standards bodies and a Web consortium were the farthest thing from anyone's mind. But as browser creators — independently and somewhat frivolously — tossed in new features (e.g., blinking text), as governments and corporations started to take notice and stake out their territory and vie for control, and as many people wondered if anyone would take responsibility for the future course of the Web and exert control, Berners-Lee had to make decisions to ensure that his invention had a future, and, more particularly, a future that was in line with his goals for the Web.

The Issues: A Web Unraveling

The sudden popularity of NCSA's Mosaic in 1993 brought the media's attention to the Web, but it focused more on NCSA and Mosaic than on the Web itself. Concern over this misdirected attention combined with an uneasy feeling after meeting with the Mosaic team of developers that left Berners-Lee worrying about the Web's future. At about the same time, the University of Minnesota announced that it would start charging a licensing fee for commercial use of Gopher, which had until then been entirely free for both personal and commercial use. Many people immediately expressed concern that CERN might do the same with the Web. No one knew what to expect, which, among other things, jeopardized the commercial viability of the Web.

HTML, the language that purportedly defined Web documents, was in fact not a language at all. Berners-Lee had never formally created a language specification to define what was and what was not HTML. He had simply applied his knowledge of the SGML that was used at CERN to create a simplified markup language that CERN people would find familiar. But as more browsers were built, it became clear that anyone who wanted to could, and often did, extend HTML with new features. The simplest and perhaps most notorious example was the <blink> attribute included in Netscape Navigator that caused text to blink on and off like a flashing cursor. The feature was not even documented by Netscape; it was simply there for people to find and use. It was someone's idea of a bonus.

Apart from the questions of whether such additions were wanted or not and whether they would be considered good or bad, they clearly signaled a problem that, if left unchecked, would greatly reduce the value of HTML in particular and the Web in general. It did not, for example, take long for notices to appear on Web sites indicating that they were best viewed with one browser or another. Such notices were antithetical to the very nature of the Web and to the overriding principle of interoperability on which the Internet was founded and on which both it and the Web relied. A solution was needed.

Standardization

Soon after global interest in the Web started to accelerate, Berners-Lee began thinking about how to maintain consistency in the way HTML, HTTP, and the URI were used. He looked to the Internet for guidance, and decided to start on the road to standardization through the Internet Engineering Task Force (IETF), an open membership organization where interested people could gather, start up a working group to discuss and debate issues, and, ultimately, define standards for themselves and others to use in implementing compliant products.

Berners-Lee followed IETF rules and, at the summer 1992 meeting, he held a birds-of-a-feather session to see if there was sufficient interest in forming a working group to standardize his URI specification. This meeting, and the meetings that followed of the working group that was eventually formed, introduced Berners-Lee to the political and personality conflicts that such meetings often manifest. The name itself, Universal Resource Identifier, incited much conflict, as some saw only arrogance in the use of universal, and even the use of identifier was considered to be insufficiently accurate. This is how the URI became the URL (Uniform Resource Locator). However, after nearly two years of trying and failing to reach consensus, Berners-Lee gave up his pursuit of an IETF standard and instead issued his own URI specification for the Web as Request For Comments 1630 in June, 1994.

In terms of outstanding issues, HTML offered the greatest challenges. Many people and organizations were proposing extensions that either suited their specific needs or at least favored some specific design goal. But rather than create a formal standard, Berners-Lee and the W3C decided to follow the Internet maxim of "rough consensus and running code" and issue a formal recommendation for HTML conformance. It was hoped that this would at least constrain the growing divergence in HTML coding and limit further browser incompatibilities.

One individual, Dan Connolly, identified very early on the kinds of conformance problems that would (and did) occur if some effort was not made to standardize HTML. He regarded HTML as a type of SGML. But it was missing a key SGML component called a Document Type Definition (DTD) that formally prescribed what the language consisted of and how it was structured. With a DTD, an individual (or a program working on behalf of an individual) could easily check HTML files to determine if they were conforming or non-conforming. In addition to the interoperability benefits it provided (e.g., knowing that conforming files would display the same through conforming browsers), a DTD made it possible for programs other than browsers to make use of the HTML files. Such uses of HTML files are explored later in this book.

Through Connolly's work, and later the work of many others, a series of HTML specifications did emerge under the banner of the W3C. These specifications gradually but powerfully extended the capabilities of HTML. The fracturing of and tinkering with HTML, however, did not disappear; some companies, most notably Microsoft and Netscape, continued to develop their own unique extensions, in an attempt to extend the functionality and popularity of their particular browser implementations. As any Web developer can attest, the lack of a formal and rigid HTML standard has been responsible for a lot of extra work, headaches, and grief.

Commercial Influence and Control

One corporation that took a very early interest in the Web was the Digital Equipment Corporation (DEC). DEC representatives visited Berners-Lee in 1994 at CERN shortly after he had started talking with Michael Dertouzos, Director of MIT's Laboratory for Computer Science (MIT/LCS), about forming a Web consortium. DEC was planning to use the Web technology for substantial changes within the company, and they were eager to know how committed CERN was to the Web's future and how decisions were being made.

Like many who understood the Web's potential, they wanted some assurance that any effort they put into developing and using the Web would not be wasted or undone through some sudden or unexpected change in the Web's path. They wanted to know if there were plans for a governing body at CERN to oversee the Web. When Berners-Lee explained that efforts were being made to establish a consortium along the lines of the one created for X-Windows, the DEC representatives were pleased.

When the W3C was formed several months later, DEC was one of the first companies called and invited to join. They accepted, as did Netscape, Hewlett-Packard, IBM, and others. The interests of all these companies were, in one way, the same. Standardization and control through a governing body like the W3C meant that they could bank on the Web's future. They could develop products and strategies to make use of the Web without fear that something was going to change without their knowing about it.

Ownership and Leadership

When CERN first looked at the Web and tried to evaluate its worth, it decided that charging for the Web software would probably not cover the administrative costs for the paperwork. This was in 1991 and, while the original code and associated information were now accessible on the Internet, oversight of the Web and its future was unambiguously held by Berners-Lee and CERN.

Just two short years later, in 1993, there was a modest but quickly growing community of Web enthusiasts. Questions were being asked about the Web's future and commercial ventures had been started. Control of the Web was generally acknowledged to still be held by Berners-Lee and CERN, but it was now clear to many people, including Berners-Lee, that this situation could not last much longer.

Before 1993 ended, both CERN and Berners-Lee formally relinquished their ownership of the Web. By getting CERN to agree to freely release the code for the Web, and by deciding at the last minute not even to issue the code under the General Public License (GPL) of the Free Software Foundation, Berners-Lee managed to place the Web technology into the public domain. This effectively put to rest any concerns raised by the licensing of Gopher. It simultaneously accommodated both commercial and non-commercial interests in the Web. It also helped to promote the global and unconstrained Web that Berners-Lee envisioned.

From that point on, ownership of the Web was not an issue. No one could claim ownership in any way, shape, or form. Leadership, on the other hand, was still vested in Berners-Lee. He took his leadership, along with his vision, with him when, in 1994, he joined Michael Dertouzos and MIT/LCS to become Director of the newly created W3C in Boston.

Through the W3C, Berners-Lee planned to "lead the Web to its full potential." The W3C would coordinate and help direct activities related to the growth and development of the Web. It would develop and distribute protocols for the Web, produce standards documents and recommendations, and provide reference code and general help implementing these standards. It functions today in exactly this capacity, with Berners-Lee still its Director.

The Mechanics of the Web

2

The Mechanics of the Web

Whereas previous chapters focused on the Web's history and on the history and relevance of hypertext and other information management systems, this chapter explains the mechanics of the Web. It describes, for example, what happens when a hyperlink is clicked, how a Web file is coded, what a Web server consists of and how it operates, and how information submitted through a Web form is read, interpreted, and used.

The functionality of the Web can be more easily presented and understood by dividing its technology into its building blocks — the underlying components that remain predominantly hidden or obscured from most individuals — and its applications — the tools and services that individuals directly and indirectly interact with when they use the Web. The core underlying components of the Web consist of: the Web's protocol for negotiating and exchanging information across the Internet, HTTP; its mechanism for addressing resources, the URL; and its markup language for encoding its primary, or native, resources, HTML. Understanding the functions that these core components perform and how they generally operate is necessary to understanding the overall functionality of the Web. Fortunately, the engineering behind these components and how they interact with one another was kept purposefully simple and straightforward. Each of these components is described at length in the following section.

The principal applications and programming services of the Web give form to the Web's information space and provide access to that space through their implementation of HTTP, the URL, and HTML. These tools consist of: a Web server application to manage a site's information resources and access to those resources; a Web browser application to manage a user's interaction with the Web's resources; and various types of Web programming services to bridge the gap between the Web and all the other types of computer applications that house or produce information or perform calculations, such as databases and project management tools. The functioning of these tools, like that of the Internet applications presented in *The Internet Revolution* (e.g., FTP and email), primarily consists of negotiating how to communicate and handling the transfer of data (e.g., sending and receiving the contents of an HTML file). While they share this basic functionality, however, each takes on a different role and different responsibilities in performing their collective job of delivering the Web's distributed and diverse information resources to the individual. Each of these tools is described at length in the final section.

The Building Blocks of the Web

Every networked information management system must satisfy the following basic requirements. First, a system must be able to read and interpret information content for the purpose of displaying that information to a user. Just as common conventions used in formatting information enable a reader to recognize the beginning of a new paragraph through the use of an indented first line or recognize the title of a chapter or the heading of a new section of text through the use of a boldface font or a larger typeface, an information management system must be able to store and display information in a way that distinguishes its form or format from its content. It must handle the representation of information in some way that captures the raw data or content (e.g., the words and punctuation of a paragraph) as it records additional information, often referred to as metadata, that describes and categorizes the content (e.g., where a paragraph begins and ends).

Although not all computer information is stored in files (databases, for example, store information in tables consisting of rows and columns), information that is displayed to a user either resides in some type of file format or it is arranged into a file on demand (i.e., created dynamically, on-the-fly, as needed). There are dozens of different file formats, many of which are proprietary in nature, like Microsoft Word files. It would be impractical to create a system to accommodate all of these different file formats, especially given that new file formats continue to be created. One option is to accommodate a subset of these existing file formats; but that would, from the outset, limit the interoperability of such a system. A simpler and smarter option is to create an openly defined, generic file format that would, if done correctly, effect interoperability in two important ways. It would enable files in this format to be accessible from any number of different computer platforms and different types of devices and display in much the same way across these various platforms and devices; and it would allow others to create filters to translate existing file formats, even proprietary formats, into this new, generic file format.

Once a system has a means to read and interpret information through one or more file formats, it needs a way to identify and locate information, which constitutes its second requirement. Each file and information resource in an information system needs a unique name and address, just as each individual needs a unique postal or email address in order for the respective mail systems to work. If an information system is being designed to function over the Internet, it can take advantage of an existing address system to partly satisfy this requirement. The Internet's Domain Name System (DNS), which was examined in *The Internet Revolution*, comprises an address mechanism and location service for uniquely identifying and locating any computer on the Internet. By using DNS, an information management system would only need to add the means to locate a specific file or resource in order to access information on any computer connected to the Internet.

The third and final requirement of an information management system is that it needs a way to access information once that information has been identified and located. Every request to access information through a computer amounts to copying that information from its original, source location to some other location specified by the program making the request. An information system, therefore, needs to include a methodology or protocol for making such a request, performing the copy operation, and storing the copied information.

The World Wide Web satisfies these fundamental information management system requirements through its three core components:

- **HTML**: the language used to encode Web files.

- **URL**: the generic syntax used to encode Web file and resource locations as well as other information resources available through the Internet.

- **HTTP**: the protocol (i.e., set of rules) that allows computers to communicate across the Internet, exchange Web-related messages, and copy data.

Together, these components enable the Web to function as a global information space. They provide a way to publish, locate, retrieve, and display information across the Internet. There is nothing complicated about how these components work or how they interact. More than anything, it was the simplicity of their design and operation that was responsible for the speed with which they were adopted by so many individuals and organizations and the extent to which they have become integrated into so many computer system environments and applications. The following sections describe each in some detail.

HTML: The Language of Web Files

Information available on the World Wide Web is contained in files that are waiting to be accessed and displayed. It is also generated dynamically, on demand, when separately stored information fragments are retrieved from such sources as database tables and time-sensitive news feeds in response to such actions as executing a query or logging into an account and are then assembled into a file. Either way, this information is predominantly coded in HTML, the HyperText Markup Language, so that it can be quickly and efficiently displayed by any number of Web browsers.

HTML is the *lingua franca* of the Web: the common, openly defined (as opposed to proprietary) file language specification designed to represent and interconnect all types of information on the Web. HTML fulfills three critically important needs of the Web. First, it provides a small and straightforward framework for creating viewable and printable documents, a framework that is sufficiently simple and generic that it allows other types of documents to be translated into HTML with little to no information lost in the process. Second, it allows any existing (or future) type of file to be referenced by and incorporated into an HTML document, thereby greatly extending the types of information that can be part of an HTML document. Third, it provides a simple, but all-important means to encode hypertext links, the threads of the Web that tie information together. The Web is not limited to handling HTML files; it includes the capability to access and display a wide variety of file types and to interact with other types of Internet sites, as the next section on the URL explains. But HTML provides the expected and much needed baseline interoperability that serves to unify information on the Web, no matter its source or composition. This information interoperability of the Web complements the communication interoperability of the Internet. Moreover, it constitutes one of the principal factors behind the Web's success as a service on the Internet.

All HTML files contain two types of information: plain text that is meant to be displayed and embedded tags enclosed by less than (<) and greater than (>) signs that constitute the control codes, or directives, of the markup language. The control codes enable a browser to distinguish text that is part of a heading from, for example, text that belongs to a paragraph or text that constitutes a hyperlink. The following is a simple, but complete example of an HTML file.

```
<!-- this is a comment and will not be displayed -->
<html>
<head>
<title>Defining the American Lobster</title>
</head>
<body>
<h1>The American Lobster</h1>
<img src="images/lobster.gif">
<p>
The American lobster, known as <i>Homarus Americanus</i>,
resides largely in the Northwest Atlantic ocean from Labrador
to Cape Hatteras. For more information, see:
<a href="http://www.lobsterusa.org/lobsterdef.html">
the full lobster definition page</a>.
</p>
</body>
</html>
```

Figure 1. Sample HTML file

The first thing to note about HTML files is that most of the tags occur in pairs, such as `<title>` and `</title>`. These pairs enclose, and thereby unambiguously identify, associated text by marking its beginning and end. The `<title>` code, for instance, identifies the text for the title element of the Web page, which is typically displayed at the very top of the browser's window and is also used as the text for a bookmark. Note that the second element of a pair includes a slash (/) that distinguishes the end tag from the start tag.

The second thing to note about HTML files is that they always contain certain mandatory tags that identify the file as an HTML file and divide the file into two distinct parts. The `<html>` and `</html>` tags at the file's top and bottom identify that this is an HTML file and formally demarcate its beginning and end. The `<head>` and `</head>` tags identify the file's header portion, which is used to define information about the file, like its title. Information contained in the header portion of an HTML file is never displayed as part of the page. Often the header area also includes meta tag information (i.e., information that describes or categorizes the file and that is used by search engines and other Web tools). The `<body>` and `</body>` tags identify the file's body portion, which is used to contain all the information that constitutes the page displayed by a browser.

The reason that HTML files are divided this way is easier to appreciate when the file is viewed from the browser's perspective. By separating the page contents from information that describes the page or affects its processing in some way, HTML enables the browser to load and interpret all of the page's general instructions before it begins the process of interpreting and displaying its contents. This approach is more efficient than if these same instructions were distributed throughout the file in terms of the work the browser needs to perform before it can display the page, and it contributes to the speed in which a typical HTML file is displayed. Although the header portion of an HTML file may only include its title, as in the sample file, a common use of the header is to define general presentation-related information and specific typographic settings, often in the form of something called a style sheet. This information may indicate, for instance, that headings labeled `<h1>` are to be displayed using a 16 point Helvetica typeface, if it is available. When the browser comes across text demarcated by `<h1>` tags, it already knows exactly how to render it in the browser's window.

Unfortunately, even the small and simple HTML file shown above will not necessarily display the same way in all browsers, or even in different versions of the same browser; and the more complex the file, the more disparities there are likely to be. The reason for this is explained below. The sample HTML file should, however, display more or less as follows:

The American Lobster

The American Lobster, known as Homarus Americanus, resides largely in the Northwest Atlantic Ocean from Labrador to Cape Hatteras. For more information, see: the full lobster definition page.

Figure 2. The Rendered HTML FILE

The sample file includes two other commonly used HTML elements. First is the image tag, `<img>`, which identifies the location of a graphics file containing the image of a lobster. Here the image file happens to be local, which means that it resides on the same machine as the HTML file that references it. Part of the power of the Web, however, is that this image file might reside elsewhere on the Internet; for example, it might just as easily reside on another machine attached to the same local network or on a remote Web server located in another state or country. If this were the case, its location would be specified differently in the `<img>` tag, but the image would display in exactly the same way; and the difference in the location of the file would be transparent to the user.

The other HTML element included in the sample file is in many respects the most significant of all the HTML tags. The anchor tags, `<a>` and `</a>`, are the principal means of specifying hyperlinks. They are used to connect the information contents of one document to other documents, to associated information in the same document, or to any number of other resources, local or remote. The general syntax of the anchor tag is as follows:

```
<a href="Link-Location">Display-Text</a>
```

The hyperlink location is known as the destination of the hyperlink. In the sample file, the destination is the address, or URL, of another HTML file. But the destination could be any type of file, resource, or program, as explained in the following section. The display text is the anchor or label that appears on the Web page; the anchor may appear as underlined text or text highlighted by a different color or font, or it may even appear as an image. Clicking on the highlighted display text (or image) activates the hyperlink, which causes the browser to locate, retrieve, and display the specified file, resource, etc.

Hyperlinks are what make **the** Web **a** web. It is by means of hyperlinks, which are the way that HTML implements hypertext, that information on the Web is interconnected. There are no limits on the types of hyperlink destinations that may exist; any type of file or information resources can be specified in a hyperlink. Accordingly, hyperlinks can be used to display a weather forecast for a particular city or region, start playing a movie or a song, start up a game of tic-tac-toe, or simply take a reader from the top of a file to its middle or end as is commonly done through a table of contents composed of hyperlinks. There is nothing complicated about how hyperlinks are coded into an HTML file or what happens when they are activated. The hyperlink in the sample file above is probably the most common form of hyperlink. Its destination consists of three parts: the protocol to use in order to access the resource, the site where the resource resides, and the local name and location of the resource. Clicking on its anchor will cause the browser to use the HyperText Transfer Protocol, http, to contact the referenced Web server, www.lobsterinfo.org, retrieve the file, lobsterdef.html, and then display it. There is nothing more to it.

When Berners-Lee first created HTML, he never considered that anyone would view HTML code directly. Instead, he expected people to use some tool, like the browser/editor of his NeXT, to create and edit Web pages; doing so would shield them from the details of the language's syntax. As he anticipated, most people today use their browser or a specialized Web builder application to create and edit HTML files, making it unnecessary to learn the specific syntax of HTML. Moreover, many desktop publishing tools now allow users to export documents as HTML files for publication on the Web. And yet some people still choose to learn the language and work directly with the HTML tags to manually mark-up their documents. They do this for two reasons: first, the language is relatively simple and files can be created and edited with the most basic tools, and second, humans produce better, cleaner HTML code than any program can create.

Since its creation, HTML has grown and changed considerably. The basics of HTML, as illustrated above, have remained stable. But the language has been extended by both individual companies, like Netscape and Microsoft, and by the W3C. The W3C continues to publish formal recommendations that represent a consensus among its members regarding changes and enhancements to the language. There is, however, no single standard for HTML. For this reason, some files display differently on different browsers, and features that function correctly in one browser may not, unfortunately, work at all in another. Despite the lack of a standard, HTML has proven itself an invaluable resource for unifying information. It has done so by introducing a common file format that anyone can use and by establishing a simple, powerful, highly effective way to interconnect information through hypertext.

URL: The Location of Web (and other) Resources

While HTML is the language of Web files, it is the URL (Uniform Resource Locator) that defines how to reference the location of those files. The URL is a simple, but highly extensible, addressing scheme; it locates HTML files and all types of other files and resources that are available through the Web or through virtually any other service that operates on the Internet.

Several HTML tags accept a URL as an attribute in addition to the anchor (<a>) tag used for hyperlinks, including the image tag (<img>) used for specifying the location of a graphics file and the form tag (<form>) used for specifying the location of a program that handles the processing of information submitted on a Web form. The basic form or syntax of a URL is the same no matter the type of file or resource being specified or where the URL is being used (i.e., in an anchor tag, some other HTML tag, or manually entered in a browser window). The sample file presented earlier includes the following URL as a hyperlink:

```
http://www.lobsterusa.org/lobsterdef.html
```

This URL, like all URLs, contains two basic components. The first component appears before the colon and specifies what is known as the *scheme*. The second component, which follows the colon, specifies the location of the file or resource and sometimes includes additional information; the exact syntax and optional parameters that may be used in conjunction with the location varies according to the scheme that has been specified. The purpose of the scheme is to identify the type of object that resides at the URL's location. Typically the scheme refers to a particular Internet service and the scheme's name is the name of that service's protocol, as is the case with such services as FTP, WAIS, and Gopher. This URL specifies its scheme as `http`, which stands for the HyperText Transfer Protocol (presented below) and is the principal protocol of the Web. In this instance, the scheme indicates to a browser that the URL points to an object that is accessible on the Web and that the browser should use HTTP in order to retrieve it. The remainder of the URL uses syntax specific to the HTTP scheme to indicate that the object is available at the network address, www.lobsterusa.org, and is named (or located at) /lobsterdef.html on that machine.

As is the case with many key components of both the Internet and the Web, the power of the URL lies in its simplicity and in its generic, all-encompassing composition. The following sample URLs are representative of the type and diversity of URLs that can be commonly found on the Web.

Sample URL Usage	
Scheme	Sample URLs
HTTP	http://www.lobsterusa.org/ http://www.lobsterusa.org:8080/ http://www.lobsterusa.org/lobster.html#photo http://www.lobsterusa.org/find.pl?t=american
FTP	ftp://www.snowfiles.org/USA/snowflake.gif ftp://fred:iluvlucy@sitcoms.net/ILY/lucille.jpg
GOPHER	gopher://lobster.net/pubg/main.txt
WAIS	wais://lobster.net/pubw/info.txt
FILE	file://localhost/home/lucy/lobsterrecipe.html file:///home/lucy/lobsterrecipe.html
TELNET	telnet:fred:iluvlucy@crustaceansrus.net:848
USENET	news:comp.infosys.www.announce nntp://news.lobsterusa.org/alt.lobster.usa/388
EMAIL	mailto:crusty@crustaceansrus.net
APPLICATION	pnm://lobmusic.com/lobstersong.rm

While these sample URLs present only minor differences in their syntax, the actions associated with them differ substantially. The first four — HTTP, FTP, GOPHER, and WAIS — retrieve files, but from four entirely different file management systems. The FILE URL provides a more generic mechanism for retrieving files; it is typically used for linking to files on the local computer rather than to remote files accessible on the Internet. The TELNET URL provides terminal (login) access to a remote machine; its syntax includes options for a valid username and password, eliminating the need to be prompted for this information before access is granted. (Including authentication information as part of a URL, particularly a password, is not a smart thing to do given the obvious security implications; but the option to do so with this type of URL illustrates how a URL's syntax is adaptable to the particular scheme being used.) The USENET URL provides access to individual news articles or entire newsgroups. The EMAIL URL, a very common Web page hyperlink, allows an email address to be treated as a special email object (as opposed to being treated as ordinary text, like a postal address or a phone number); clicking on an EMAIL URL typically signals the local computer to launch its default email application, open a mail composition window, and fill in the recipient's address with the address from the URL. Finally, the APPLICATION URL is a generic scheme meant to accommodate any type of application, such as an audio application that plays music files, a document viewer application that displays PostScript files, or a productivity application that displays spreadsheets and bar charts.

The URL may have begun its existence as part of the infrastructure of the Web's technology, but since it filled a void in the infrastructure of the Internet, it was quickly adopted as an Internet-wide mechanism for identifying and locating files and resources. For example, an email message that contains a URL to a downloadable file from an FTP site or to an audio file from a radio station's music on-demand site may have nothing whatsoever to do with the Web. The email application, like a Web browser, reads and interprets the URL in order to locate and retrieve the specified file; neither its interpreting the URL nor its retrieval of the resource involves the Web. The Web's power, however, lies in its ability to use the URL in conjunction with HTML to unify and simplify access to all the different types of files and resources that are available on the Internet.

The versatility of the URL specification extends beyond the types of services and schemes that it already accommodates. It was designed with the future in mind. The syntax of the URL is sufficiently general that it can accommodate new services, resources, and file types as they are created. More importantly, by including the Domain Name System (DNS), the Internet's network addressing mechanism, as part of the URL's specification, Berners-Lee created a resource addressing mechanism that would grow as the Internet grew. The simplicity of HTML further ensured that anyone would be easily able to specify these URLs. It's one thing to define a system to locate resources and quite another to make such a system easy to use. But, with HTML and the URL, Berners-Lee did both and, in doing so, he removed any lingering boundaries and uncertainty relating to where or how information was stored on the Internet.

HTTP: The Protocol of Web Files

HTTP, the HyperText Transfer Protocol, is what powers the Web; that is, HTTP is the mechanism that enables a computer to reach out across the Internet, negotiate with a remote computer regarding a particular file or resource, and retrieve a copy of that information so that it can be displayed, or otherwise used, on the local computer.

HTTP is an application-layer Internet protocol; it runs over TCP/IP, using the default TCP port number 80. (Each established service on the Internet is assigned a different default port number to help simplify interoperability; and each port acts like a separate telephone line that waits for and only accepts incoming requests for that one associated service.) Like other application-layer Internet protocols, such as FTP or the email protocols, POP3 and IMAP4, HTTP's job is to control the handshaking between two computers and to communicate and resolve issues related to the location of the requested data, permissions for access to that data, and any special requirements for packaging the data before it is sent. TCP/IP takes responsibility for the handling and transportation of the data, as it does for most of the traffic over the Internet.

HTTP, like many other Internet protocols, functions according to a client-server model, with a browser acting as the client and making the requests and a Web server answering the requests and providing the data. HTTP defines the rules in order for Web applications to do the following:

1. Establish a connection between the client and server.

2. Issue the request for data.

3. Wait for a response from the server, followed by the requested data or a message.

4. Close the connection.

This process of exchanging information was designed to be as simple and as fast as possible. Most browsers indicate the state of this conversation as it progresses somewhere in their window. After clicking on a hyperlink, the following sequence of messages will typically be displayed: "Connecting to ...," followed by "Sending request ...," followed by "Transferring data ...," and often ending with "Document done." The following sample conversation shows the type of data exchanged by a client and server when requesting an HTML file through a Web browser. Comments appear in boldface and are enclosed in square brackets.

```
[client requests file lobsterdef.html]
GET /lobsterdef.html HTTP/1.0
Connection: Keep-Alive
User-Agent: Mozilla/4.75 [en] (X11; U; Linux 2.2.14-5.0 i686)
Host: fmertz.iluvlucy.com
Accept: image/gif, image/x-xbitmap, image/jpeg, */*
Accept-Encoding: gzip
Accept-Language: en
Accept-Charset: iso-8859-1,*,utf-8

[client signals end of information with blank line]
[server replies with OK, followed by the file contents]
HTTP/1.1 200 OK
Date: Thu, 13 Sep 2001 03:06:26 GMT
Server: Apache/1.3.21-dev (Unix) DDQ/1.0.3
Content-Location: /lobsterdef.html
Connection: close
Content-Type: text/html

<html>
[remainder of file]
</html>
```

Figure 3. Sample HTTP Conversation

The heart of the conversation consists of the client's GET command, which communicates the specific request, and the server's 200 OK response, which signals that the file exists, permission is granted to send it, and its transmission follows. The 200 OK message may seem familiar (see *The Internet Revolution*); it is exactly the same message used by other protocols, such as FTP and SMTP, and it is used to communicate the same basic information in all of the protocols. A common Web server response that most people encounter from time to time is the 404 Not Found message. This is the response returned by a server when a requested file or resource does not exist on the server.

The other lines in the sample conversation represent additional header information that gets exchanged in the process. This information varies considerably, depending on which version of HTTP is being used and on the type of client and server. The header information serves a variety of purposes. It is used primarily to facilitate the exchange of data between client and server by allowing each to tell the other any specific requirements or limitations it may have. This, too, may seem familiar since it is another common feature shared by many application-level protocols. Information from the client's header lines also helps to populate log files on the Web server, providing a record of who requested which files and when.

HTTP functions as what is known as a *stateless* protocol. This means that HTTP treats each connection, each click of a hyperlink, separately, with no regard for or understanding of what transpired before and no concern for what may come next. For example, if a person fills out a Web form and then clicks its button to submit the form, this action results in one complete HTTP process. If the Web site brings up a second page of the form requesting some additional information, when the button on this page is clicked to submit the form an entirely independent HTTP process occurs. HTTP has no means to connect the information or actions on the first page of the form with those of the second page. The data transmissions are treated as separate events, and this is why HTTP is called a stateless protocol. It is its stateless nature that helps make HTTP such a fast protocol. Its design was singularly focused on retrieving Web objects as quickly as possible.

But what HTTP lacks, other technologies and services have provided. As discussed later in the book, data about people in general and about an individual's use of the Web in particular is captured and tracked in other ways, such as through the use of browser cookies, CGI programming, and Java applications. As a person surfs the Web, logs on to Web portals (a portal is a large and diverse Internet site, such as Yahoo! and MSN, that offers a variety of information feeds, services, and tools and that acts as a gateway to the Internet's resources), adds items to a shopping cart, etc., his or her independent HTTP transmissions are collected, examined, and interpreted behind the scenes in order for those actions to be connected and information to be carried from one Web click to the next. This is not part of HTTP, but the information collected and communicated by HTTP makes these sorts of activities possible.

HTTP has matured considerably since it was first created in 1990, and it continues to evolve today as new Web-enabled devices are created (e.g., Web-enabled cell phones) and concerns over controlling information access and security continue to grow. Recent versions of the protocol have added features for hierarchical proxy servers, file caching, persistent connections, and virtual hosts. All of these features have helped to improve the performance of the Web by expanding the capabilities of HTTP and by enabling the operation of HTTP to be more finely configured for its intended use on any one server. Some of these features are discussed in later chapters.

The security of information transmitted over HTTP was an early concern of Web site creators. The Web first became popular just as commercialization of the Internet began; and Internet commerce required a means to protect sensitive information from being stolen or exposed. But, as illustrated above, the data transmitted by HTTP in both the header information and file content is sent in plain text. How could credit card information be collected in the process of purchasing a product on a Web site if it was going to be transmitted in plain text that anyone could read? How could any type of personal or confidential information, for that matter, be collected through the Web and transmitted by HTTP if no assurances could be provided about the security and privacy of that information? Neither merchants nor customers would consider such conditions acceptable, which meant that commerce via the Web could not move forward until this problem was solved.

The immediate solution was found in data encryption, which turns plain text into an unintelligible code that only the intended recipient can decipher and therefore understand. Netscape was the first to provide the technical means to implement this solution on the Web through its creation of something called Secure Sockets Layer (SSL) and its variant of HTTP called HTTPS. This was followed by the W3C's development of the specification for S-HTTP (Secure HTTP), a more generalized extension to HTTP that incorporates standard ways to provide for the secure transmission of data across the World Wide Web. Both approaches encrypt sensitive data, such as credit card information, before the data is transmitted; only the Web server collecting the information has the cipher (i.e., key) to decrypt the data. The two approaches differ only in the details of how the authentication and encryption/decryption process is performed.

The Applications of the Web

While HTML, HTTP, and the URL represent the building blocks of the Web, they would not have amounted to much without an application for building the information content sites of the Web and another for visiting those sites. The Web is an information management system, but HTML, HTTP, and the URL do not include any functionality for creating or managing document collections or other information resources. At a minimum, the Web also needed the following tools to be created before it could function as a complete system:

■ **Web Servers**: a server-side tool for information suppliers to store, organize, and manage access to a site's HTML files and other information resources.

■ **Web Browsers**: a client-side tool for users to store and manage the addresses of information resources (e.g., through bookmarks) and to view Web content.

■ **Web Programming**: specialized programming designed to share information between the Web and other types of information storage systems, such as databases and business applications, or between the Web and legacy systems. (Legacy systems are typically older computers or applications that predate the Web or the Internet and therefore have no means to share information on the Web.)

Berners-Lee was the first to create all these tools in order to get the Web up and running and to integrate its operation into the computing environment at CERN. He released all of his work freely onto the Internet, which allowed others to build more easily on what he had created and to understand all the inner workings of the Web. Each of these tools is discussed below.

Web Servers

Web servers are essentially file servers, but they are designed specifically with the Internet and with Web resources, such as HTML files, in mind. As their name suggests, they serve up the information that constitutes most, but not all, of the Web's information space. Other services and other types of file servers contribute their own collections of information and resources to the Web's larger information space. Common examples of these other services are listed above, represented by the different types of URL schemes; they include the considerable information resources found on FTP, WAIS, and USENET Internet sites.

What makes these other services, file servers, and the information they contain also part of the Web's information space has to do with the URL and the functioning of Web browsers. The URL identifies the location of the Internet's files and resources, not just those of Web servers; and browsers can read and interpret all types of URLs, not just those URLs related to the Web (e.g., with a scheme of http or https). But HTML and Web servers also play an essential role in unifying these diverse and distributed information resources and establishing the Web's information space. HTML files and the use of hyperlinks create the interconnections that define the matrix of the Web's spatial construction, and Web servers provide access to that space.

Web servers are the essential counterpart to Web browsers, constituting the server side in the client-server architecture of the Web. They are designed to manage a collection of information resources and control access to those resources, whether from across the Internet or from within a company's internal computer network or intranet. All Web servers are built around HTTP, the Web's communication protocol, just as FTP and TELNET servers are built around their respective protocols. A Web server's primary function is to answer requests for information and, when permissible, provide that information according to the data transfer rules specified by HTTP.

The simplest Web servers manage a collection of independent, static HTML files. Such collections typically consist of information that does not need to accommodate any personalization or customization, and their information normally remains unaffected by the passage of time. A Web server managing a collection of recipes is a good example of this type of simple site. The HTML files containing the recipes reside on the Web server's file system. The server waits and listens for any incoming HTTP requests for one of these files. It grants or denies access based on its programmed conditions. It might, for instance, be configured to require authentication through a login and password before it will grant access to any file on the server or to one or more selected groups of files. Once permission to access the requested file has been established, the server sends a copy of the file's contents through the HTTP connection. If permission is denied or a problem is encountered in locating or accessing the requested file, the server instead replies with a message explaining why it cannot fulfill the request, such as the 404 Not Found message. In the simplest and most general terms, this sequence of operations makes up the core functionality of all Web servers.

Many slightly more advanced Web servers interface with a database of information, often in addition to managing a collection of HTML files. One reason for configuring a Web server to interact with a database is that storing information in databases is a common and established practice, particularly in environments that house large quantities of data, and converting such information and storing it in HTML files is neither practical nor cost effective. Another reason is that databases offer an extremely efficient way to store information objects of all types. They can also be used to manage access to information (i.e., control which users can retrieve which types of information) and to manage changes to the data. It makes good sense, from the perspective of information management, to let a database operate as it always has, performing the functions that it does best, while configuring a Web server to act as an intermediary between a user's requests for information and the database's store of data.

An early example of this type of server, which was introduced in the previous chapter, was the Stanford Linear Accelerator Center (SLAC) Web server, http://slacvm.slac.stanford.edu, the very first Web site in the U.S. The database at SLAC housed a large collection of document preprints for the physics community. A Web server was built at SLAC to provide global Internet access to that existing store of data, leaving the database itself unchanged. The project included the creation of simple HTML files that provided forms through which a user could enter search criteria to locate and retrieve specific documents. The Web server would interpret the criteria provided by the user on one of these Web forms and, using programs written expressly for interacting with the preprint database (like those described later in this chapter), it would use this information to query the database, which would locate any documents that matched the search criteria and extract them from the database. The server would then send the extracted file data to the user's computer via HTTP.

A larger, more advanced Web site of recipes would benefit from the same approach. A database could be set up to store the recipes and categorize the information they contained according to any number of parameters, including type of cuisine, preparation and cooking times, ingredients, and difficulty level. The database would greatly simplify and enhance the Web site owner's ability to maintain and update the recipes. Instead of manually updating hundreds or thousands of simple HTML files, standard database functions could be used to make single, multiple, or global updates to the information as needed. The Web server would be modified to interact with the database, instead of listing the HTML file recipes stored on the site; and HTML files would be created to provide users with a way to enter search criteria and sort recipes. The difference in how the recipe information was stored and accessed would remain entirely hidden from the users accessing the site. The Web server would absorb all the changes, enabling the users to enjoy their improved access to the recipes while they continued to receive the same data in the same format (HTML files) that they received before.

A more advanced and sophisticated type of Web server is one that generates HTML pages dynamically from a variety of different information sources and in response to a variety of different factors or conditions. Such Web servers build HTML files on-the-fly, often every time a request is made. These dynamically created HTML files frequently contain data that is unique in its content, format, or both, which is why the pages must be generated on demand and why a more sophisticated type of Web server is required to manage the information on such a site. The data contained in these pages may be the result of a specific search request, preconfigured account preferences on a site, demographic information that has been stored on a site or that is being tracked without the user's knowledge, or any number of other factors or conditions that the

Web server is capable of reading, interpreting, and applying to the pages it is generating. Web site advertisements known as banners are often one information component on dynamically generated pages. Depending on the level of sophistication of the Web server, the advertisements shown to a user may be generated randomly or they also may be based on some known criteria like the gender and age of the user. A simple example of a common type of Web server that produces dynamically generated content is that of a search engine. A user enters one or more words or phrases that get submitted to the site's search engine. The resulting page is assembled from various components, some static and common, like the page headers and footers, and others dynamically built and unique, like the listing of the Web pages matching the search criteria.

This type of Web server is used by many e-commerce sites. An e-commerce site, such as an online bookstore, retains information on its Web server about every individual who visits the site. For those who create an account, this includes basic demographic information as well as stated buying preferences. For those who buy products, this includes transaction information about specific purchases and inferred information about buying preferences. For those who only browse the site (i.e., they have no account and have not made a purchase), thereby limiting the information that the Web server can retain, the server can deposit information on the user's computer — typically in an information fragment known as a cookie — to store such information as the date of their visit and the products or categories of products that were examined. All of this information, stored on the Web server and on the user's computer, functions to identify and profile the user for when he or she next returns to the site. The server will use this profiled information to build Web pages specifically for that user upon his or her return. This personalized information content might include the user's name, news about an ongoing sale for a product that was previously purchased, or a reminder about products that were examined during the prior visit to the site but were not purchased.

On the extreme end of the spectrum of Web servers, there is an ever-increasing number of Internet portal sites that want to cater to a user's every online need. These sites provide numerous degrees and types of information customization by enabling a user to create his or her own personalized home page. An individual selects the type of news, sports, stock information, weather, television listings, etc., that will be part of his or her home page; the arrangement and typography can sometimes also be selected, thereby further personalizing the page. Additionally, such sites provide a wide range of communication, scheduling, and productivity tools for their users. A calendar application, for example, is a popular tool on these sites; appointments and reminders entered into the calendar adds another personalized element to the page. The intent of these Web sites is to bring the Internet and the rest of the Web to their users in a familiar, pre-packaged form, keeping each user on their site for as long as possible. The Web servers that manage these sites rely on powerful, complex, highly configurable engines to manage such a large and diverse repository of information and generate such highly individualized Web pages. Nevertheless, the output created by these servers is at least in one respect no different than that created by any other Web server: it consists of data in the form of a compliant HTML file sent via HTTP to a waiting browser.

There is no limit to the types of Web servers that can be created, any more than there is a limit to the type of information that can be published on the Web. This is part of the power and versatility of the Web. Moreover, just about any computer can be configured as a Web server, even basic laptops and PCs. Berners-Lee envisioned the Web as being as much an environment for publishing as a means for global information access. Everyone who has access to the Internet also has the opportunity to create their own, personal Web site, either by subscribing to an Internet service and paying a small monthly fee to host their site on the Internet, or by installing a Web server on their personal computer, even if the information it contains will not be shared across the network. Fortunately, there is an abundance of well written, free Web server software available that can be easily downloaded from the Internet. Some of these free Web servers, such as the Apache server, date back to the first server software created for the Web. They contain the contributions of individuals who believe, like Berners-Lee, that the Web should remain a free and open information space equally accessible to all for both retrieving and publishing information. To this day a large percentage of commercial Web enterprises use this same free software to manage their Web files and resources.

Despite their differences, all Web servers perform the following basic tasks. They listen for incoming HTTP client requests from browsers or other sources. They answer these requests by starting an HTTP conversation with the client. They check for the existence of the requested file or resource and for any restrictions on granting access to it. If the request cannot be fulfilled, a message is returned stating the reason, and the HTTP conversation is closed. Otherwise, the requested data is sent to the client and the HTTP conversation is closed. In the process, they enter one or more entries into a log file to record the request, information about the client, and the outcome of the request.

An important aspect of every Web server is its configuration. Even the simplest Web servers include dozens of configurable parameters. These parameters define where resources are located, whether they are restricted and, if so, who they are restricted to, the types of files that the server can provide or exclude, what name or multiple names the Web server will be known by, and many other things. Each time a request is made — and it is not uncommon for some of the busiest Web servers to receive hundreds of thousands of requests or more every day — a Web server must check that request against all of its various configured conditions and rules before it can reply. All this in a mere fraction of a second.

Web Browsers

Web browsers are the principal client-side application in the client-server architecture of the Web. They bring together the Web's core components — HTML, HTTP, and the URL — for the purpose of accessing the Web's content and navigating the Web's information space. All Web browsers read and interpret HTML files to display the Web's information content, present URLs in some selectable form (typically a clickable hyperlink) to interconnect the information content of the Web, and initiate HTTP sessions to retrieve requested Web files and resources. Most Web browsers, however, do considerably more.

The confusion over what is the Web and what is the Internet, where one stops and the other begins, probably has more to do with the engineering and functionality of Web browsers than any other single application. All Web browsers do more than navigate the information content of the Web and display HTML files. Even the earliest browsers functioned more as Internet navigation tools than Web-specific tools, given their ability to access FTP, Gopher, WAIS, and USENET sites in addition to Web sites. Berners-Lee's goal was to create a global, all-encompassing information system; from the beginning, Web resources were considered only part of that larger information space. The versatility of Web browsers and the engineered flexibility of the URL proved key to reaching this goal, due in large part to their capacity to interact with the widest variety of sites, services, information systems, and information objects that could be found on the Internet. Without the URL, the Web would have remained a small, but effective information management system, one of many such systems coexisting on the Internet. But the generic design of the URL, combined with the URL's incorporation into Web browsers, enabled the Web's space to be superimposed on any type of information space existing anywhere on the Internet. More exactly, browsers make it appear this way.

The very first sources of information on the Web were the existing information services of the Internet, which were provided by FTP, Gopher, WAIS, and newsgroups. Each of these services was separate, distinctly different in operation, and unique in the content of its information and the manner in which it stored that information; and users interacted with each service separately, individually, each through its own client and interface. The introduction of the URL and the first Web browser collected all of these separate and unique information services into a larger, all-encompassing information space along with the Web's own information service consisting of HTML files served by its communication protocol, HTTP. The Web became a service on the Internet, like FTP, WAIS, and the others; but, at the same time, it treated the Internet and its other services and resources as information content for its own service. In the process, the Internet became the ultimate purveyor of information, while the Web established a single point of access. The Web, therefore, can be seen as two distinct entities: an information space superimposed on the Internet and a distinct service in its own right, providing Web pages and Web resources. Web browsers serve to encapsulate both entities, further blurring the distinction between where the Web ends and the Internet begins.

The introduction of Web browsers caused a surge of interest in the Internet. They succeeded in making the Internet's resources far more accessible to far more people, including, for the first time, people outside of the computer field with little, and sometimes no, understanding of the workings of computers or of the Internet. Web browsers quickly established themselves as the interface to the Internet and have become one of the most commonly used computer applications. Web browsers are not only free, but they provide a single, multipurpose, easy-to-operate application that meets the needs of most computer users. They allow users to send, receive, and organize email, shop online, access news, weather, and other changing information, play games, create and organize documents, and many other things. It's not difficult to imagine a future in which Web browsers or their next-generation replacements displace computer operating systems and provide a single, intuitive, customizable interface to all of our information needs, both personal and public.

The core functionality of every Web browser is its ability to interpret and display HTML files, the Web's native file format, and its corollary ability to handle multimedia files through something called the Multi-purpose Internet Mail Extension (MIME), a standard for identifying file types that was described in the chapter on email in *The Internet Revolution*. As explained above, each browser recognizes and interprets HTML somewhat differently. Most, however, generally conform to one of the standards issued by the W3C. How HTML files are displayed on any one computer is generally determined by the following factors:

- What was coded by the author of the HTML page. Web page creators can include as much or as little information as they want regarding how the browser should display the page with respect to typefaces, font sizes, colors, background images, text alignment, and more.

- The default settings the browser uses to interpret a page's code with respect to such things as typefaces, colors, and font sizes.

- The browser settings configured by the user that augment or override features set by the page author or that affect the browser's default settings.

- The presentation features that the computer's operating system makes available to the browser; for example, the page author may specify a typeface of Helvetica, but if the computer does not have this typeface installed, it must substitute another.

Despite all these differences, most browsers manage to do a relatively good job at displaying HTML files in a way that is consistent with the author's intentions. Fortunately, there are many guidelines and tools to help authors produce HTML code that avoids pitfalls and maximizes a file's interoperability.

Not all the files requested through a browser, however, are HTML files. Consequently, MIME was integrated into the operation of Web servers — just as it had been into other applications and even into operating systems — to help identify different types of files and to automate the handling of files through associated helper applications. (Email uses MIME for the purpose of automating the handling of email attachments.) For instance, in the sample HTTP conversation presented earlier, the client's `Accept:` line is there to tell the Web server which file types it is configured to handle, including such image files as GIF (Graphics Interchange Format) and JPEG (Joint Photographic Experts Group). Similarly, the server's response includes a `Content-Type:` line that formally identifies that the file it is about to send is an HTML file. This information is then used by the browser to help it identify the data it is about to receive and determine exactly how to handle that data.

Since MIME types also enable browsers to start helper applications, they serve to extend the apparent seamlessness of the Web to encompass all types of files. A Web server can send any type of file over an HTTP connection. It uses MIME to tell the browser what type of file it is sending and, optionally, what application should be used to display the file. The browser uses this information in conjunction with its own MIME settings to start up the appropriate application for the file and, using it, display the file in the browser's window. For instance, if a user clicks on a URL that identifies a PDF (Portable Document Format) file (i.e., a type of formatted document typically created from a PostScript file), the browser will start up a helper application, such as Adobe Acrobat, to interpret and display the PDF file. Similarly, if a user clicks on a URL that identifies a movie clip, the browser will start up a local program that plays movie files.

One way a browser identifies these different file types is through the filename extension in the URL; a .pdf extension, for instance, normally identifies a PDF file. But Web servers also use MIME in their configuration parameters and may communicate additional MIME-related information to the browser to assist the browser in its handling of the file. When a Web browser and a Web server are talking, therefore, they may be negotiating issues on how best to handle the file that was requested on behalf of the user. The desired goals of the process are to hide the complexities of the technology from the user and to maximize interoperability, the two most common and most important goals of any Internet service.

Web Programming

Web servers rely on specialized programming to provide the kind of functionality that was deliberately omitted from the core specification of the Web. The Web makes no demands on the kind of information it serves, just as the Internet makes no demands on the kind of data it transmits. It is, therefore, largely up to programming efforts engineered for the particular needs of the Web to fill this void. Web programming bridges the gap between the expectations of Web servers and Web browsers and all the various methods, applications, and systems that store information.

As described in the previous chapter, it was Web programming that first brought the Web to the scientists at CERN through the construction of an interface, or gateway, between existing information services at CERN, like the CERN phone book and XFIND, and Berners-Lee's Web server. HTML pages on CERN's Web server allowed a user to select an information source, like the phone book, and then either enter search criteria or select an item from a listing. The job of the Web server was simply to hand off the information from the HTML page to another program and wait for a response from that program that it could then send back to the user's browser through the HTTP connection.

The tasks required of the Web server were designed to be performed quickly and efficiently. More importantly, they were generalized in such a way to allow the server to interact with any type of information system, provided two conditions were met. One, the server handed off information to the waiting program in a prescribed and consistent manner. Two, the program returned an HTML file in response. These conditions dictate how information between the Web server and a program — any program — could be exchanged in a fast, simple, and uniform manner. The Web program interpreted and evaluated the information it received from the Web server, used this information to query the associated database of information (in the CERN example), retrieved the data, and converted it into HTML, before forwarding it to the Web server.

The efficiency of the Web's operation is a direct result of the modular design of its components, as is illustrated by the exchange of information described above. The request for information is communicated through the Web browser, which knows nothing about how the data will be retrieved, how it might be stored, or where it might be stored; it simply waits for a response from the Web server. The Web server receives the request and recognizes, through settings in its configuration, that the requested information is stored elsewhere (i.e., not in one of its managed files). Accordingly, the Web server acts as an intermediary between the browser and the source of the requested information; it passes the information it received through the browser on to the configured program, and passes the information returned from the program on to the waiting browser. Like the browser, the server knows nothing about how or where the data is stored. Conversely, the database that stores the requested information knows nothing about the waiting Web browser and server, and nothing about HTML. It functions just as it always has, storing information in its tables and retrieving information in response to a properly prepared query.

The Web program bridges the gap, converting the information for the request from the Web into a proper query for the database, submitting the query to the database, converting the retrieved data into an HTML file, and sending that file back to the Web server. All four components perform their individual assigned tasks, but only the Web program contains any specialized instructions relating specifically to the task at hand. It acts as a gateway between the Web and the database. As such, it localizes all of the data translation and interface instructions specific to this task in its code, just as a network gateway (router) localizes all of the data translation and interface instructions for passing data between two dissimilar networks in its programming code.

Before the Web and HTML, this type of programming paradigm was commonly used, but with one very large difference: there was no common, uniform way to represent the retrieved data that would work for many different types of computer platforms and operating systems. Instead, it was necessary to accommodate each type of hardware and operating system individually, and doing so represented a significant portion of any development effort. The creation of browsers and the simple file markup defined by HTML changed all this. For the first time, it was possible to focus programming efforts on better access to and manipulation of information content, rather than on how that information would be displayed or how many different types of files needed to be created for the various systems that had to be supported. A single, simple HTML file could be created to represent virtually any type of information from any type of information system; and Web browsers would display that HTML file roughly the same way on whatever type of computer was being used. The programming community caught on quickly to the new, liberating, modular approach to information access offered by the Web. Moreover, it did so with fervor.

Since the early 1990s, many different programming models for the Web have been developed. Two of the largest, most all-encompassing models, Java (from Sun Microsystems) and .NET (from Microsoft), have extended the power of the Web and the Internet to such a degree that they may some day eclipse the Web altogether and provide a new paradigm for information management, access, and control. (Java is described at length in *The Technology Revolution*.) But one of the first common Web programming models — called the Common Gateway Interface (CGI) — offers a simpler illustration of how this aspect of the Web actually works.

CGI programs bridge the gap between a Web server and any service, database, or information resource one wants to make accessible through the Web. They can be written in any language supported by the local computing environment. Common, early languages used were the Unix shell, C/C++, and Perl. Information is typically gathered from a user through some type of HTML Web form. The form may prompt the user to make selections from one or more lists, such as checkboxes for selecting color choices for a sweater or dropdown lists for selecting a car manufacturer and model type. Or it may require the user to enter text for a query, such as keywords for a search. It all depends on the related application. The form itself may be a simple, static HTML file on the Web site, or it may consist of HTML code generated dynamically by the CGI program itself.

Once the form is submitted for processing, which occurs as soon as the user presses its 'Submit,' 'Go,' 'Search,' or other similarly named button, its information is passed to the form's associated CGI program along with additional information about the user that has been collected automatically by the Web server. This additional information typically includes the IP address of the user's computer, the computer's name (if available), and the type of browser that was used. The Web server packages this user-specific and computer-specific information, as well as the information the user entered through the form, into environment variables, which are essentially named containers that hold all of the data. Some of these named containers or variables are defined by the person who wrote the CGI program. There might, for instance, be one called TELNO to hold the telephone number the user was required to enter. Other variables, such as REMOTE_ADDR (for recording the user's IP address) and QUERY_STRING (for recording all of the user-specified data), are defined by HTTP itself and are recognized as part of its standard; these variables constitute the 'Common' component of CGI.

Every CGI program relies on this common packaging of the data to perform its first and most fundamental task: to extract and interpret all the information captured by the Web form. The specific content of this information will vary from form to form, since each form is designed to capture information specific to its purpose. By packaging this information in a consistent, uniform, predefined manner, however, the Web server enables a CGI program to use standardized code to read and interpret that information (as in the example below). This type of standardization, like the standardization of HTML, greatly simplifies the writing of CGI programs and other types of programs for the Web.

After the CGI program has extracted the needed information and used it to perform its assigned task (e.g., look up a database entry or update a record), it replies to the Web server. Its response is typically (but is in no way limited to) an HTML document that the CGI program produces dynamically, as shown below. Before sending this response, however, the CGI program must first send a MIME-related line specifying the content type of the file it is about to send, as shown here, which must be followed by an empty line:

```
Content-Type: text/html;
```

This line indicates that the file contents it is about to send is an HTML file.

The following code samples illustrate how simple this type of programming can be. Presented first is the code for an HTML form that asks the user to enter his or her first name, last name, and favorite type of food.

```
<html>
<head>
<title>Favorite Food Form</title>
</head>
<body>
<form action="/cgi-bin/favfood.pl">
Your First Name: <input type="text" name="fname">
Your Last Name: <input type="text" name="lname">
Your Favorite Food: <input type="text" name="food">
<input type="submit" value="Press Me!">
</body>
</html>
```

Figure 4. Sample HTML Form Code

The form names the CGI program, `favfood.pl`, that the Web server will call once the user clicks on the `Press Me!` submit button. It includes three text fields, indicated by the designation of `input type` as `text`. These would appear on the form as empty boxes into which the user would enter text. Each of the text fields includes its own, uniquely named variable, indicated by the `name` element. These variables will store the data entered for the user's first and last name and favorite food (`fname`, `lname`, and `food`, respectively). As far as the HTML coding is concerned, that's all there is to this form.

The following figure shows the complete code for the CGI program. Comments are included on the right side, separated by a pound (#) sign.

```
#!/usr/local/bin/perl  # locates the perl program interpreter
# favfood.pl            # simple comment line with program name
require 'cgi-lib.pl'    # a perl library with common functions
&ReadParse(*input);     # perl function that reads the data entered
                        # and stores it in a variable named $input

                        # the remainder of the program prints the
                        # HTML code, dynamically inserting the
                        # three values entered in the form
print "Content-Type: text/html\r\n\r\n";
print "<html>";
print "<head>";
print "<title>Your Name and Food Preference</title>";
print "</head>";
print "<body>";
print "Hi " . $input{'fname'} . " " . $input{'lname'};
print "Your favorite food is: " . $input{'food'};
print "</body>";
print "</html>";
```

Figure 5.   The favfood.pl CGI Program

The program was written in the Perl programming language. This same program, however, could have been written in any number of different programming languages commonly used in creating programs for the Web. The program uses a library function (i.e., a small, reusable program or code fragment that performs a commonly requested operation) called ReadParse to interpret, evaluate, and store all of the information passed along by the Web server. This one, deceptively simple line of code, &ReadParse(*input);, hides the detailed but standardized information processing that every Web form must perform.

This CGI program really only does two things. First, it reads and interprets the common environment variable that captures all the pieces of information entered by the user and it stores this information in its own variable called $input. Second, it produces a simple, but complete HTML file to send back to the user, repeatedly using the print function to print one line at a time. It is these lines — starting with the MIME Content-Type line — that are received by the Web server from the CGI program and are used, in turn, as its response to the user's browser. Included in these lines are tokens that reference the information entered by the user, such as fname for first name and food for favorite food. The CGI program replaces these tokens with the associated text that it interpreted and stored through the `ReadParse` function as it prints the lines and sends them to the Web server. The resulting page would contain something like:

```
Hi Fred Mertz
Your favorite food is: Banana Cream Pie
```

This simple example demonstrates the flow of information common to all Web programming. A user provides some data and initiates a process, typically by clicking on a URL or the button on a form. The Web server packages up the information that was entered along with additional information it collected from the user's browser and passes it along to the CGI program. The program then interprets the data, hopefully does some validation checking (for example, making sure the user entered a first and last name if that was required), performs any additional work, and replies to the Web server with properly coded HTML, or perhaps with some other type of acceptable file format.

The HTML form and CGI program shown above illustrate how information is captured on a Web form, how that information can be stored and used, and how a Web program returns information to a Web server. But the Web routinely captures and processes a lot more information about people than most Web forms suggest or than most people realize. It also captures data about people while they are simply surfing the Web. Even without the use of a Web form to explicitly solicit information, a Web site may be configured to capture and record information as people browse the site and retrieve information. Any number of intermediate events can be triggered on a Web server when a person clicks on one of its URLs, each one collecting and/or passing on various types of personal information. This all happens quietly, behind the scenes. As is described in more detail in later chapters, there are few, if any, constraints on the type of information being collected by the Web or how it is being used; and there is a growing use (and some argue misuse) of this information by both commercial interests and government agencies.

The Information Web

The Information Web

The World Wide Web was created to house, share, and interconnect information on the Internet. In the process of introducing an information management system to the Internet commensurate with the Internet's global reach and consonant with its goal of interoperability, the Web managed to equate finding information about Internet resources with finding information in general. Our principal activity on the Web, consequently, is the pursuit of this information. How the Web has empowered us to go about finding information, therefore, is worth some investigation.

Before information can be found on the Web, information purveyors must first store and represent the information they want to make accessible. HTML was created to simplify these tasks. But the Web makes very few demands in this area. From the earliest days of the Web, therefore, a wide variety of methodologies and applications have been developed for and employed in the business of information storage. Using databases for this purpose, for example, is one common and highly efficient approach. Building online libraries — virtual representations of the brick-and-mortar institutions adapted in form and functionality for information access over the Web — is another. Search engines also fulfill this purpose, because before they can assist us in locating resources on the Web, they must first discover and copy information about those resources and store that information on their site in a form that their application can use in performing searches.

The information stored on the Web comprises more than the files and resources that are made available to us, just as the process of finding and retrieving that information often entails more than simply entering search criteria on a Web form or clicking on a hyperlink. Accessing information on the Web also — and always — results in depositing information on the Web. Consequently, a large portion of the information stored on the Web is generated by us and our movements on the Web, and the majority of this information is collected without our knowledge or explicit consent. We provide information about ourselves willingly when we enter our name and address into a Web form, perhaps to enter a sweepstakes or to make a purchase. But we also leave a trail of information on the Web, as the pages we view, the preferences we express, and the advertisements we see and respond to are recorded for subsequent warehousing and analysis. The information generated and collected by our use of the Web may some day even dwarf the information created for our retrieval. As we shall see below and as is explained further in a later chapter, all of the information generated through our use of the Web is of considerable interest to many commercial organizations and even to certain government agencies. Where information is concerned, it is important to recognize and remember that the Web is a two-way street.

Over a relatively short period of time, the expanse of the Web's information space has already become vast; it continues to grow at an exponential rate. The Web's size and the dynamic nature of its composition and contents have resulted in the creation of new technologies designed to improve both access to and control over its information. One of these new technologies consists of automated agents known as Web robots that travel the Web in search of information according to predefined preferences or rules. Another consists of Internet devices that serve to finely control information access and protect information assets. These technologies rely on programmed intelligence to identify and distinguish different types and categories of information. Therefore, the more concretely and uniformly information is structured and represented on the Web, the better these tools can perform their assigned tasks on behalf of their operators.

Many people consider the success of these tools and others like them as essential to managing the Web's information space; the tools are expected to enable the Web to continue to grow while they extend the capabilities of the Web's users and its information providers. But, for such tools to succeed, the representation of information on the Web must change; HTML is too small and simple a file format specification to fulfill the requirements of these tools. This need has, among other things, led to the development and growing acceptance of a new, standardized methodology — called the Extensible Markup Language (XML) — for identifying and categorizing information.

The following sections cover the fundamentals of the information Web. The first section explores how individuals go about finding information, the forms in which information is made available, or served, how information is filtered, and how information can be customized. The second section presents subjects related to information storage and structure, including an explanation of XML and the operation and significance of cookies. The final section describes information agents that travel the Web carrying out our requests for information and how devices such as proxy servers and firewalls are being used to manage and control Web access and to protect information resources.

Finding Information

For most of us, the process of locating information is our first and most common interaction with the Web. Whatever the type of information being sought — the day's news headlines or sporting event scores, the definition for a word, or the lowest airfare for a flight to Kathmandu — the information must first be found before it can be put to use. Given that the Web is an information space — something superimposed on the Internet that provides a means to locate, dispense, and interconnect information — the question arises about how one goes about finding information contained in this space? People already familiar with the Web who have bookmarked sites that routinely fulfill their information needs and are adept at using one or more of the Web's popular search engines to seek out other types of information may think that there is not much to this question. But it is important to recognize that there is no single or best way to locate information on the Web. Moreover, as the business of helping us find information on the Web continues to grow, more and more questions are emerging about how and why information is being filtered and otherwise manipulated before it reaches our eyes.

Unlike a library that has a record for every book, periodical, and information resource housed within the walls of its information space, no single map or portal or search engine exists that lists or knows about all of the Web's information sources or that can fulfill all of our information requests. Even the largest search engines reach only a small fraction of the information resources accessible through the World Wide Web. How one navigates the information space of the Web, therefore, is different for everyone and may even vary considerably from one day to the next. Fortunately, the services, tools, and methods one can choose from are virtually limitless, and they are increasing every day. Unfortunately, sometimes having too many options to select from and too much information to sift through can make it harder to find the information we are after.

One factor affecting our ability to find information on the Web is that the information space of the Web is changing all the time. The Web's information management system was created on a non-commercial Internet owned and operated largely by the U.S. government. Today's Internet is privatized, highly commercialized, and regulated to some extent by each of the countries in which it operates, as is today's Web. The information space of today's Web, therefore, differs substantially from that of the early Web. In part, these differences relate to several obvious changes: the great increase in the quantity and diversity of information, the introduction of an endless number and variety of products and services that can be purchased, and the addition of greatly improved facilities for searching the Web and its contents.

What may be less obvious changes, however, are also responsible for considerable differences in the content of the Web's information space and for differences in how people interact with the Web and locate information each and every day. These changes include: rampant Web site advertising, monopolization of the browser market by Netscape and Microsoft, and the popularity of Web-based Internet portals such as those operated by Yahoo!, Netscape, and Microsoft. The impact of all these changes is evident both in how we find information on the Web and in how information manages to find us. As explained in the following sections, finding information on the Web entails more than executing a search and clicking on a hyperlink. Information is the primary commodity of the Web and getting you to visit one Web site as opposed to another is a highly competitive business. Therefore, how you go about finding information, how information can be directed to you, and how information can be extracted from you are all part of the information Web.

Surfing, Searching, and Sifting

The process of finding information on the Web can be categorized as surfing, searching, or sifting through the Web's information space. Surfing the Web is an uncharted and dynamic way to navigate its information space that evokes the loosely tied information associations described so well by Vannevar Bush. Surfing for information is like going out for a Sunday drive just to wander or explore, without concerning yourself with reaching a destination. You let the Web pages and hyperlinks take you from place to place, and the trip becomes a journey of discovery. The experience of surfing the Web recalls the book-based information browsing of picking up an encyclopedia or dictionary and flipping the pages or following cross-references in the simple pursuit of self-edification or entertainment.

Searching the Web, on the other hand, while commonly intermixed with surfing, is a very different sort of experience, one that is targeted and filled with expectations. Unlike surfing the Web, searching for information contained in the Web's information space is an experience that requires the use of specialized tools; these tools are designed to transform the distributed and disparate information resources of the Web into a single, searchable body of information that will yield results quickly, efficiently, and intelligently. Accordingly, it is also an experience that has attracted the attention of the business community and has become the focus of many business ventures on the Web. Services for searching the Web — like those for providing information to

Internet users and capturing information about the habits and preferences of Internet users — are one of the Web's most lucrative and growing types of revenue streams.

There are three principal ways to search for information on the Web: search engines, hierarchical (tree-organized) subject matter listings, and specialized, searchable databases. These approaches differ considerably with respect to both how they collect, or pool, the body of data that is used in performing a search and how search criteria are applied to this data. Each approach has its own strengths and weaknesses, as described below.

Search engines, such as Google and Alta Vista, do not actually search the Web when you submit a search request on their Web sites (www.google.com and www.altavista.com, respectively). Instead, they apply the supplied search criteria against a collection of data stored locally, on their own computer systems, that has been gathered by specialized, automated programs commonly called spiders. Spiders navigate the information space of the Web, following links from one page to another, in order to discover the location of information on the Web and record and categorize its contents. The longer and further they crawl through the Web, the more of the Web they discover and the greater the volume of data they can use in performing a search. These spiders, as well as other types of automated information agents on the Web, are discussed in more detail later in this chapter.

The benefits of using search engines are that they can search the contents of billions of Web pages and that, because they have stored and indexed these pages locally, searches typically complete in a few seconds or less. The disadvantages of using search engines are that these billions of pages are not organized in any way (nor are they evaluated for content) and that the information they contain may not be current. Crawling through the Web and copying pages takes time, therefore many pages will have changed between the time they were copied and the time a search is executed. Furthermore, no matter how many billions of pages these search engines have found, they represent only a fraction of the Web as a whole, because some parts of the Web cannot be found or indexed by such automated mechanisms and the Web is growing and changing every day.

Each search engine ranks the pages that match the supplied criteria according to some algorithm, in an effort to distinguish more relevant from less relevant results. It then displays the resulting pages in this ranked order. Better search engines allow a user to refine their initial search by applying additional criteria in a second search that is performed against the first search's returned results. This may help narrow and focus the search results; it does not, however, change the fact that no intelligence, other than the user's, has been applied in conducting the search for information. Search engines are very good at returning results, which is their primary function, but the resulting pages will always contain the good, the bad, and the ugly. This is one reason why sifting information — distinguishing and separating the good from the bad from the ugly — has become an integral part of finding information on the Web.

Subject matter listings, like those found on Yahoo! (www.yahoo.com) and About.com (www.about.com), offer a more personal, guided approach to helping users find information on the Web. These hierarchical listings are created by individuals who are continuously exploring, cataloging, and categorizing the Web on behalf of the users who visit their sites. Users conduct and refine their search by selecting categories and subcategories until they come across the listings they want to search or the pages they want to visit. For instance, a user might select a main category called 'News and Media,' then the subcategory 'Television,' then 'Networks,' and then 'Movie Channels' in an effort to find information on the broadcast times and channels for a particular movie genre or title. This simple, step-by-step process of refining the information area enables the user to surf or search a far smaller and more concise body of data than any body of data that a search engine could use in conducting one of its searches. Moreover, most of the bad and ugly results will have been avoided, leaving the user with a much higher percentage of good results to show for his or her efforts.

The benefits of these hierarchically-organized subject matter directories are that they are created, researched, and maintained by people rather than programs and that subject matter experts are often employed to further refine and add value to the information they contain. This personal attention to and customization of the data helps to eliminate the large part of the

Web that contains unwanted, dated, or replicated information. Moreover, the hierarchical organization allows a user to navigate easily to and confine his or her search to the most appropriate area of information. It also offers the added benefit of enticing a user to browse a specific subject, a behavior not supported by other search mechanisms. Unlike search engines, however, subject matter directories offer a very narrow view of the contents of the Web; and because of the way they are created, they are highly subjective in terms of both their content and organization. Accordingly, each of these searchable subject matter sites is unique. Finding the one that best covers your particular area of interest may itself be something of a search.

Searchable databases provide the most specialized and focused type of information search on the Web. The CERN phone book is the first example of this approach to using the Web as a generic gateway or information delivery service to retrieving highly specific types of information. A simple Web form allowed search queries to be entered. The Web server passed the search criteria on to a custom program that interpreted this information and executed a query on the existing database system that held the names, locations, and phone numbers of the CERN scientists. The database returned the results of the query to the program, and the program packaged those results into an HTML file that it passed to the Web server and that the server, in turn, sent to the user's browser. Such information cannot be found by search engine spiders or be easily categorized by hierarchical subject matter listings, because it is not contained in accessible Web pages. The data is stored elsewhere, outside of the Web's information space (e.g., in a database) and is then retrieved and formatted into a Web page on demand.

A vast amount of information accessible on the Web exists outside the scope of simple HTML files. This information cannot be located, bookmarked, or categorized. Sometimes this is due to the fact that the information content needs to be stored in a way that can accommodate frequent updates, as is true of a large phone book or a catalogue that lists the contents of a library. Sometimes the information is stored in an older system that knows nothing about HTML or the Web, and the fastest way to make that information available is simply to provide a Web interface from which listings or searches can be performed. Sometimes the data itself is highly fragmentary in nature, like census data. Such information must wait for some sort of catalyst, for instance the specific criteria of a query, before individual pieces of information can be retrieved and assembled into some usable form. In any event, these less visible and more dynamic information resources (e.g., the Thomas search facility provided by the U.S. Library of Congress, described below) are worth discovering. They represent a growing, highly valuable, and often overlooked type of information resource on the Web that the other more generalized and commercialized types of search mechanisms tend to obscure.

Whatever type of search engine you choose to use, it is worth investing a few minutes in learning a little about its expectations and its limitations before executing that first search. No two search engines work precisely the same way; and the more you understand about how an engine will interpret your search criteria, the more likely it will return the information you seek. You should always begin by carefully choosing the words or phrases for your query. The more specific the better, although it is possible to be too specific; and spelling does count, although some services will catch basic misspellings and bring them to your attention. Then you must determine such things as whether or not the search engine is case sensitive, how it handles phrases as opposed to individual words, how it handles boolean (true/false) operators to distinguish matching *any* as opposed to *all* words, how it lets you exclude specific words or phrases, and how it handles special characters called *wildcards* that enable you to specify partial words. The list goes on. Simple differences in how you conduct a search for information may lead to profound differences in the quantity and content of the information returned by any search mechanism. For instance, if you are looking for the "Little Bo Peep" nursery rhyme, you may see a large difference between the results returned when you enter the three words surrounded by quotation marks and when you enter them without quotation marks.

As the information content of the Web continues to grow, trying to locate what you want may become more difficult rather than less. If nothing else, you will be confronted with more and more information resources, larger listings returned by searches, and an increasing number of sites and subject matter listings, making your ability to sift through this information that much more important. Sifting through information on the Web is something you become accustomed to quickly, but experienced at slowly. It is not difficult to become inundated with search results or to feel you've lost track of where you've been and what you were originally looking for. Moreover, there is a lot of purposeful misdirection on the Web: sites that represent themselves as one thing but turn out to be something else entirely, or sites with names that are close in spelling to those of popular sites that are waiting to prey on people who enter a typo or misspell a word. Sifting through the Web's mass and maze of information can be a challenge. One increasingly popular way to confront this challenge relies on information filtering, which is described below. Another, more advanced approach related to information sifting involves personal information agents, which are described later in this chapter.

Information Filtering: You versus Them

When you go in search of information on the Web, you should not assume that all potential matches for your search are necessarily being returned and shown to you. Because no matter how you go about locating information on the Web, every site and every tool filters information in some way before it reaches your browser. The process of filtering may be overt and may even be promoted as a feature, as in a search engine excluding known pornographic sites from the searches it conducts, or it may be covert and may be done to promote the site's business interests, as in a search engine moving references to sites hosted by its sponsors or partners to the top of the list of sites it returns. The most important things to know about information filtering on the Web is that it is already commonly used and its use is growing.

There are ways to use information filtering to your advantage, to use it as a tool to reduce the amount of information sifting you need to do with respect to trying to locate information on the Web. But the same process of filtering, instigated by you or by someone or something else, can just as easily prevent you from accessing specific types of information or specific information providers without your knowledge or consent. Some governments, for example, are determined to restrict access to certain types of information that are available on the Web. One way they achieve this control is by disabling all Internet communication to specific sites, such as Web sites controlled by the British Broadcasting Corporation, from computer networks operating within the country's borders. It is impossible for any user to know the extent of such efforts to control and filter information access on the Web.

Information filtering can occur either on the Web server providing you with information, on your computer through specialized software that excludes specific sites or types of information, or on some intermediary network device like a proxy server. (Proxy servers are discussed later in this chapter.) The most obvious and prevalent use of information filtering relates to preventing access to Web sites that contain or promote pornography, which is a large, growing, and commercially successful part of the Web. But given that the Web is largely an uncensored environment, there is a lot more than pornography that many people want to make inaccessible from their home and business environments.

For parents, information filtering begins at home. More and more companies are providing software that allows parents to categorize Web sites, adding some to a list of prohibited sites, others to a list of acceptable sites, and so on. This type of software typically includes content filtering algorithms and techniques to deny or allow access to sites based on certain criteria, as well as prepared site listings that categorize many existing sites for users. But even with all the software and information that is commonly available to help a parent or guardian create a safe and appropriate information environment on the family's shared-use personal computer, doing so is not as easy or effective as one might think (or demand).

Configuring the information filtering settings correctly for everyone who uses a specific computer is one challenge that many people find insurmountable. Another involves keeping the site listings and the filtering criteria current, which is critical given the dynamic nature of the Web's information space. Finally, it is important to realize that no software is capable of filtering all the information on the Web that you might consider objectionable or of providing the intelligence to do the job exactly as you would expect. By excluding one category of information, you may well be inadvertently eliminating access to information that you never meant to exclude. For instance, methods used to identify some pornographic sites often misidentify medical sites, such as ones dealing with breast cancer, and restrict access to them.

Information filtering takes on a different meaning and raises different questions when you take into account the public Internet terminals available in libraries throughout the world. Governments, local communities, librarians, teachers, parents, and children all have different views on whether or not such terminals should, or even legally can, filter information available over the Web. Equally vocal parties are arguing in favor of and against installing filtering software on such terminals to prevent or restrict access to pornographic, prejudicial, and violence-filled Web sites. A lot of creative and collaborative work will be necessary to resolve this problem to everyone's satisfaction, if it is even possible to do so.

Business operators, especially large organizations, are faced with similar questions and problems related to filtering information content on the Web. Many companies have found that unrestricted access to the Web leads to a significant amount of lost work time, because employees visit sites unrelated to the performance of their job. Centrally located devices can easily restrict network access to specific Web sites or to specific types of information; they can also track employee behavior on the network to alert management of possible abuses. These devices, however, can be expensive to purchase and maintain. Their use also raises questions relating to how and where a business draws the line for information filtering; how do you create and implement a corporate policy that works for everyone in the organization and does not negatively impact the work environment or the work being performed?

The larger issue of information filtering, however, is one of technology versus information access. The technology of the Web and the Internet makes no distinctions about the type of information that it stores, publishes, and transmits. Information is data; and data is composed of zeros and ones. On some level, all of this data is considered equal, varying only in size. There is no Web content rating system like the one that exists for movies and television. No agency exists, or even could exist, to oversee the information content of the Web. The decentralized nature of the Web and its global reach make this impossible. How then do you protect children, for instance, who represent a considerable percentage of frequent Web users, from deliberately or inadvertently coming into contact with information that simply is not meant for their eyes? How do you help yourself, your business?

If nothing else, you should be aware that information filtering exists. It is used by sites that help you search and navigate through the growing information space of the Web. It is part of Internet devices that may reside on the network through which you are connected to the Internet. It is a commonly installed application that may reside on the computer you use at home, the office, or in a public facility such as a hotel or library. Many questions and problems surround the use of information filtering; and these questions and problems exist at all levels: personal, professional, and societal. The consequences and controversies related to the use of information filtering on the Internet, and more specifically on the Web, are explored at greater length in *The Technology Revolution.*

Information Give and Take: Pull versus Push

The Web has turned some of us into information gluttons. We spend more and more of our time actively seeking out and *pulling down* information on demand as we use the Web to pursue information on our terms, according to our individual needs and schedules. At the same time, the Web has created a sort of subculture of information panderers *pushing down* their information to us whether we want it or not: consider the Web's incessant advertising banners, popups, and unsolicited emails, as well as the efforts of traditional broadcast media and advertisers to incite us to visit them on the Web. This pull-push dynamic imparts a difficult-to-define but prominent and distinct vitality to the Web's information space.

Prior to the Web, we relied on city or university libraries and the books, periodicals, and reference materials they housed to find the information we needed. This was the pre-Web equivalent to our pulling information on demand, as we searched for answers to questions, researched topics of interest, and otherwise tried to educate and entertain ourselves. Similarly, we relied on the broadcast media and the publishers of books, periodicals, and newspapers to supply mass-produced information to us on a schedule of their choosing. This pushed information allowed us to choose from a selection of news, sports, entertainment, and other sources of information, but the selection was relatively small and the content was typically produced for a particular geographic region or generalized audience. Also prior to the Web, information providers were very limited in their ability to know the preferences of their audience or their demographic makeup and to produce and distribute different information content for small, but distinctively different audiences. And we, as individuals, were very limited in our ability to publish and distribute the information we wanted to share.

The arrival of the Web effectively turned the tables on the information providers, the libraries, the publishers, and the broadcasters. It did so by empowering us as individuals to express and follow our uniquely individual wants and needs for information. We could find and access the information we wanted from an endless variety of global information sources, instead of being confined to the limited and local information sources of our area. We could also have our individual needs catered to, enabling information providers to supply us with the information we wanted and only that information.

The Web also turned the tables on the information providers by enabling us to publish in a way that was never before possible, to push our information into the world by making it openly accessible in the Web's information space. The contributions made by individuals in the form of home pages, journal entries (known as blogs), newsletters, and newsgroup postings (to name only a few ways in which to publish information on the Web) constitute a large and popular segment of the Web's information space. The size and diversity of this self-published information on the Web clearly demonstrates how much information individuals have to share when given the opportunity and freedom to do so.

Our ability to pull information content according to our individual needs and schedules is as empowering to us as it is beneficial to the information providers; and its benefits for them can be seen both in their greater capacity to push information down to us and in their newfound ability to pull information from us. For example, information providers can create and distribute information as they always have (e.g., in books, periodicals, newspapers, and television broadcasts) and, with very little additional effort, they can distribute that same information on the Web to reach a far larger and more geographically dispersed audience than is possible with any other type of publishing environment. We also benefit through such Web-publishing efforts by having a larger, more diverse selection of information sources available to us; we can access the radio station broadcasts and newspaper editorials from the town we grew up in, for example, even if we live thousands of miles away. But this example represents the simplest and perhaps least significant form of Web publishing.

Before the Web, when information providers broadcast or printed and distributed information entirely on their terms and according to their schedule, we either caught or missed that information as a result of any number of changing conditions in our busy lives. It was possible to locate some of this missed information by visiting a library or contacting the information provider directly and requesting a copy or a transcript; but doing so was time consuming and more the exception than the rule. But when the Web changed the way in which people could access information, it also changed the way in which information providers could distribute their information. The producer of a radio show, for example, can place the show's broadcasts on a Web site in the form of downloadable audio files for individuals to pull down and listen to on demand. Similarly, a newspaper can maintain archives of its articles, editorials, and other information on a Web site so that subscribers to the paper (or others) can easily access information they may have missed.

Because the Web makes it possible for information providers to learn about us, our browsing and buying habits, and the types of information we routinely access, it enables them to push information customized for our particular wants and needs. Consequently, the majority of information published on the Web is produced specifically for distribution on the Web, and much of this information is distributed in channels that are designed to appeal to a specific group of individuals, such as generation X, science fiction fans, dieters, or war protesters. The greater the number and diversity of channels, the larger and more diverse an audience a site may serve; and the more a site knows about the users who visit it, the greater its ability to select or suggest information channels for each user.

Because we pull this information down, either by visiting the sites that house the type of information that interests us or by requesting it be delivered to us (e.g., through email or through a Web portal's customizable home page), the costs for publishing this information are minimal. The combination of reduced costs for publishing information, the ability to reach a larger, more diverse audience than ever before possible, and the enhanced capacity to target information for smaller, more narrowly defined audiences has resulted in a revolution in information publishing. Organizations (in addition to individuals) that could never have afforded to publish information and reach their intended audience can use the Web to do so, no matter how esoteric the subject matter or how radical the viewpoint.

Information publishers are not the only ones to benefit from the economies of distributing information on the Web and the ability to pull information from users and recognize the preferences of individuals. Product manufacturers, service suppliers, advertisers, marketers, and others also benefit from the pull-push give-and-take of information on the Web. The same practice of information customization and audience targeting used in publishing information on the Web can be found in how advertising is conducted on the Web. When Web site owners know the individuals who visit their site, for example, they can choose to display a cat food advertisement to someone with two Siamese kittens and a pet store advertisement about adopting a cat to someone who has no pets on a Web page that is otherwise identical. For better or worse, this new capability of targeting specific information content for a specific audience is made possible by the Web and its two-way exchange of information, and it is changing the way information providers and advertisers develop and distribute their information.

Consider how information is still pushed indiscriminately down to us, through phone solicitations, junk mail, print and broadcast advertising, and other means. Consider the costs of such efforts alongside the hit-or-miss nature of the attempts. Now consider the Web from this perspective. We identify ourselves on the Web whenever we create an account on a site before buying a product or using a service. We willingly provide more information about ourselves when we fill out a Web form for a survey, a sweepstakes, or some type of promotional contest. We supply still more information about our preferences and browsing habits as we navigate the Web and unknowingly deposit data that can be used to retrace our movements through the Web's information space. The information about ourselves that we willingly supply, along with other information about us that is covertly gleaned from our use of the Web, is being collected in ever-increasing quantities and mined by more organizations and for more purposes each and every day. This information is being used to sell more cat food; but its value far exceeds its usefulness in selling products and services.

Where once existed an information gap — a separation between the information providers and the individual, due largely to the anonymity of the individual — the Web has introduced a type of information matrix that is responsible for capturing and collecting all forms of information about us and our lives, both on and off the Internet. The dynamics of how we get information and how information gets to us has changed, as the information we pull from the Web and the information being pushed at us is now being customized, even personalized. The Web has empowered us by turning us into information operators (and publishers). At the same time, however, it has transformed us into information targets and into sources of information that can be mined for any purpose imaginable.

Refining the Data Stream: Your Web

Information is an integral part of all of our lives; we consume information. We expect open and easy access to all types of information, and we rely on our various information suppliers so that we can stay informed, learn new things, make decisions, and be entertained. Each of us has our own unique wants and needs with respect to the types of information we routinely seek out. When the Sunday paper arrives, for instance, it is not uncommon for one person to grab the comics, another the sports section, another the front page news, and another the magazine. The Web has a similar effect on us with respect to its frequently changing information: each of us gravitates towards different information sources, including comics, sports, and headline news reports.

Unlike the Sunday paper, the Web is far more than the sum of its information. In addition to widening our access to information, the Web is transforming our expectations, demands, and dependence on information. This effect can be seen by examining how the Web enables you to customize information in an effort to suit your individual needs. Once you overcome that initial feeling of angst in navigating the Web and gain some familiarity with the Web's resources and an appreciation for the diversity of its information, it is not uncommon to realize that many of your information needs are recurring. This is when you take the next step on the information Web and refine the data stream according to your tastes. You make the Web *your* Web.

One of the most common and easiest ways to customize information on the Web is to create an account on one of the many Web portals, such as those provided by Yahoo!, Netscape, and Microsoft. Once you become a member (membership is typically free), you can choose from a wide selection of information channels, tools, and services. You can select news headlines from various sources, local (or remote) weather reports, financial news and stock quotes, entertainment news and local television and movie listings, your daily horoscope, sporting event scores, ski resort conditions, and more. You can customize calendar tools, see your appointments, and receive reminders for meetings, birthdays, and other events. You can create a Web email account and build your address book pages. You can store your real or imagined stock portfolios and watch their value sink and rise daily, weekly, monthly, and yearly. You can sign up for shopping specials and be notified when certain items go on sale, when auctions start, or when the list of best selling books changes. You can pay your bills and sign up to be notified when mortgage or auto loan rates drop below a certain level. You can elect to get daily tips on a wide assortment of subjects from parenting, to cooking, to exercising. After you select the information content that you want to receive, you can also personalize how you want it displayed by choosing from different page layouts and colors.

Customizing information sources and tools is an effective way to make the vastness of the Web's information space seem more welcoming. The effect of all this customization is that the Web's information is now channeled to you. You have created an online, personalized Web presence; and, in a way, you have now become part of the information Web. You have defined the information that is important to you, simplified your ability to locate some percentage of the information you routinely use, and enhanced what you can do with this information.

Even though creating an account may be free, there is a cost involved in using one of these Web portals. As described in the previous section, your information preferences are a source of information for others to use. While it may or may not matter to you, the fact that you like reading the Doonesbury comic strip or enjoy receiving a new recipe every day has both meaning for and value to others. Making others aware of this information might, for instance, result in your being shown more advertisements for a new cooking show on television or for a line of pots and pans that just went on sale at one of the Web portal's sponsored Web sites. The information that is collected about you in no way diminishes the value of using one of these sites. But it may be helpful to remember that you and your preferences are a commodity on the Web and, the more of your information you make known, the more you personally become part of the information Web.

Storing and Representing Information

Finding and accessing information on the Web is one thing. Where and how that information is stored is something else entirely. The technology of the Web does an excellent job of hiding all the nuts and bolts — the wires, protocols, computers, and applications — responsible for managing the information accessed through the Web and bringing this vast store of information to us. This effect, however, does not diminish the need for Web servers, Web browsers, and other applications to perform such frequent and fundamental tasks as recording information, storing it on some device for retrieval and use at a later date, and representing it in a way best suited to how the information is used or what it contains.

The simplest Web sites store information in a collection of HTML files on the hard drive of a Web server. This approach suits relatively small sites that contain infrequently updated information. More complex sites, however, typically store information in a variety of different file types, including one called XML that has been engineered to make up for the deficiencies of HTML; and they use applications designed for the storage and management of information, such as relational databases, to store and maintain information that needs to be updated, searched, sorted, combined, or collected into reports. It is not apparent or relevant to a user how a site stores and represents its information; any two sites can use radically different approaches and yet look and behave like they have few if any operational differences. This engineering flexibility is a significant contributing factor to the Web's success.

The Web also needs to store and represent the information we provide, record, and request to be remembered as we browse the Web, fill out a Web form, bookmark a site, and add items to a shopping cart. This type of information can also be collected, stored, represented, and used in any number of ways. But because this information is related directly to us and our use of the Web and, moreover, because some of it is stored on our computers as opposed to a Web server, how a Web site handles this information is relevant to us. It impacts the nature of our presence in the Web's information space and has implications for the privacy and security of our personal information.

The following sections describe some of the ways in which the Web's information is stored, what this information looks like, how it is collected, and how it is remembered. In addition to an explanation of how databases are used and how online libraries catalog information, Web forms, XML, bookmarks, and cookies are presented.

Storing Information with Databases

Databases are the information warehouses of the Web. Amazon.com, for instance, is more database than shopping mall or bookstore; all the products lining its virtual shelves derive from the information stored in its database. Just as the Web makes no demands on how information is stored or where it exists, databases make no demands on how information is used, combined, or presented. They store vast amounts of information, broken down into its smallest, constituent elements; and they allow this information to be easily and quickly changed, deleted, added to, or combined.

Databases store information in tables that effectively consist of columns and rows. Think of your checkbook's ledger with its columns of date, check number, description, and amount, with each row or record listing a separate check or transaction. When you fill out a membership form on a Web site, your information is typically stored as a new row of data in one or more database tables. Your first name, last name, address, and telephone number will all be stored in separate columns. Information that is selected from lists rather than typed in, such as your marital status or years of education, will also be stored in separate columns. But here your selection may be represented referentially, perhaps with a simple number or code. This referential data is then linked to another table that stores all the associated details. For instance, the number 1 might indicate single, the number 2 divorced, and so on. Storing information as simply as possible and establishing relationships between tables of information is at the heart of relational databases, which are used throughout the Web to store persistent data (i.e., data that needs to be recalled at a later date).

If you look at Amazon.com, you can quickly appreciate the importance of storing information in databases. The site contains information about many thousands of items to purchase, many thousands of accounts, and many thousands of transactions, all of which are stored in one or more databases. When you log in, the site's Web server checks that your login and password information match what it has stored in its database. It may retrieve preferences you specified previously and additional information relating to prior purchases from its database, so that it can suggest items that you may be more likely to buy. It then combines this information with other information derived from its database about current sales and promotions to build a Web page exclusively for you. Every Web page on the site is built much the same way, dynamically, with most of the information retrieved from a database. The process of building these pages typically takes a matter of seconds. Databases make this speed and efficiency possible.

It is not just storefronts that rely on databases for information storage on the Web. The information displayed on most larger, more sophisticated Web sites changes periodically; and whether a site displays the same content to everyone, or different content on demand as search engines do, or different content based on user preferences as Web portals do, the storage and updating of this information is greatly simplified through the use of databases. Even displaying something as basic as the copyright information that appears at the bottom of all the pages on a site can benefit from storing that information in a database. When it needs to be changed, the information can be updated once in the database, rather than a dozen or a hundred or a thousand times in each of the site's static HTML pages. Without databases, the Web would be a slower, smaller, poorer, and far less dynamic information space.

Cataloging Information with Libraries

While databases provide a highly efficient way to store, organize, and associate pieces of information, libraries on the Web serve much the same function, only on a different level. Databases work with data fragments and remain hidden from view, storing and retrieving information in a way that best suits the data. But online libraries catalog information in a form that we are familiar with — as articles, periodicals, and books — and they are designed to interact directly with a user to facilitate access to their information resources. Despite differences between an online library and its brick-and-mortar counterpart in terms of how we visit them and access information, both serve the same purpose of providing repositories of information that are open to the public.

Libraries on the Web represent a major information resource for students, educators, researchers, scientists, and others. They vary tremendously, however, with respect to both form and function. Many are online extensions of their physical counterparts, enabling us to do such things as search their card catalogs for books or periodicals, find out about lectures or special events, and renew borrowed books. Some are information catalogs about particular subjects, like the Ornithological Web Library (www.aves.net/the-owl/) that organizes and presents information on Web sites devoted to wild birds and their study. Others are general-purpose online research collections, like questia (www.questia.com) that houses a large number of fully searchable books, journals, and articles and includes tools for writing notes in the page margins, highlighting text, and creating footnotes and bibliographies. What all of these online libraries have in common, however, is that they collect and catalog some type of information and use the Web to make this information easily and widely accessible.

Consider the Library of Congress in Washington D.C., the largest library in the world, containing more than 120 million items stored on roughly 530 miles of bookshelves. Its presence on the Web (www.loc.gov) allows it to better fulfill its purpose of making its resources freely available to both Congress and to us. Through its Web site, we can learn about the Library and its history, explore American history and culture, find resources, and ask questions of a librarian, from the comfort of our home or office and anytime of the day or night. Without the Web, or had the Library not created its site, access to the extensive resources of the Library of Congress would have remained limited to those who could travel to and visit its physical location. Its virtual location in the Web's information space exemplifies what both the Library and the Web were originally built to do: to facilitate the open, free, unrestricted sharing of information.

The Library also promotes an initiative called the National Digital Library Program. Its focus is to digitize selected contents of the Library for electronic access and distribution. Already, millions of the Library's records are available online, including its entire card catalog. An associated service called Thomas, in tribute to Thomas Jefferson, provides an interface and search facility for current and past activities of the Congress, its legislation, the congressional record, and committee information. Also cataloged and available are current and past Library exhibitions and millions of images taken from over one hundred of the Library's historical collections.

Some argue that online libraries do more harm than good, that they diminish the use of our public libraries, divert funds from their maintenance, and serve to promote a more superficial type of online reading at the expense of traditional book reading. Others see them as complementary institutions, expanding the reach of libraries and the knowledge they contain, providing easy and equal access to remote resources, and helping to preserve the rich and often unique information they house for future generations. In the end, our behavior will decide this issue.

Collecting Information with Forms

Web forms are common throughout the Web. They are used to collect information from us and often about us. For instance, search engines use a simple Web form to collect our search criteria; they also typically provide a more advanced form that includes an assortment of text fields, selectable options that employ dropdown lists and checkboxes, and on/off buttons, that allow us to specify greater precision in our search. Web stores use these same forms, first to record the merchandise we want to purchase and finally to collect our payment and shipping information.

What all these forms have in common is that they collect and temporarily store our information before they hand it off to an associated program for validation and processing. They do this by recording each piece of information (e.g., the contents of a text field that holds your last name, your selection of a state or country from a dropdown list, and your choice of yes or no with respect to gift wrapping) in individual variables specified in the HTML page that constitutes the form. Depending on how a form is written, you may see these variables and your associated information appear as part of the URL displayed by your browser after you submit the form. If so they will appear as name/value pairs separated by ampersands, as in:

```
last_name=Mertz&state=NY&giftwrap=NO
```

As you may have guessed, information collected through Web forms typically ends up being stored in a database. The information may first be *massaged* or *normalized* in order to make the data more uniform, perhaps by removing excessive spacing or turning all entered text into uppercase letters. But in order for this information to be retained, it must be recorded in some persistent storage device, such as a database. Sometimes this information is also stored in a persistent form on your computer. This is where *cookies* come into play on the Web; they are discussed in a separate section below.

Representing Information with XML

For some, the Extensible Markup Language (XML) represents the next-generation replacement for HTML. But it is a lot more than that. While some consider XML a new and more powerful way to represent data, it is actually a smartly done repackaging of the Standard Generalized Markup Language (SGML), which was introduced in the chapter on the history of the Web. SGML was used widely at CERN and many other places as a means to customize information templates with something called Document Type Definitions (DTDs) in an effort to define and identify all elements in a document. What this means is that an SGML DTD specifies a set of rules, like the syntax for a language, and a strict vocabulary that can be used when identifying document elements, like <TITLE> and <PARAGRAPH> and <SECTIONHEAD>.

Consider HTML the Web's DTD. It contains a static, well-defined number of markup elements; and HTML files must conform to certain basic structural rules if they are to be correctly interpreted. The problem is that HTML is a weak DTD; it cannot do everything people want it to do. It is also diluted with elements that are purely typographic. Instead of identifying the content type of the information, these elements identify how the information will appear when displayed or printed. For example, HTML elements are commonly used to identify text as boldface or italic, instead of marking the information according to its specific type of content (e.g., new terminology, a book title, or the name of a command). Worst of all, HTML is not adaptable. It does not include a mechanism for adding and defining new elements, which means that complex and simple documents must both conform to the same lowest-common-denominator approach to markup.

XML is meant to fix all of these problems, and not simply for new and improved Web page documents. As its name indicates, XML is extensible, which means that it is what you make of it. You build a vocabulary. You define the rules that determine which elements are required, which are optional, what order things need to be in, and so on. XML allows you to create documents with terminology that makes sense to you and that matches your particular type of information and the specific needs of your application. The best part is that your XML files can be used for any number of purposes. You can display them on the Web; you can use them to build other types of files; and you can filter them through any number of formatting templates to produce different output for different audiences or media.

Imagine for a moment that you have a Web site devoted to recipes. Recipes contain a small set of well-defined types of information. Each recipe has a title, a list of ingredients, a set of instructions, perhaps some notes or warnings, and an author. With XML you can document each recipe file with descriptive terms that exactly match the types of information that the recipe contains: <TITLE>, <INGREDIENT>, <INSTRUCTION>, <NOTE>, <AUTHOR>. To begin with, using this type of customized markup allows your files to read like recipes. Instead of marking up the content with general terms that identify paragraphs, headings, and bullet lists, you have identified exactly what type of information each text area contains. This simple, but fundamental operation allows you to do a lot more with your recipe files than would have been possible had they remained coded in HTML. Programs can be written to distinguish the different types of data stored in each file. You could, for example, write a program to search all recipes for those that call for olives as an ingredient. You could also produce a cookbook by easily collecting all the recipes from one or more of the recipe authors, or all the vegetarian recipes.

What XML brings to the Web is a new and rich environment for developing and representing information. Through the use of XML, information can be developed independently of any concern for presentation or format. Information can be more easily reused: one source file can be used to populate a Web page, produce an internal company report, or help generate statistical information for inclusion in a spreadsheet. Information can be identified using terms that make sense for the type of information being represented, rather than through weaker, less useful generic terms. The final chapter in this part of the book, "The Semantic Web," provides a more detailed look at how and why XML may be integral to the future of the Web and, more generally, to information management on the Internet.

Recording Locations with Bookmarks

There is nothing complicated about bookmarks. Their purpose is to make our favorite Web locations more easily accessible. They do this by storing Web page locations, identified by their URL, and presenting them to the browser as a standard hyperlink. One click and the page is located and loaded. Bookmarks also typically store additional information, such as your name for the location (the page's title is used by default, but you have the option to change it), when the bookmark was added, the last time the page was accessed, and the last time the page was modified. Bookmarks differ from the other ways in which information is stored and represented on the Web discussed above in two areas. One, bookmarks are stored and managed on an individual's computer — on the client side — instead of on a Web server. Two, bookmarks are entirely browser-dependent; each browser developed its own methodology to add, delete, edit, and organize bookmarks, which means there is no standardized way in which this information is stored and represented.

Netscape was the first to introduce the term *bookmark* in its Navigator browser and to apply it to the storage of Web page addresses. Microsoft included the same basic functionality in its Internet Explorer browser, but it used the term *favorites* to name the feature. While the browsers from Netscape and Microsoft store bookmark information differently, how their respective bookmarking features are used and what they are used for are the same: both enable the user to record a Web page address in a single click and to organize the stored listing of addresses into categories.

Some people spend a fair amount of time and energy collecting and organizing bookmarks. They use their bookmarks as a type of personal map of the Web and its resources. It is not uncommon for such people to create elaborate, personal home pages to more effectively organize their maps of the Web and to make them more readily accessible. Such efforts are reminiscent of Berners-Lee's original Enquire program, with its internal and external links and its idea that one's personal information space intersected the larger, remote information space of others.

The problem with bookmarks is that they can become stale, as occurs when a Web page changes its location or is removed entirely. To counter this problem, some people employ personal programs or agents that automatically read through their collected bookmarks, connect to the specified addresses, record whether or not the page is still active, and then update their bookmarks accordingly. Personal agents like this are described in more detail below. But a more basic solution to this problem is already long overdue.

Remembering Us with Cookies

Just as databases store persistent information about your visit to a Web site on the Web site itself, cookies were designed as a simple means of storing persistent information about you on your computer. They enable a Web server to recognize your identity upon your return and to recall preferences, selections, and other information that was captured and stored on your computer from an earlier visit.

Cookies store relatively small and simple pieces of information. They consist of name/value pairs that store data, such as:

```
CUSTOMER=FRED_MERTZ
SHIPPING=FEDEX
```

They include additional information, such as a date when the cookie will expire and what Internet domain it is used with.

A common use for cookies involves storing your user name and password for a particular site so that the next time you visit you will not need to go through its login form. The Web site will automatically read the previously stored cookie information, submit your login and password information to the program that authenticates users for access to the system, and redirect you accordingly. Of course, it is not you that the program is authenticating for access; it is whoever is sitting at your computer and is using your browser. This is one reason why security-sensitive sites will ask you to supply your password when you attempt to enter an area that might affect or display sensitive information, like your credit card information.

Another use for cookies involves storing information used with shopping cart applications, a component found on most commerce-based Web sites. Cookies are used to store information about the items you have selected for purchase, instead of using an application or database on the Web site to track your selections. The cookies allow you to put and retain items in a shopping cart while you browse a site (i.e., without logging in or otherwise identifying yourself on the site), something that would be impossible to do on the Web site without your opening an account and logging in. You can then return at some later time and, provided the cookies have not expired (depending on their intended use, cookies are created to last hours, days, months, or years), your shopping cart contents will be read and interpreted by the Web server as if you had never left the site. The only way this type of information storage could be achieved was by recording information about your selections on your computer. You bring the information that constitutes the contents of the shopping cart with you when you next visit the site.

Web cookies have confused and even alarmed many people since they were first introduced by Netscape. Like bookmarks, cookies store information on an individual's computer instead of on a Web server, and the information contained in cookies is browser-specific (i.e., a cookie can only be accessed and used by the same browser that stored it). But unlike bookmarks, this information is created and deposited on your computer as a result of an action initiated by a Web server, not because of an action performed by you. This is part of the perceived problem. Furthermore, the information stored in cookies can be easily accessed by that Web server sometime in the future; this is why they were created. The retrieval of the information stored in a cookie by a Web server may occur, and most often does occur, entirely without your knowledge or explicit consent. This is the other part of the perceived problem.

Cookies that store login information and shopping cart items are by themselves relatively innocuous. It is the potential for abuse, however, that alarms many people. Since cookies are created and later read by Web servers without our consent or knowledge, we have no control over the types of information that Web sites choose to remember about us. Cookies can be used to store any type of information that a Web site wishes to track; they are in no way limited to storing information that directly benefits us in using a Web site. Web sites use cookies to track the frequency of our visits to their site and other related information that can be used to assist them in the running of their site. Another common use of cookies is to record which advertisements a Web site has shown to us and which pages and products we have viewed. Cookies are, therefore, a major factor contributing to the erosion of our privacy while we browse the Web.

Another privacy issue related to cookies involves Web site advertising and the business of affiliate management that goes along with it. It is very likely that cookies have been deposited on your computer from Web sites that you never realized you visited, storing personal information about you that you never consented to reveal. When you click on an advertisement, for example, you frequently do not go directly to that advertiser's Web site. Instead, you are directed to a Web site run by an affiliate management company that records information about your click as part of a process of paying the Web site owner for your click; the Web site run by the affiliate management company then forwards you on to the advertiser's site. Oftentimes, the information collected by these affiliate management companies (which can be considerable) is used to track your browsing and buying habits. Therefore, the concern with this type of cookie use is largely one of awareness. Very few people know that this type of information is being collected and that, through cookies, our computers are being used as part of the process. This privacy issue and the technology surrounding it is discussed at length in a chapter entitled, "The Shadow Web."

Cookies were designed to meet a specific need: to retain information that the Web itself was not designed to collect and store. They serve this purpose well by storing small, simple pieces of information with our computer and browser. Abuse of this technology, however, has left us all vulnerable to its exploitation by organizations that want to try to track our movements through the Web. The question remains about how we can obtain control over the type of information others store on our computers in order to simplify and enhance our interaction with the information Web and, at the same time, assert control over the privacy of our information.

Soon after the use of cookies became controversial, browsers began providing configurable options relating to the handling of cookies. These options included whether or not the browser would accept cookies, if the user would be prompted before accepting a cookie, and the ability to delete cookies. These options, while a step in the right direction, are very limited in their ability to help the typical user safely navigate the Web, retain control over his or her privacy, and still be able to buy products, use Web portal sites, or do any number of other things on the Web that depend on cookies to function. Somehow the eventual solution will need to come from the technology itself.

Automating the Discovery and Protection of Information

The Web succeeded so well at creating an information management system that complemented the interoperability of the Internet, fulfilled the diverse needs of virtually every type of information provider, and still managed to be fast and easy to use that it defied all attempts to accurately forecast how fast or far it would grow or how it would be used. The Web charted its own path and its information space quickly developed into something far removed from its simple and humble beginnings at CERN. Consequently, as the amount of information on the Web grew, as more and more people became active on the Web, and as privacy and security issues took on greater importance for both individuals and businesses, innovative Web technology was developed to solve emerging problems, improve the overall performance of the Web, and provide better overall information management.

Much of this technology was directed at automating the discovery of information on a Web that was growing exponentially and that was housing more and more dynamic information. It was also directed at refining control over information access, to protect information from unauthorized access and to protect people from being exposed to certain types of information (e.g., pornography). In general, this technology set out to address the following questions. How do you map the contents of the Web? How do you help people find the information they need? Conversely, how do you keep parts of the Web that may be considered offensive or dangerous isolated from a particular audience? What can be done to help individuals use the vast information resources of the Web and not be overwhelmed by too much information? What can be done to help businesses limit their employees' exposure to the Web, protect their company's data and computers, and even reduce their networking costs? Some of the answers to these questions are presented below.

Web Agents: Bots and Spiders

Automated agents, generally referred to as *bots*, an abbreviation of robots, roam the Web in search of information and provide a variety of other services. The most common form of web bot is called a spider. Spiders are principally used by various types of search engines to locate information dispersed throughout the ever-growing Web by crawling from link to link; they return some or all of the information they find to the spider's point of origin so that it can be used as data against which searches can be performed. Their goal is to discover and map the information contents of the Web, thereby making the Web more accessible and its information easier to locate.

If someone publishes a Web site on the mating habits of lobsters or creates a Web store containing models of every lighthouse in the world, you need a way to know that these sites exist and know something about what they offer if you are to make use of them. If you cannot locate these sites when you are looking for information on lobsters or when you want to purchase a lighthouse model, what use will they be? Spiders were designed to discover such information for exactly this purpose: to automate the mapping of and assist in the classification of information on the Web, so that when you search for information on lobsters, lighthouses, or anything else, the sites that contain the requested information have already been located, categorized, and, therefore, made findable. Without spiders and their tireless efforts to crawl through the Web's information space on our behalf, information on the Web would be far less manageable and much of the Web would remain undiscovered.

Bots residing on Web sites perform a wide variety of information management tasks. Generally, they automate repetitive work that would otherwise need to be performed by individuals. Some act like spiders, but crawl through a local Web site (as opposed to the Web at large) in order to index a site's contents and provide various ways for users to browse and locate information stored on that site. Other bots focus on auditing the performance and operation of Web sites. One class of these auditing bots focuses on external audits that compare one site's ranking on various search engines and other informational sites with those of its competitors. Another class focuses on internal audits that check a site for a wide range of hardware, software, and file problems in an effort to prevent problems or to locate problems before they get worse. Some bots are used to check the continued validity of links by testing that their addresses still exist and return valid pages. There are even bots to help individuals create their own Web sites, upload files to a Web service provider, and monitor the performance of Web sites.

Web bots were originally created for large Web sites, especially those in the business of providing Web resources to others. But now individuals can employ various types of bots to do their bidding on the Web. Bot software can be purchased on the Internet, either in the form of engineered bots that perform a specific function or, for the more advanced user, as an application that allows you to build your own specific type of bot. There are also many sites that offer bot software that can be freely downloaded from the Internet.

There are personal search bots for finding and downloading image files or music files, others that perform searches by simultaneously consulting several search engines or visiting sites directly, some that are specifically designed to search newsgroup information, and some that act like private detectives and search people directories and databases for individuals or for genealogical information. There are also bots that track computer usage behavior, news stories, and weather reports.

Email bots can be used to automatically check any number of email accounts and notify you if any new mail has arrived, saving you the trouble of first visiting those sites yourself. Email bots can also be used to eliminate unwanted email, relieving you of the growing problem of spam. Tracking bots can be used to watch specific sites and Web pages, letting you know when they have been updated, and even retrieving pages automatically when they have changed. Surfing bots can be used to eliminate annoying pop-up Web advertisements, monitor and limit browser behavior, block certain types of sites or specific Web sites, and periodically clean your computer records in order to protect your privacy.

Shopping bots can be used to search the Web as your personal buyer. They will check various auction sites for specific merchandise or conduct exhaustive comparison shopping for new merchandise. Many bots are geared specifically to the stock market; they watch for rising or falling stock prices and market trends, and seek out new company stories and events. There are even artificial life bots that can be used in Internet chat rooms and for other communication purposes. They can, for instance, take the form of cartoon characters or pets and provide an animated presence to help present online information or tutorials, or act as personal assistants in order to help you work or organize information, or simply to accompany you when you are browsing the Web.

As you may have guessed, there is a future in bot technology and bot usage. They provide control, perform routine, but necessary tasks, tirelessly monitor systems and situations, map information, and generally reduce the overhead of performing many recurring Web-related activities. As the Web continues to expand in both size and influence, these Web agents will become responsible for performing more work and providing more services for both individuals and information providers.

Proxy Servers and Information Caching

Proxy servers are networking devices that are installed at many business locations to help reduce external Internet traffic by means of what are called *store-and-forward caches*. What this means is that, if your browser is configured to use a proxy server, as is common practice at many business locations, your computer never directly connects to a Web site. Instead, it connects to the proxy server and passes it the URL you are requesting; the proxy server then retrieves the page and forwards it to your computer's browser. As explained below, a proxy server may be performing any of several important tasks in acting as an intermediary between your computer and the Internet at large.

Proxy servers are typically configured as cache servers, which means they store retrieved Web pages locally on their system. When a proxy server receives a request to retrieve a URL, it first checks its local cache of pages for a valid copy of the one being requested. If it finds the page locally, it forwards it to the computer that made the request without generating any traffic outside of the company's intranet. If there is no local copy, it connects to the Web site specified in the URL and retrieves the page on behalf of the local computer, stores the page for future requests, and forwards it to the local computer. Even relatively small companies can profit from such simple, but powerful efficiencies; and, in turn, the Internet as a whole profits through greatly reduced traffic. Since Web pages can quickly become dated, however, particularly those that contain frequently updated information such as news headlines and weather reports, time stamps are used with the cached pages, along with other configurable parameters, to control how long certain pages are cached and when they should expire. These controls signal when the proxy server should retrieve a fresh copy of any particular Web page.

Most people do not know, or care, whether or not they use a proxy server at work. Unless the proxy server configuration was done incorrectly and the pages being retrieved are stale, or the proxy server is unable to take into account site personalization features, such as those provided by Web portals, the use of a proxy server, like its benefits, remain transparent to users on the network. Generally, proxy servers reduce the time it takes to retrieve pages, eliminate the duplicated effort of many people accessing the same resources, reduce overall network bandwidth requirements, and enhance security by minimizing direct interaction between the Internet and individual company computers.

Proxy servers are also becoming more common in home computer environments. They are being used to hide a computer's IP address from the Internet, thereby providing an additional layer of security. Also, many proxy servers offer the added feature of Web site and information filtering. They are, therefore, also being used by families to restrict information access to objectionable Web sites.

Firewalls and Information Protection

Firewalls are a different sort of networking device, geared more towards security, although it is not uncommon for a single device to act as both a firewall and a proxy server. Firewalls provide precise control over incoming and outgoing traffic between your computer — or your company's computers — and the Internet. Their job is to receive, inspect, and then either accept or reject all incoming data before it reaches your computer; and they can regulate outgoing data, too. As the name implies, their purpose is to prevent any harm coming to your computer or your network.

One of the most important and common tasks for firewalls is packet filtering. The data that travels through the Internet is contained in Internet packets that are defined by the TCP/IP specifications. Firewalls examine each and every one of these little packets, but only in two areas: the address information (i.e., the IP addresses and ports of the origination point and destination) and the protocol. They then check this information against the list of rules (called policies) that have been configured to determine whether to accept or reject the packet in question. The most common policy is one that blocks packets from one IP address or from a range of IP addresses. IP addresses are routinely blocked when it is discovered that someone is attempting to, or has succeeding in, breaking into one of the computers on the local network.

Another function of firewalls is to act as a circuit relay or circuit-level gateway. This means the firewall validates individual computer connections as they attempt to perform specific types of operations, such as starting a TELNET or FTP session. In this case, the firewall not only uses address and protocol information in making its determination, it also checks settings for user and password information as well as the time of day. Once the connection is allowed, the firewall passes the data back and forth across the connection, hiding the local computer from the Internet. A common use for this service is to enable outgoing connections while denying incoming ones, working under the assumption that the local computer users can be trusted. This protects you and the network from an external attack, while leaving you free to reach the Internet.

Firewalls can also function as application gateways. This means they serve as a proxy for applications. Like a proxy server, the firewall becomes the intermediary between the local computer and one on the Internet, handling the data exchanges on behalf of the local computer and keeping it entirely hidden from the Internet. This enables the firewall to allow use of some commands while denying others, allow or deny access based on file type, and configure different levels of access for different users. As an application gateway, it can also create detailed access logs to record networking traffic, monitor events looking for suspicious or troublesome behavior, and sound alarms in case of problems. Security on the Web, and on the Internet in general, is largely dependent on the existence of firewalls.

The Multimedia Web

The Multimedia Web

The term multimedia predates the Web. It describes the use of several forms of communication media to convey information. It is commonly applied to devices (e.g., CDROMs) and information storage systems (e.g., computers and the Web) that deliver information using some combination of text, graphics, animation, audio, and video; but it also refers to an approach to presenting information that regards the combined effect of several forms of media as a more engaging and powerful way to educate and entertain than is possible through any single form of media. A common example of the use of multimedia is a presentation that combines text and graphics with voice-over narration.

The invention in 1985 of the CDROM device (a piece of computer hardware that reads data from a compact disk, or CD) was responsible for introducing multimedia to computers. A single CD can store several hundred megabytes of information; by comparison, a floppy disk, which was then the only other common type of removable storage, can at most store about 1.5 megabytes. The large storage capacity of a CD made it possible to distribute multimedia content for the first time; this content took the form of games, self-paced courses, product demonstrations, and documentation that were designed to take advantage of the associated advances made in video and sound card technology. But it was the Internet, largely by means of the Web, that popularized the use of multimedia and greatly expanded its influence. Through its use of multimedia content, the Web transformed the Internet from an environment that was predominantly text-only to one that was rich with photos and artwork, animations and movies, and audio clips and live radio.

Although multimedia content on the Internet exists independently of the Web, the Web greatly simplifies its delivery. That's because the Web is an ideal platform on which to combine different types of media easily and effectively, as was demonstrated by the Web site described in chapter 1 that merged text with photos, audio, and video to create a virtual tour of Honolulu Community College's dinosaur exhibit. Creating a site that uses multimedia effectively, however, is a lot more challenging than simply using the technology. A site like the dinosaur exhibit is still more the exception than the rule.

Multimedia Web documents are HTML files that include hypermedia links. Unlike Web documents that only include hypertext links, which interconnect text-based information with other text-based information, documents that include hypermedia links interconnect text-based information and other types of document elements with multimedia objects, like photos, audio recordings, and animations. Many of these multimedia objects are stored as files; they contain a digital representation of an image, an audio clip, or a video recording.

A commonly used multimedia object included in many Web documents are the animations displayed as part of Web page advertisements. Animation files are typically built from a series of separate images arranged in a sequence and encapsulated into a single file, such as a GIF (Graphics Interchange Format) image file. They are the computer equivalent of the little booklets children create by stacking a series of drawings and then flipping the pages to produce the illusion of movement. Another type of multimedia object that is becoming more common on Web sites consists of streaming content, such as broadcast radio. Streaming content, as the name suggests, contains live or recorded information that is played or displayed as the data stream continues to be delivered across the Internet to the user's computer. Streaming audio and video content are two more examples of the Web acting as a point of convergence for different types of information distribution. Like the distribution of other multimedia objects, streaming content does not rely on the Web to be distributed or played. But Web sites simplify how we access these resources, hypermedia links contained in Web documents collect and interconnect these multimedia objects, and Web browsers seamlessly manage how we retrieve these various types of information objects and how they are displayed or played on our computers (e.g., starting up an application to play a video).

Early Web sites limited their use of multimedia objects, mostly because of a lack of network bandwidth. Bandwidth determines how much data can be transferred from one network location to another in a given amount of time; more than any other factor, bandwidth affects how much time it takes for a browser to retrieve and display a Web page. Generally speaking, the greater the bandwidth the faster data may be transferred. Bandwidth is a critical concern for Web sites that want to include multimedia objects because these objects are typically much larger in size than text objects, like HTML files. If a large percentage of a Web site's visitors are connecting to the Internet over a low-bandwidth service, such as a 28.8 Kbps modem, the site's pages will display reasonably quickly only if the pages' content are limited to text or text mixed with small graphics files. If, instead, the site's pages include animations, large graphics files, and other multimedia objects, visitors may need to wait minutes, rather than seconds, as the data transfers to their computers; and many will likely go elsewhere before the data transfer completes.

Concerns over the use of multimedia objects having an adverse impact on the delivery of information have been addressed recently in two ways. First, higher bandwidth Internet services, such as those provided by DSL (Digital Subscriber Lines), cable, and satellite, have been made available and are becoming more affordable. Many more home Internet users and businesses are, therefore, connecting to the Internet using these faster services. Second, more sophisticated methods have been developed to reduce the size of multimedia files and speed up the transmission of streaming content without sacrificing their quality. Such methods include techniques for compressing data before transmitting it and uncompressing it after it has been received and specialized algorithms that resample the original data in order to reduce its size. (Resampling data means taking a multimedia object, like a high-fidelity audio recording, and using a program to carefully examine its data and remove selected segments that are not absolutely needed for it to be displayed or played on a computer.) As bandwidth becomes less and less of an issue, the use of multimedia content will probably increase as more and different types of multimedia services appear on the Internet.

Through its distribution of multimedia content, the Web is transforming parts of the publishing industry, such as the publication of magazines and newspapers, augmenting the businesses of radio broadcasting and music sales, and threatens to change much of the entertainment and news industry forever by radically altering how its content reaches audiences and by allowing that content to be retrieved on demand. The sections below explore the current state of multimedia content on the Web and some of the history behind the growth of related technologies, like Java applets and 3D modeling.

Publications

The Web seems like it was purposely designed for much of the publishing industry, and especially for newspapers and magazines. Establish a connection to the Internet, configure a Web server, convert your publication's existing information to HTML, and suddenly you have a whole new channel through which to distribute your articles, stories, photos, artwork, job and merchandise advertisements, and so on. Additionally, you don't incur the expense of printing and distribution; and you don't have to delay the release of time-sensitive information because of production schedules. Publication of the news in general, and of stories of breaking events in particular, takes on a whole new level of immediacy, a level approaching that of broadcast radio and television. What could be a better advancement for the publishing industry?

The Web, and Web browsers, were originally engineered and subsequently refined with publishing in mind. Existing publications, like popular, weekly magazines and daily newspapers, seemed likely businesses to recognize the Web's potential for the publishing industry and create an early presence on the Web. After all, they possessed the single most important and highly prized commodity for publishing on the Web; they controlled information that people already paid for. Moreover, by the time the Web was first becoming popular in the mid 1990s, these publishing operations were already largely computerized, which meant that their stories and the images associated with them were stored as files, and typesetting was done electronically rather than mechanically. They had incurred considerable expense to computerize their publishing operations in the expectation of reduced printing costs, less time to write, edit, approve, and typeset information, and greater efficiencies in handling and sharing information. In the process, they had also unknowingly completed most of the difficult work that would be needed to get their information onto the Web.

But the publishers had to resolve a number of unfamiliar and challenging problems before they could consider publishing on the Web. Would they charge for this new service, and if so, how? What would happen to their existing subscription base if the same information was now available electronically? What changes would they need to make to their existing advertising structure? Not least, where would they obtain the expertise to create a Web site that would match the quality and standards of their printed publication? Moreover, there were those in the industry who believed that the Web was a fad (some still believe this), and investing time, energy, and money in a venture that might not last seemed ill advised.

While the mainstream publishing establishment waited, wondered, and considered its options, something new and strikingly different appeared on the Web: publications created and designed exclusively for the Web. One of the first such online publications was called HotWired. It appeared in 1994, when the NCSA Mosaic browser was used by the vast majority of people on the Web and a few short weeks before the official release of Netscape's first browser, Navigator. HotWired was created by the avant-garde publishers of *Wired* magazine. The content of Wired was focused on the advances and cultural changes brought about by new technology; it had debuted a short year and half earlier.

The HotWired Web site and its online publication, like the printed magazine, positioned itself as the chronicler of the digital revolution. But HotWired was not simply an online version of the magazine. It was, instead, an associated publication that presented entirely new content and that demonstrated through its use of the Web the exciting, new multimedia technology of the Web. From the very beginning, the guiding principle of HotWired was "no shovelware." Unlike many of the Web sites that were to follow, the design of their site and its contents were ruled by and subject to the unique qualities of the Web's online forum. The publishers of HotWired were not interested in another way to rebroadcast (i.e., shovel) their existing information. They wanted to create content that was exclusively for the online publication and present that content in a form that was designed specifically for its delivery over the Web. Moreover, they were interested in not only informing and entertaining their audience, but also in building a new type of online community.

When the HotWired online publication was launched, you had to register to become a member of the site before you could access its resources. Registration was free; this allowed the publishers of HotWired to promote the long-standing, commonplace expectation that information resources published on the Internet were freely accessible. Meanwhile, they collected demographic information from the registration process that they could use for any number of purposes, including customizing content and advertising. In association with site membership, they used weekly emails to their members in order to build a sense of community. Email was simply another channel through which they could distribute information to their readership. Later, site membership became optional when they learned that many people turned away from filling out and submitting the registration form.

As with their printed magazine, the publishers of HotWired generated revenues through advertising. Here, though, advertising took the form of banners at the top of each page. Banners are rectangular areas containing text, graphics, or animations that function as hypermedia links; a user clicks on a banner and is taken to the advertiser's site or to information about the advertised product or service. HotWired pioneered this form of Web advertising and, given the site's demographic of a young, affluent readership, they attracted advertisers with deep pockets, such as Zima, Volvo, and Club Med. Ironically, one of the problems HotWired encountered in pioneering the use of Web banners to generate revenues and direct traffic to their advertisers was that most of their advertisers did not yet have any presence on the Web, which meant that there was no where to which to direct an interested individual. The Web was still in its infancy and very few companies had taken notice of its existence or considered its potential for conducting business. So, in order for the banner advertising to have any effect, HotWired not only had to create the banners but they also had to arrange for Web sites to be built for their advertisers.

The creators of HotWired did not limit their online publication to the same type of journalistic, commercial, and academic content that appeared in their magazine. Instead, they created several distinctly different channels of content that were developed exclusively for their Web readership and the Web's unique multimedia environment. One of these channels was called The Piazza and acted as a virtual meeting place. The Piazza consisted of a chat environment that members could use to exchange and debate ideas in real time and bulletin boards that allowed for asynchronous information sharing. It also included a virtual auditorium where guests could lead discussions in an open forum; this exchange of information was broadcast both as text and as live audio. These mechanisms allowed HotWired to engage and interact with its audience and also allowed members to interact with one another. This had the effect of turning the online, Web publication into something more far-reaching and more intimately connected to its audience than any traditional printed magazine could ever achieve.

The publishers of HotWired established the guidelines that many other online publications would follow. They adeptly used the Web's multimedia environment to extend their publication's reach and to expand how they interacted with their readership. Their printed and online publications complemented rather than competed with each other. Moreover, the two publications served to illustrate the sharp differences between the *push* effect of the printed media, which gave every individual the same information on a predetermined schedule, and the *pull* effect of the online media, which allowed individuals to choose the information they wanted on a schedule that suited them.

In many ways, HotWired deftly showed what an online Web publication could accomplish, provided, of course, the desired time, funding, and expertise were readily available and plentiful. But HotWired represented one extreme of publishing on the Web. The economics of the Web, unlike the economics of the print media, do not demand deep pockets and a large staff. The Web is first and foremost a medium for distributing information; it facilitates the sharing of news, ideas, research, commentary, and other forms of information. To start a publication does not, however, require a large investment of capital, prior publishing experience, or the approval (or licensing) of a government agency. A single individual or a small organization with a modest amount of money can create a popular and effective Web publication equal to any other on the Web. The Web's information management system simplifies the process of self-publication by providing the tools and the platform that allow anyone to have a voice and to be heard from anywhere in the world and concerning any subject imaginable. An individual publishing a personal Web log or journal — a process called blogging — exemplifies this point. (Blogging is described in detail in a later chapter.) Ultimately, whether a Web publication will succeed and find an audience depends more on the quality and desirability of its content than its presentation.

The empowering and equalizing effect produced by the Web's open and economical publishing environment does, however, come at a cost. Some topics and some forms of expression are simply not suitable for all audiences. When you take into account how many children are surfing the Web and how few of their parents understand what is out there for them to encounter, the benefits of the Web's publishing environment are, at the very least, diminished by the lingering and perhaps unsolvable controversy over protecting free speech and protecting young, impressionable minds.

Despite the clear and significant differences between online and printed publications, many people still believe that the multimedia capabilities of the Web, combined with the immediacy of its published information and its generally free availability, will ultimately transform, if not eliminate, the contemporary, conventional businesses of the print media. As more and more people turn to the Internet for their information, will newspapers and magazines retain a sufficient number of subscribers to survive? Will they adapt and provide a service that the Web cannot also provide faster and cheaper? Consumers will ultimately decide what happens. For the foreseeable future, at any rate, there is no reason why both cannot successfully coexist; and those who marry their printed media with the multimedia capabilities of the Web will likely make their publications into something bigger and better than they were before the Web. There is no denying, however, that conventional printers and publishers will need to change with the times if they want to survive and thrive.

Audio

Audio on the Web can present itself in many forms, ranging from a small, simple file with a sound effect, like an oinking pig or meowing cat, to a continuous, real-time channel feed from a broadcast radio station. Including some type of audio feature on a Web site can be as straightforward as including a photo. You use a URL to identify the location of the audio file, which can exist in one of several common audio file formats. You can then choose to include the URL as part of a hyperlink, which will enable the user to retrieve and play the audio file on demand. Or you can choose to embed the audio file in the Web page, which will cause the audio file to download to the user automatically, like a graphics file, and start playing without any user intervention. The difficult part of including audio on a Web site is choosing the type of audio you are going to provide and deciding how you are going to integrate it with your other information.

Audio exists as an adjunct source of information in the Web's information space. This was clearly demonstrated by its use on the Web site with the dinosaur exhibit where each page included an audio icon that, when clicked, caused a narrative audio file to be downloaded and played. But the most far-reaching effects of audio on the Web can be found in the growing popularity of Web-distributed broadcast radio and in the controversial distribution of CD-quality music in the form of MP3 files.

One thing that all types of audio distributed over the Internet have in common is that the higher the quality, the larger the file size or data source. For instance, CD-quality audio can require as much as 10 megabytes of space per minute of audio. Even with the greater availability of higher bandwidth connections to the Internet, such large transfers of data posed what seemed an insurmountable problem to those who wanted to distribute high-quality audio content over the Web. Two approaches were developed to solve this problem: reducing the file size at the expense of sound quality; and employing specialized data compression methodologies that encode and decode audio data and still retain a reasonable level of sound quality. The popular MP3 file format is the result of one of these data compression methodologies.

The following sections describe three very different ways in which audio information and entertainment are handled by computers and by the Internet and the Web.

MIDI Files

A somewhat different approach to audio on computers than those mentioned above was implemented with Musical Instrument Digital Interface (MIDI) files. Unlike other audio files, MIDI files are small by design. That is because, instead of containing a digital representation of recorded audio, they contain instructions in the form of a music definition language — very like a musical score — that specify to MIDI devices (e.g., a PC's sound card) how to generate the required sounds through electronic synthesis. This means, among other things, that you cannot record MIDI files. Accordingly, they are incapable of capturing the quality of someone's voice or that of a musical performance.

Many different types of software applications and hardware components handle MIDI files. The advantage of MIDI files is that they are very small and therefore transfer quickly over the Internet. The disadvantage is that neither the creator of the audio content distributed in a MIDI file nor the individual playing the file has any control over the audio's quality. Quality is entirely dependent on the MIDI device playing the file, and it may vary considerably from computer to computer.

RealAudio and Streaming Audio

Audio for the Web and Internet was largely pioneered by a company called Progressive Networks (later renamed RealNetworks) and its product, RealAudio, which was first released in April, 1995. RealAudio brought audio-on-demand to the Internet. Audio-on-demand gave people access to broadcast radio and recorded programs for the first time; it stood in sharp contrast to the type of audio content people had become accustomed to on the Web, which consisted of downloading files that contained short recordings or sound effects. Key to RealAudio's success, especially early on when bandwidth was much more limited for both businesses and home Internet users, was how its engineers combined audio data compression with the new concept of streaming audio.

Streaming audio enabled audio content, whether a song or a radio broadcast, to start playing after only a small portion of the data was transferred over the network. Before streaming audio, an audio file had to be downloaded in its entirety before it could be played; and with relatively small bandwidth, it was not uncommon for it to take five times longer to download a file than to play it. Few people were willing to accept these conditions. So downloading most types of audio files was limited to a small minority of Internet users with high-bandwidth connections; and such a limited audience meant that the business of providing audio content over the Internet was not feasible.

With streaming audio, however, playback begins as soon as the data fills a small file buffer on the receiving computer and continues as the data continues to arrive. The first version of RealAudio produced very low sound quality, because it had to use a very high data compression ratio of 176 to 1 in order to accommodate the typical modem speed at that time. Subsequent versions of RealAudio provided more data by using lower compression ratios, thereby producing higher sound quality. Version 3.0, which became available in the fall of 1996, included for the first time a variable-speed component that enabled FM-quality sound at higher connection speeds. Suddenly, the Internet was capable of bringing its users high fidelity radio and music, and a new door swung open on the Web.

The business model for RealAudio was to give away the players (i.e., the client-side software application that played the audio files), much as Netscape was giving away its browsers, but to sell the server component to Web site owners who wanted to provide audio as a resource for their visitors. Deals were also reached with browser companies like Microsoft, Spyglass, and Netscape, enabling them to integrate the audio facilities of RealAudio into their browser's capabilities. Since RealAudio specified its own Internet protocol extensions and file formats, its data was classified as a new type of Internet media rather than simply another Web resource or another type of audio file. This classification made it easier to integrate RealAudio into existing applications, like Web browsers, because it ensured that the traffic of RealAudio data was kept distinct and separate from other types of data. Other benefits of classifying RealAudio as its own media type were that it simplified and hastened the process of creating new types of stand-alone applications or browser plug-ins, and it simplified the task of tracking and charging for RealAudio services.

In addition to establishing audio as a viable multimedia component on the Internet and providing a compelling new type of information resource for Web sites, RealAudio subtly but irrevocably changed the business of radio broadcasting. This change manifested itself in two distinct ways. First, radio stations were no longer restricted to their broadcast area; they could feed their live broadcasts through a Web site, and anyone with Internet access anywhere in the world could listen to their broadcasts. Second, radio stations could now make it possible for their audiences to listen to shows when each listener wanted rather than only when the shows were broadcast by recording the shows into files and making the files available through a Web site. Here, as elsewhere on the Web, a traditional broadcast (or push) medium (i.e., radio) was being transformed into an on-demand (or pull) medium that individuals could access and use according to their schedules and needs. This was a new and powerful paradigm for radio.

MP3

An audio file compression technology called Moving Picture Experts Group, Audio Layer 3, more commonly known as MP3, has changed the way many people listen to music. The term MP3 applies to both the file type and the compression technology used in creating and playing the files. Because the data compression of MP3 files has only a marginal impact on sound quality, it quickly became the de facto standard for both the legal, and illegal, distribution of music over the Web.

While the MP3 file compression rate is adjustable, a compression ratio of 10 to 1 is fairly typical. This means that a 4 minute song can be recorded and saved in a 4 megabyte file rather than in a 40 megabyte file. This was precisely the kind of file size reduction that many individuals and corporations were waiting for before they would consider releasing their audio content over the Web. When you consider the following conditions that existed in the late 1990s when the MP3 technology arrived on the Internet — higher bandwidth Internet service was becoming more common; the capacity of file storage devices (e.g., hard disk drives) was increasing in leaps and bounds, while the size and cost of the devices were sharply decreasing; and writeable CD devices were becoming affordable and popular — it is easier to understand how the relatively small, high quality audio files of MP3 acted as a catalyst for a revolution in marketing, distributing, and listening to music.

The MP3 technology was developed in Germany in the 1980s, but it wasn't until 1998, which saw the introduction of the first free MP3 music player (called Winamp), that interest in MP3 started to manifest itself. As interest increased, more and more MP3 devices and software started to appear. These included MP3 encoders that created MP3 files from audio CDs and other sources, CD rippers that created libraries of MP3 files from CDs, software to transfer MP3 files to a CD, and more MP3 players in the form of new software and self-contained hardware devices similar to personal CD players.

Then, in 1999, Napster arrived and changed the MP3 world, the Internet, and the recording industry. Napster was a Web site that used peer-to-peer file sharing to seamlessly interconnect the computers of individuals across the Internet, enabling people to easily make their MP3 file collections available for others on the Internet to download. In effect, Napster created a virtual community of shareable MP3 files by turning the standard, desktop computers of individuals into file servers. In this way, Napster established its own decentralized network of machines within the larger confines of the Internet, thereby simplifying the task of searching for, locating, and copying just about any song imaginable.

After a lot of publicity and heated debate, the Recording Industry Association of American (RIAA) managed to get Napster shut down over the issue of copyright infringement. The record companies and artists represented by RIAA won the immediate battle, but they did not succeed in changing people's behavior; the downloading and sharing of MP3 files continues unabated. The technology of digitally-encoded audio files promotes such behavior, whether the files are in an MP3 format or some other type of file; computer files were designed to be easily copied and shared, and digitally encoding information preserves that information in a way that prevents it from decaying over time or through use. It will, therefore, take new technology to reassert the copyright laws.

The surge of interest in MP3 audio files was responsible for a large increase in the number of Web sites devoted to music, the music industry, and the technology for recording and playing music. While Napster was operational, and even afterwards, MP3 file transfers accounted for a significant amount of the traffic on the Internet. MP3 files and other popular audio file formats will continue to shape the Web as the multimedia content of Web sites grows and more information is produced through audio channels or made available in audio files. No less important, the dynamics of peer-to-peer networked communication will also continue to shape the Web and the Internet. Unrestricted and decentralized file sharing is part of the foundation of the Internet. Peer-to-peer networking will probably evolve and gain wider acceptance for the same reasons that brought success to the Internet. Instead of large corporations and governments establishing the networks and creating the rules, peer-to-peer will allow individuals and small groups to form networks of their own design and for their own purposes.

Just as the multimedia information produced in online publications can just as easily be distributed on the Web by individuals as by large corporations, the same holds true for the distribution of audio over the Web. Distributing audio content over the Web is more than simply another channel for broadcasting music and information and more than another means for existing media companies to expand their influence and market share. For example, established recording artists can use the Web to connect directly with their fans and promote and distribute their own songs without the expense and intervention of a recording studio; and new artists can use the Web to make their music accessible to others in the hopes of finding and building an audience. Streaming audio over the Web offers noncommercial broadcasters a wider, richer sphere of influence, creating, in fact a whole new type of personal broadcaster that is outside the mainstream and independent of commercial affiliations.

Video

There are a lot of similarities between audio content and video content on the Web. Video can be easily stored in files and placed on a Web site for simple retrieval and playback. Video can also be distributed as streaming content that plays as it downloads. Additionally, video can be broadcast live, offering another distribution channel for television broadcasters, a cost-effective tool for video business conferencing, and even a means of making video phone calls.

Programs also exist that allow you to make video emails. These messages are sent just like any other type of email, but they combine your video with a Java applet (a small computer program) that plays the video message automatically when the recipient opens the message. This approach of combining video content with an associated application not only enables the data to be compressed to a more acceptable size for transfer over the Internet, but it also solves the problem of not knowing if the recipient's computer can play the message by packaging the means to play it together with the message contents.

Two of the most popular Web programs that play streaming video content are browser plug-ins. One, from the company that created RealAudio, is called RealPlayer. The other was developed by Apple and is called QuickTime Player. Both are available on multiple platforms and handle the playback of several different video file types, including the open standard called MPEG (Moving Picture Experts Group). Both have their particular technical strengths and weaknesses.

The transmission of video content over the Internet makes greater demands on network bandwidth than other types of multimedia content. Video files are large and nothing comparable to the MP3 technology has been created to facilitate the storage and distribution of video content on the Internet. The use of video on the Web is still in an early stage of development and integration, as was true of audio prior to the introduction of MP3. The technology exists for creating, downloading, and playing various types of video files, but due to a lack of standardization and insufficient data compression to make retrieving video information from the Internet feasible, the audience has remained small and its use remains limited. There are, nonetheless, several fast-growing and inventive uses of video, such as small and inexpensive Web-connected cameras called web-cams and video recordings that interact with virtual reality software to produce something called interactive video. These video technologies are presented in the following sections.

Interactive Video

An extension to QuickTime called QuickTime Virtual Reality (QTVR) nicely illustrates how the accessibility of multimedia video content through the Web is not simply providing another distribution channel for video information and entertainment, but is altering the experience of viewing videos by enlarging and enriching what video can do and how it can be used.

QTVR supplies something called a panoramic scene experience, in which you explore locations by moving through them. As you move, your perspective changes, allowing you to control your experience of and interaction with the filmed scene. For instance, QTVR enables you to take a walking tour of a museum; you control your movements through the filmed environment by walking from room to room, pausing in front of the objects that you want to study, and even finely adjusting your perspective to focus in on a particular detail or to look at an object from different angles. QTVR also allows objects to be embedded in scenes; these objects can perform predefined actions when selected, such as narrating the history of an artist or one of the artist's specific paintings or sculptures. QTVR makes video content both interactive and individualized; each person charts his or her own path through the information it contains.

This sort of video technology, simple to operate and highly effective and personalized, lends itself to many different sorts of applications. For example, a real estate Web site can include interactive videos of each home it lists for sale. Interested buyers can download a video and take a virtual walking tour through the home. They can walk from room to room, turn to see a 360 degree view from where they are standing, climb the stairs to the second floor, and examine specific features, like a stove or a fireplace, in more detail. Another example where this type of multimedia content would prove useful is a Web site that sells used cars.

Interactive videos of each car would allow interested buyers to sit in the driver's seat, open the hood or the trunk, and examine a car for superficial damage or cosmetic repairs. The technology of interactive video is simple to use, its applications are endless, and the Web provides an ideal environment in which to distribute this type of multimedia information and to integrate its use with the selling of merchandise, educational pursuits, or entertainment.

Streaming Video

The most popular use of video on the Web involves streaming video services. Just as with streaming audio, the sites that offer streaming video can be divided into two categories. One is a business-to-business type of site; the operators of these sites develop and sell the technology that allows Web site owners to provide assorted Web-accessible video services and to create streaming video content. The other is a business-to-consumer type of site; the operators of these sites sell streaming video content and promote subscription services that include news and entertainment broadcasts, interactive video gaming, and video conferencing.

Streaming video, like streaming audio, incorporates a buffer to allow the video to start playing while the data continues to download. It is used for distributing video files that, for example, contain short movie clips or animations, and for making live video broadcasts accessible over the Internet. Two types of video streaming services can be commonly found on the Web. One is called progressive or HTTP streaming; the other is called real-time streaming. Progressive streaming handles on-demand video file downloads; it uses HTTP to transfer the file, so it does not require a streaming video server to control the data feed, and it offers video quality superior to that offered by real-time streaming. Real-time streaming handles the broadcasting of live events over the Web; it requires a specialized streaming server to control the flow of data and uses a separate protocol as part of this process. Real-time streaming can also be used to transmit video files; it allows users to pause the playing of a video and return to earlier scenes.

Personal Video Cameras

Specially designed video cameras that have become popular in home surveillance systems represent another (and very different) type of video content that is becoming accessible through the Web. These cameras operate in conjunction with other components as part of a system that monitors a home's security, detects smoke, fire, and carbon monoxide, senses mechanical systems failures like leaking water or a broken furnace, and controls lighting, a thermostat, and other common home devices. The cameras and the other components are controlled by a computer application that is installed on a home's personal computer or is part of a dedicated computing device delivered with the system.

These applications are now being designed to be accessed over a network, and many include a Web interface as a standard feature. The intent of integrating network access into these systems is to put a home and its surveillance/monitoring features on its own integrated home network, interconnecting video from the cameras, audio from an intercom, telephones, mechanical systems, and so on. By extension, this home network and all the information and controls it interconnects can be accessible on the Internet through the home's connection to an Internet service provider (ISP). This means, among other things, that such systems allow you to watch live video or recorded images from your home while on vacation or at work or see who is ringing your door bell from the laptop in your upstairs bedroom. Such systems have clear business applications, too, given their ability to simplify and centralize security for a large property or building.

Small cameras that broadcast their signals over a network and that can be accessed on the Web, commonly called web-cams, have existed since the Web's earliest days. The first, a web-cam that monitored the coffee pot in the Trojan Room (part of the computer laboratory at the University of Cambridge) and aptly named the Coffee Cam, became accessible on the Web in November, 1993. The camera had been installed over two years earlier so that researchers at the lab would know when a fresh pot of coffee was available, thereby saving themselves a tiresome trip to the Trojan Room when no coffee was to be had. Later, when the Web arrived at Cambridge, the researchers provided access to the camera's images through a Web page and it quickly garnered a large international audience. The second such web-cam was called the Fish Cam and was installed in 1995 at Netscape's headquarters. This camera was positioned to take pictures of a fish tank; it is still in operation and available over the Web, unlike the Trojan Room's web-cam, which went offline when the lab was moved in 2001. Both web-cams have been counted, at one time or another, among the most visited sites on the Web.

The inclusion of images from these early cameras — the images were updated according to some programmed frequency, ranging from every second to several minutes — on otherwise static Web pages that contained only text and graphics was key to demonstrating the versatility of the Web. The use of web-cams also represented one of the first ways in which people tried to turn the Web into a more dynamic, multimedia environment. The millions of visits that these early sites received because of their web-cams were unrelated to the subjects that these cameras photographed. What people were coming to see was how different technologies were being integrated and converging on the Web. To click on a Web page and watch a coffee pot or a fish tank from virtually any location on the planet was something provocative, and it made many people wonder where this new technology and these new capabilities were going to take us.

Television and the Web

The Internet and television are two very different types of information delivery systems that seem destined to meet. The multimedia content of the Web continues to grow and already includes broadcast television as one of its realtime streaming video services; and television is growing increasingly interactive due to the introduction of digital television distribution through satellite and cable. Large-scale attempts to integrate the Internet with television using specialized set-top boxes date back to before the Web's creation. An early attempt — called ITV — was later considered "the Web that never happened," and other attempts that followed proved equally unsuccessful at gaining market share. But it is only a matter of time before alliances form among television subscription providers, hardware manufacturers, and media companies for the purpose of integrating the Web, Internet access, and video-on-demand services. The necessary technology already exists. Moreover, the higher bandwidth supplied by satellite and cable television services can now be put to work to handle a home's Internet connectivity.

The Web offers television channel broadcasters and the content creators of television programs and films the same benefits it offers radio station broadcasters and radio program producers. The most significant of these benefits is the ability to know their audiences as was never before possible. They will also be able to provide content designed to appeal to a smaller, narrowly defined audience, test out new shows and solicit viewer feedback more easily, and distribute both old and new programs in the form of files that can be retrieved by users on demand. Users benefit, too, in having access to a larger and more diverse selection of programs and film from which to choose, far exceeding what can be provided by traditional television, and being able to watch what they want according to their schedule.

Existing add-on products for television (e.g., Tivo and Replay TV) provide a glimpse of this type of new service. These products represent the next generation of video recorders, but they do far more than record television programs and movies. They store video on a large disk drive, eliminating the need for tapes; and, more importantly, they can be programmed to record programs based on a title or category, instead of basing the recording on a specific channel and time. They can automatically record all episodes of your favorite shows, or a single episode, or only first-run episodes (as opposed to reruns). They can also recognize the types of programs you like to watch, such as westerns or biographies, and record these types of programs on your behalf without your making a specific request. Because their programming interacts directly with your television service provider's program guide, they know when your shows start and end and which channels they are broadcast on; they also know which films have been categorized as westerns and which programs are biographies. This means that you no longer need to know or care about program schedules. The films and programs stored on these products effectively become your personal television channel; the shows are waiting for you and you can watch them at your convenience.

These same products also allow you to pause live TV, so that you can answer the phone or prepare a snack without missing a minute. They accomplish this by automatically recording whatever you are watching on the disk drive and delaying display by a few seconds. So, you think you are watching live TV, but the device is actually playing the video from the disk drive. When you press the pause button, you are simply pausing this playback; meanwhile, the device continues to record what is being broadcast. This subtle but clever innovation illustrates how the simple combination or integration of technologies can have an impact greater than the sum of its parts, much like the Web itself.

The very features that make Tivo and Replay TV so popular are at least partly responsible for delaying television's integration with the Web. The economics of television broadcasting is based on advertising revenue and that revenue structure is tied to specific time slots when shows are broadcast and to expectations regarding the demographic makeup of a show's audience. Products that eliminate the need to watch a show when it is broadcast, allow for commercials to be ignored by fast forwarding over them, and, moreover, eliminate the need even to know when a show is broadcast or on which station, undermine these economics and threaten to render them obsolete. In this instance, the technology has outpaced the economics and it will probably require the creation of a new economic model for television broadcasting before television programming and the Web will find a way to coexist on the Internet.

Standardization

No single video file standard or architecture has emerged to dominate the growing interest in video services on the Web. MPEG files are one of the few open standard video formats that continues to evolve and gain wider acceptance. But, overall, standardization has been elusive and consumers remain waiting for some type of catalyst — something equivalent to the MP3 technology — to make video a viable commodity and information resource on the Web. The work needed to arrive at video standardization will have to take into account existing bandwidth restrictions and the relationship between video resolution, file compression, and other factors that directly impact video quality. Only after bandwidth restrictions have been reduced or eliminated and some type of video file standardization has been achieved will video be able to have a transforming effect on the Web.

In response to the technical difficulties involved in providing video content over the Web, many companies have developed their own proprietary tools and file formats in the hope of establishing a de facto standard and gaining the greatest market share. Meanwhile, organizations such as the Internet Streaming Media Alliance (ISMA) have formed in an attempt to deal with the lack of standardization. They want to establish one or more specifications that will openly define an interoperable implementation of streaming rich media and, in doing so, they hope to stimulate growth in the industry by simplifying the task of producing and maintaining video, audio, and other multimedia content. Without such standardization, content providers must either limit themselves to one or two of the more established video file formats, or create five or more different files for everything they wish to distribute.

Remarkably different types of video applications — simple, short movie files and animations, web-cam surveillance, video-on-demand services, and broadcast television through the Internet — can be easily and effectively brought together by the Web. The Web provides a single point of access through a browser and associated plug-ins that effectively hides the technology and unifies all the various and very different sources of video. But how and when the Internet, Web, video, and television will eventually come together is impossible to predict. The technology has reached the point where some sort of fusion is possible. The Internet is capable of distributing virtually any type of multimedia content, including realtime television broadcasting, and television services providers are capable of providing Internet and Web access (e.g., WebTV and AOLTV) through their set-top boxes. It will not be long before consumers who currently pay for both services through separate Internet and television providers will insist on paying only for one, provided that a single service can accommodate all of their needs.

Multimedia Built for the Web: Applets, Flash, and 3D

The Web has proven to be an excellent platform on which to establish new types of publications and from which to provide new ways to distribute audio and video content. But the Web has also been responsible for the evolution and widespread use of new types of multimedia. These new types of multimedia, which include Java applets, Macromedia Flash, and three-dimensional (3D) modeling, greatly enrich the multimedia power of the Web because they were developed with the Web in mind. They possess the capabilities needed to bring truly interactive content to the Web. They also bring tools to the Web that can be applied to a wide range of activities, such as working with a spreadsheet application, following a self-guided tutorial, or interacting with a computer-generated animation.

Java Applets

Most people who have heard of the Web have heard of Java. Java is an object-oriented programming language that was developed by Sun Microsystems and incorporated interoperability as the driving force behind its design and engineering. The promise of programming in Java is: write code once, run it anywhere. The history of Java and the influence of its technology are, in many respects, as compelling as the history of the Internet and the Web. *The Technology Revolution* includes a chapter on the history, technology, and use of Java.

Much as the Web empowered information providers to simplify the distribution of information and greatly extend its interoperability through the architecture-independent file format of HTML, Java empowered application developers through its architecture-independent programming language. For the first time, a developer could write one set of instructions in one language and have those instructions run on a Windows PC, a Macintosh, a Unix workstation, or any number of other platforms. A developer could now focus more time and effort on designing a program's features and functionality, because the vagaries of a specific operating system or hardware platform could be ignored.

When Java was combined with the Web, which was made possible by Java applets, suddenly developers could produce executable programs that ran on any platform and were accessible from anywhere in the world.

Java applets are a specific type of Java programming designed to run in the confines of a Web browser. They are mini-applications, small in scale and highly focused in terms of their purpose. There are restrictions on what they can be built to do (e.g., Java applets are not allowed to read or write files on the client computers' disk drive); these restrictions have not, however, limited the effectiveness or impacted the wide variety of animations, games, productivity tools, and communication tools that have been created as Java applets.

Java applets are identified by the `<object>` HTML tag and they reside in compiled files typically named with a .class file name extension. When a browser interprets an HTML page that includes an applet, it retrieves the specified Java .class file just as it retrieves any other embedded objects in the page, such as files that contain photos or drawings. The browser then uses its Java virtual machine (JVM), which is a small application incorporated into the browser environment or installed as part of the computer's operating system, to interpret and then run the code contained in the applet file. The JVM, incidentally, is where general application instructions, like those to draw a line or display text, meet the specific requirements and vagaries of the local computer hardware and operating system; the JVM understands both the Java programming language and the local computer environment and, therefore, it is through the JVM that Java's interoperability is implemented.

It is important to understand that Java applets are executable programs and that they run locally, on your computer. In order to ensure that they would be safe and secure to execute on an individual's computer, restrictions were imposed on the types of operations they could perform. As noted above, for example, Java applets cannot read or write files on the hard disk of an individual's computer. They do, however, use the local resources of your computer when they run. If, therefore, your computer has a lot of memory and a fast processor, a Java applet will probably function a lot better on it than it will on an older, slower system.

The client-side approach to program execution of Java applets is quite a bit different than the client-server model used by other types of programs and applications. The client-sever model can take advantage of the greater resources and processing power of the server and it primarily uses the client computer as an output device for displaying information. The client-server model helps to ensure that an application runs as quickly and efficiently for one client as for another, even if the clients differ considerably in terms of their processing power and resources. But the client-server model makes far more demands on the network than a Java applet, which runs entirely on the client computer, and it is vulnerable to increased demands on the server's and the network's resources as more and more people connect to the server.

Java applets can have a transforming effect on any Web site. Among other things, they can be used to introduce dynamic content that updates itself automatically. For example, a simple ticker-tape applet will scroll information alongside other content in a browser window or in its own popup window. But unlike a standard HTML page that would need to be reloaded for any dynamic content to be updated, the applet is a self-contained program and it can be designed to update its information periodically, thereby providing new information every thirty seconds, every minute, or every five minutes. Such a ticker-tape program on a sports-related Web site might easily contain updates with scores for ongoing games; on a financial Web site it might contain stock quotes. The applet's purpose is to enhance the Web site owner's ability to keep the attention of visitors on the site for as long as possible; the success of most commercial Web sites depends on visitors remaining on the site for an extended period of time and returning periodically. Java applets that automatically display and refresh frequently changing information, such as news headlines, sports scores, and stock prices, are an effective way to accomplish this.

Java applets turn static images into moving animations. They also play movies and music. Most significantly, they allow you to interact with information, tools, and other people. For instance, a crossword puzzle Java applet allows you to fill out a puzzle in your browser window; and you control whether it remains silent, or tells you when you answer incorrectly, or provides hints when you are stuck. You could even do the crossword with a friend across the

Internet, with each of you seeing what the other has filled in. Java applets are frequently used as Internet chat clients, enabling people to communicate directly with friends, family, and business associates by exchanging typed-in messages. Java applets also have widespread business applications, providing common tools that are easy to upgrade across the company.

When applets first became available in the mid 1990s, not long after the Web started gaining popularity, the Java language was young and still needed considerable refinement. Also, the Java virtual machines were generally slow and contained some serious limitations that caused even well-written applets to perform poorly or not work at all. The result was a great idea with immense potential that was not quite ready for any serious applications. Now, however, the Java language and associated applications have matured into a rich and powerful development environment, and Java applets can supply the Web with just about any type of multimedia object you can imagine.

Flash

Java applets are one approach to making Web sites more exciting, more useful, and more powerful. Flash, a Web development program created by Macromedia, offers a different approach to bringing multimedia and dynamic content to the Web. Flash, unlike Java, is a proprietary platform that uses vector graphics (i.e., mathematical commands and formulas that define graphical objects) to create rich, dynamic content. It is a popular choice for such things as sophisticated advertising animations, self-guided tutorials and learning applications, and interactive streaming video.

Since Flash is proprietary, a programmer must use Macromedia's development tools to create Flash applications and a free Flash browser plug-in must first be downloaded on a client computer before any Flash application will run. The benefits of Flash are that it offers a powerful and intuitive environment for creating simple programs, like animations, as well as customized, feature-rich applications. Like Java applets, these programs can easily include audio and video components, graphics and lively animations, and can enable a user to interact with the program through a keyboard and mouse. An advantage of Flash is that the proprietary format allows files to be smaller, enabling Flash animations and applications to start playing quickly.

The powerful tools and advanced features of Flash, however, come at a price, both literally and figuratively. Unlike Java, which is a rich programming language that allows a developer to build virtually any type and size application, the Flash development environment limits what a programmer can create. More importantly, content developers that use Flash are tied to a single company's vision of multimedia on the Web. This approach clashes with the open standards development environment of the Web and the Internet. Nevertheless, Flash remains a popular choice for providing sophisticated and engaging multimedia content for the Web.

3D Modeling and VRML

Creating, distributing, and interacting with three-dimensional (3D) objects over the Web has been a serious and passionate pursuit since the early days of the Web, as evidenced by the creation of the Virtual Reality Modeling Language (VRML). VRML is an open standards development language specifically geared towards modeling 3D objects. Like HTML and Java, VRML is platform independent. In general terms, the language describes the geometry and behavior of 3D objects and scenes and enables the creation of virtual environments by allowing its objects and scenes to be interconnected, shared, and interacted with.

VRML dates back to 1994; it was introduced by its creator, Mark Pesce, at the first World Wide Web Conference held at CERN. In the following years, it developed in a series of specifications in which its functionality grew from the simple, static display of 3D objects, to enabling animations, the inclusion of audio components, and direct user interaction with the objects. Through VRML, you could build virtual worlds with sounds that could be tied to specific objects, movement, or backgrounds, scripts that defined animations and object behavior, and sensors that triggered actions based on what was occurring in a scene.

While VRML still exists on the Web, and plug-ins are freely available for viewing and interacting with VRML 3D objects, 3D multimedia on the Web has been migrating to a newer, open standard called Extensible 3D (X3D). X3D hopes to solve some of the performance and file format problems that were keeping 3D modeling from becoming more prevalent on the Web.

3D modeling offers a wide variety of new and exciting content and interaction on the Web. For example, 3D modeling can enhance the presentation of all types of information on the Web, from a storefront's display of a sweater to a scientific report describing the molecular makeup of a compound. With 3D modeling, you can view objects from any angle and acquire a better appreciation of their form and characteristics. It also makes an excellent environment for building and conducting demos and simulations, allowing you to try out products from a virtual storefront or view a model of your home, and even walk through it with your architect as it goes through its various design stages. The introduction of 3D modeling into gaming and communication applications on the Web will change them into far more engaging experiences, as virtual worlds are built across the Internet to further people's ability to interact.

Unlike many other types of multimedia components on the Web, VRML and 3D object rendering are still relatively scarce. One basic reason for this is that the computational power needed to display and manipulate 3D elements is greater than it is for other types of multimedia components; and many existing video boards possess only rudimentary 3D imaging features. Also, while VRML browsers and plug-ins have been developed, none has been adopted in any large-scale way, perhaps because relatively little has been done by way of producing 3D content for the Web. Nevertheless, 3D object modeling and virtual reality applications already exist on the Web; their use includes merchandising, marketing, education, entertainment, medicine, and training.

The Business Web

The Business Web

What is it about the Web that has, in a matter of a few short years, managed to transform the way so many companies conduct business? The packaging for a roll of toilet paper promotes the manufacturer's Web site. Web site addresses (URLs) are printed on cereal boxes and milk cartons, prompting us to visit their sites. Nearly every product that has the space to display a URL includes the manufacturer's address on the Web. Radio and television broadcasts promote Web sites to their audiences that are associated with their channel or with a particular program, encouraging audience members to visit them on the Web after the broadcast to access additional information, take part in a poll, or participate in a community forum. Advertisements that are a part of these broadcasts beckon us in much the same way with respect to their products and services; few commercials fail to include a URL where interested individuals can go to make a purchase or learn more about the advertised item, company, or organization.

This change in how business is conducted and promoted represents a radical departure in how businesses and consumers interact with each other and in how businesses interact with one another. It took several years for the business community to recognize what the Web had to offer and a few more years for it to fully embrace the Web as a new place (and space) in which to make money. Yet, because the change was so radical, it somehow feels as if it took place overnight. This change speaks to something fundamental about the Web, an information space that, like the Internet, started out as an exciting new tool in the community of scientists and academics but that was quickly overtaken by, and seemingly taken over by, the business community. It speaks to the Web's capacity to transform whatever comes into contact with it.

If we read any newspapers or magazines, watch television, listen to the radio, buy groceries or purchase just about any product, or if we stand on just about any city street and take a good look around us, we will encounter an address for a Web site. If we hike into the woods to get away from them, we may find, unfortunately, that we are taking them with us. They may be sewn into the labels of our clothes, printed on our backpack, squeezed onto that tiny label stuck to our apple, or printed on the paper used to wrap the sandwich we bought for lunch. How and why did this happen?

Why it happened is partly a result of the Web turning us into information operators. The Web enabled and encouraged us to find and access information according to our needs and schedules instead of waiting for information to be delivered to us. Earlier, very different advances in technology were created for much the same purpose and, like the Web, quickly became part of the daily lives of millions of people. The addition of the rotary telephone dial, which was invented in the late 1890s, turned us into operators by enabling us to make our own calls instead of waiting on a telephone company operator to make the connection on our behalf. The advertising created for one of the first of these automatic phones (as they were called) marketed the device as the "girl-less, cuss-less, and wait-less telephone," emphasizing the benefits of operating the technology oneself. Similarly, the creation of automated teller machines (ATMs) in the early 1970s — devices that are now located on every city block and can be commonly found in grocery stores, gas stations, convenience stores, and elsewhere — turned us into operators by enabling us to conduct our own banking transactions. They enabled us to withdraw cash, deposit checks, transfer money, and check account balances when and where it was convenient for us.

Making us operators reduces the cost of doing business, whether it is for banking, making telephone calls, or, as it applies to the Web, for buying products and services and locating information. Web site addresses are storefront locations on the Internet; they beckon us to visit a site, spend time there, and, very often, spend our money. Through the Web, we can access our financial accounts, transfer money, and pay bills without visiting the bank, talking with a teller, or even using an ATM. We can buy and sell stocks without contacting a broker. We can order a pizza without picking up the phone. We can make our own travel arrangements, find the cheapest flights, and rent a small villa and a red sports car for a romantic getaway outside Florence, all with a few keystrokes and mouseclicks. For businesses, turning us into operators reduces the costs of doing business. But for us, it is liberating and even empowering.

We gain access to information that was always there, but was previously beyond our reach; and through access, we gain control. Businesses gain the potential for more customers and more transactions at lower costs; storefronts on the Web can stay open twenty-four hours a day, seven days a week, while computers instead of humans answer questions, suggest merchandise to buy, and handle all transactions. In addition, the Web enables businesses to build entirely new business models, in which stores and services are more or less virtual in form. Web storefronts do not need to stock products; they only need to provide information about the products they sell and handle the various data transactions related to a purchase (e.g., payment processing, order forwarding to the product's supplier, and shipment tracking). Nor do they need to provide a service directly to a consumer; they can instead build a network of service providers and a database of information and fulfill requests by using their resources to direct a user to a service provider that can assist them.

The low cost of doing business on the Web is also a reason why Web businesses have become commonplace. For corporations that already had Internet access before the Web, creating and maintaining a presence on the Web did not necessarily require purchasing any new equipment or hiring additional staff. Although, if a corporation planned to pursue business on the Web, to develop, for example, an e-commerce Web site, it might incur startup costs for new equipment and technical staff and additional costs for operating the site, all of which would be offset (hopefully) by the income it generated on the Web. For those with more modest needs, however, the cost of having a Web site created and hosted on the Internet can be less than a dollar a day, making the Web one of the most cost-effective ways to promote a business and sell products and services, and putting the Web within reach of any business. The reasons for such low costs are many. Competition among service providers is fierce, which helps to keep costs down. Computer hardware continues to increase in terms of its processing power and storage capacity while it decreases in terms of its cost. Network costs continue to decrease. Moreover, much of the software used to host Web sites is freeware — developed by individuals or organizations and donated for others to use free of charge.

Another reason for the predominance of business Web sites has to do with geography; more specifically, it can be attributed to how the Web has helped to reduce the relevance of geography with regards to selling products and services. Consider a small business that provides a variety of smoked salmon products to local restaurants and distributors in Downeast Maine. Creating a simple Web site that lists the company's products and provides an order form enables the business to accept orders any hour of the day, any day of the week, from anywhere in Maine, the United States, or the world. Geographic boundaries are made less relevant by the Web and commerce is changing accordingly, as businesses of all types and sizes explore how they can use the Web to reach out to new customers in locations near and far. Prior to the Web, nothing existed that could promote a business to such a large, diverse, and distributed population of potential customers.

What attracts a business to the Web, however, and what enables a business to succeed are two different things. The costs of doing business on the Web are relatively small and the customer base that can potentially be reached is enormous. But in order to succeed, the operators of a Web business must recognize that the Web's basic currency is information. Whether a business is product or service based, commercial or non-commercial, profit or non-profit, small or large, what matters most is the information a site makes available and how that information and site are interconnected with other information and sites on the Web.

For example, the Web's ability to turn customers into operators — to research, compare, select, and buy products without the expense of a salesperson or even a store — fundamentally changed the way products could be marketed and sold. The sharing of information made this possible and the success or failure of a business depended on the quality of this information and how well or poorly it assisted customers in becoming informed, making a decision, and making a purchase. For a customer to learn about a product, information describing that product had to be made available and easily findable. For a customer to buy a product, information about pricing and shipping options had to be made available, and shipping and payment information had to be collected from the customer to complete the transaction. Most of this information was not new. It was largely the same information used to market and sell products through brick-and-mortar storefronts, print and broadcast advertising, phone solicitations, and mass mailings. What differed was how this information was distributed and who controlled access.

The information that companies made accessible on the Web and that in effect brought a part of their business operations onto the Web did not simply impact the consumer and the merchandising and sales of products. Its impact reached all areas of a business's operations, internal and external. The Web's information space enabled a business to manage and interconnect all of its information and enhanced the ways in which information could be shared between employees, between different organizations within a company, and between employees and customers. As more information became accessible and sharable, company managers began to discover that this growing mass of information was capable of changing the way in which they conducted business, not just in how they sold products, but in how many fundamental business operations were run, such as managing inventory.

Consider a company that manufactures personal computers. A customer using the Web site's virtual storefront sees that the model she wants is in stock, because the storefront interface is connected to the company's inventory system. The manager responsible for maintaining the company's inventory of assembled computers and parts uses her Web browser to view the same basic information through an internal interface, helping her to determine how frequently and how urgently to order new parts and to adjust the assembly line process in order to keep ahead of demand. A manager in marketing can view the same inventory information and use it to run sales reports and forecasting projections to help determine which models might need more promotion or might be best to discount. In this instance, the same basic information is viewed from three different perspectives for three distinctly different purposes. This type of shared access to basic business information, the interconnecting of this information throughout the structure of a business, and the ability to view this information from different perspectives and for different purposes was the making of e-business (electronic business), something that the Web helped to create.

In his book describing the turnaround of IBM, Lou Gerstner, Jr. wrote the following on his, and IBM's, position on e-business:

> There is a new technology here that is going to transform every kind of enterprise and every kind of interaction. But please understand that this technology — like any other technology - is a tool. It is not a secret weapon or a panacea. It has not suspended the basics of marketplace economics or consumer behavior. And the winners will be found among the institutions that skip the shortcuts and understand that e-business is just business. It is about real, disciplined, serious work. And for those willing to do the unglamorous labor of transforming a process, unifying a supply chain, or building a knowledge-based corporate culture, it will deliver tangible and sustainable benefits.[1]

By supplying customers and employees with information and access on demand, the Web provided a highly effective tool that businesses could use to increase the scope of their business while improving how they operate and, potentially, reducing costs. Implementation of this new approach to information access and integration, however, was the key to success. For every Web business success, there have been many failures, as the dot com bubble of the late 1990s made clear.

Note that the terms e-business, e-commerce, and Web business do not refer to the same things, although they are often used interchangeably in journalistic coverage of the Internet. E-business is the broadest term and generally refers to the practice of conducting business using networked computers in conjunction with the Internet. An e-business is one that has succeeded in taking all of its operational information (e.g., product information, employee information, and customer information) and its business logic (e.g., how it charges customers, manages costs, and handles transactions) and developed a computerized environment in which to store, manage, interconnect, and communicate that information.

E-commerce refers specifically to the exchange of merchandise and services via the Internet. Web business refers to conducting business specifically on the Web, such as a bookstore that sells its merchandise through a Web site. Most Web businesses use e-commerce for their business transactions; the ones that have integrated their business model, infrastructure, and their employee, customer, and product information on their computer systems can be considered e-businesses.

While the terms e-business and e-commerce connote a sudden and radical change with respect to the practices of conducting business, they are instead evolutionary. The development of the terms and their application in business derive from two far-reaching technological innovations: the digital storage of information and the networking of computers. These advances in technology fundamentally altered the way information was recorded, stored, used, shared, and communicated; and, in doing so, they enabled companies to run more efficiently, communicate better both internally (between employees) and externally (with customers and suppliers), promote themselves and their goods more effectively, fully integrate all the various types of information used in conducting business, and make that information available, and in many respects invaluable, to employees for the performance of their jobs (and to others, such as customers, for additional purposes).

It is important to note that the technology did not change the content of the information commonly used in conducting business. It changed, instead, the form of this information; and this new form is what made possible the innovative, transforming business models of e-business and e-commerce and the technology on which these models rely, the Internet and the Web. When information that is basic to the operation of a business — like the number of units currently in stock of a particular computer model or part — is made instantly available to different audiences for different purposes, the running of that business changes and all sorts of new possibilities emerge.

Where does the Web fit into this picture? It provided the missing piece of technology that took the digital information stored on computers and the communication infrastructure of the Internet and supplied an information management system to interconnect that information and simplify its access across the network. In other words, the Web acted as a catalyst that brought networking and information sharing together in one simple, non-proprietary, generalized information space. In short, it successfully and succinctly connected all the dots.

The following sections present the histories of individual Web businesses and descriptions of several categories of business that the Web was responsible for creating. The first section presents some of the better known Web business success stories. These businesses, such as Netscape and Amazon.com, were born from the Web; each staked out its own particular territory on the Web and succeeded — in very different ways — in becoming either the dominant player or one of the dominant players in the market they were pursuing. The section that follows examines some of the better known Web business failures, such as Webvan and Kozmo. It presents an overview of the type of business each company went after, how the owners went about building market share, and why they ultimately failed. The final section looks at three types of businesses that serve to build and support the operation of the Web, such as Web hosting services.

Web Business Successes

The history of the Web is full of business success stories. Many of the better known success stories describe a couple of college students and their innovative idea for a new type of Web-based service (e.g., a search engine, a directory listing of information resources, an online auction marketplace). They create a modest Web site, attract attention, and quickly discover that the traffic to their site is increasing exponentially. They turn what started as a hobby or avocation into a small business and obtain the investment of millions of dollars of venture capital. The company grows and goes public with an initial public offering (IPO) of stock that turns the college students and others into millionaires. This was, and remains, the dream of many people who, inspired by those who achieved success, view the Web as an untapped resource that is capable of rewarding entrepreneurs with inordinate wealth.

No two Web success stories are the same. What is common to them all, however, is that the Web was viewed and exploited as a new frontier for conducting business. In the early to mid 1990s, the Web as frontier was still largely undiscovered territory; being first, therefore, to introduce a service onto the Web was considered paramount to achieving success. Later, as the Web became better known, the Web as frontier came to be regarded as underdeveloped; being first became less important to achieving success than the development of a well-researched business plan, sound financing, and the experienced execution of the business plan.

The companies described below each found success in providing a service on the Web that satisfied an outstanding need or that created something fresh and provocative that many people liked once they were introduced to it and, more importantly, liked enough to use repeatedly. What these stories make clear, like those of the Web business failures that follow, is that the ways in which companies pursued business on the Web were as varied as the people who began them. Moreover, success (or failure) could not be attributed to any single factor.

Netscape

Appropriately enough, it was Netscape, which created the first commercial Web browser, that ushered in the business of Web business. First, Netscape's introduction of its Navigator browser in 1994 helped to transform the early Web from a largely scientific and academic landscape into a place for fun, education, and, most significantly for the Web's future role in the business world, commerce. Then, in 1995, the drama of the company going public with its earlier-than-expected IPO sent the lust of a gold strike into the hearts and minds of countless would-be Web millionaires. The Web business feeding frenzy had begun, and nothing could have been better for Netscape's business.

Netscape was first to envision the Web as the new frontier for conducting business, and it recognized that in order for businesses to take up residence on the Web two things needed to occur. One, the Web needed buyers; there had to be sufficient consumer traffic to warrant the expense of putting one's business on the Web.

Netscape decided to give away its browser to confront this need; free browser software, the managers of Netscape believed, would help increase use of the Web and attract the attention of business operators to the Web. Two, the Web needed a means to handle business transactions safely and securely. Netscape decided to develop and sell software to fulfill this need, setting its sights on Web commerce for its revenue stream.

Netscape's commercial software for the Web integrated data encryption into the client-server exchange of information between Web clients, or browsers, and Web servers. Netscape did this by creating a new protocol called the Secure Sockets Layer (SSL), to handle the encryption/decryption process, and a variant of HTTP called HTTPS that allowed the client-server conversation to accept this encrypted form of communication. This allowed a business to offer secure transactions, enabling information provided through a Web browser to be readable only by the one Web server that was requesting it. It made possible for the first time, for instance, the safe exchange of confidential credit card information, thereby overcoming one of the earliest and most pronounced obstacles to conducting business over the Web.

Netscape sold its Web server software for the creation and maintenance of commercial Web sites, complete with SSL and HTTPS, to businesses eager for a presence on the Web. Netscape quickly branded itself (i.e., established brand name recognition) as the driving force behind browsing the Web, a process that was made considerably easier by the fact that few alternatives existed to its technology. Sales of its Web server software constituted a sizable portion of the company's early revenues. But Netscape also made money by obtaining royalties, or licensing fees, from companies that packaged the Navigator browser with their own products. For example, Compaq included Navigator with the software supplied on its personal computers. Netscape also sold a suite of development tools to assist application programmers in creating new Web-based products and in providing access from the Web to other, existing information systems.

After achieving success in licensing its browser, selling Web server and Web development software applications, and becoming recognized as a leader in the burgeoning Web development industry, Netscape focused its attention in a new direction. Privatization and commercialization of the Internet along with rapidly growing interest in the Web had incited many large corporations to begin developing their own, private Internet-like networks called intranets. Netscape wanted to provide the software that would run on a company's intranet and it developed a product called SuiteSpot, which was an integrated, networked information management application. This type of application came to be called groupware. Groupware products unified a suite of common network-based tools such as email, a calendar, a notebook, a project planner, conferencing, and chat; and it integrated these tools and the information they contained with the Internet and the Web. Therefore, Netscape's SuiteSpot product provided businesses with a way to build and manage both their Internet and intranet services.

At the same time it was developing SuiteSpot, Netscape created a complementary client-side application that expanded the Web browser into a new type of Web-centric application. The application was called Netscape Communicator and it quickly became the new standard for Web browsers. Communicator packaged together the standard Web browser and Web page creation tools with email and address book management and assorted collaboration tools for chatting and discussion groups. The idea that Netscape was trying to convey was simple, but convincing: whether for use at home or at work, surfing the Web or building a presence on the Web, connecting people or information services, Netscape would provide the software that made all of these activities faster, more efficient, and more powerful.

When Netscape chose to give away its browsers, the practice was something new and controversial. But there was nothing new or controversial about its software application business. Its approach to sales and marketing was traditional; it managed to offer a wide range of products and licensing fee structures that appealed to small, medium, and large businesses, enabling it to succeed in capturing a healthy market share. As the Web and Internet markets changed and grew, so did Netscape. After it became a subsidiary of America Online (AOL) in 1999, Netscape started to shift its attention from information tools to information services. Web portal sites (e.g., Yahoo.com and About.com) were the latest rage for getting the attention of the growing number of Web users and, more importantly, for making sure users spent time on a site and continued to return. The portal site created by

Netscape was named Netcenter. It was an immediate success, and it continues to grow by adding new subscribers, new services, and new corporate sponsorships in the U.S. and abroad.

Netscape's business was responsible for fostering the widespread popularity of the Web, which, in turn, established it as an industry leader in all matters of commerce related to the Web. It began by enabling and enlivening the experience of Web browsing when it introduced the Web's first commercial browser. It grew and became profitable by enabling businesses to provide information and conduct commerce on the Web, and by helping businesses better integrate their information resources and communication systems. Finally, it established itself as a leading Web portal, serving up channels of information and providing an ever-growing selection of networked resources. Netscape has evolved much as the Web itself has evolved, which no doubt has contributed greatly to its success.

Amazon.com

Whereas Netscape founded its business on building the Web, Amazon.com went into business to sell merchandise on the Web and it constructed one of the earliest virtual storefronts to do just that. As its name indicates, Amazon.com is purely a commercial Internet venture; it conducts its business exclusively on the Internet. Moreover, it is a business built of the Web and for the Web; its presence is utterly dependent on the Web and the Web's core components of HTML, HTTP, and the URL.

Amazon.com opened its virtual doors for business in July, 1995, advertising itself as the ultimate bookstore, or, more exactly, the ultimate virtual bookstore. The company had been founded by Jeff Bezos, a Princeton University graduate who had studied computer science and electrical engineering. Bezos had worked as senior vice-president at a Wall Street investment bank and knew very little about the Web or the Internet. When he read, however, about how quickly the Internet was growing and that it was expected it would continue to grow at an astronomical rate, he left Wall Street and headed across the country to Seattle, Washington.

Seattle was near one of the largest book wholesalers in the U.S.; it was also home to a large crop of young, technically savvy individuals.

Without shelves to limit the number of books it could sell, or store hours to limit how long it remained open, Amazon.com began conducting business on the Web by cleverly distinguishing itself as a new, bigger, and better place to buy books. It offered a larger selection of books than any brick-and-mortar bookstore could provide and a location where the lights were always on. More significant than its vast selection of books, however, was Amazon.com's success in creating an online shopping experience that was simple, safe, fast, and fun. Amazon.com pioneered the look and feel for a Web storefront that many other stores would later emulate, if they did not copy it outright. Over the years, they expanded this storefront, as the bookstore grew into a diversified virtual mall selling clothing, music, electronics, power tools, and toys.

Unlike most of its competition, which use their Web store as adjunct to their physical stores, Amazon.com relies exclusively on the Web to interact with its customers and sell its products. Proclaiming itself to be the largest bookstore in the world and, later, advertising itself as offering the largest selection of products on earth, was enough to excite general interest in Amazon.com and, most importantly, to get customers to the site. But what they really needed to do was get customers to buy products through the Web site, convince them to bookmark the site, and, most critical of all, induce them to return again and again. To accomplish this, they focused entirely on their customer and his or her navigation through the site. Usability was essential if customers were to find the product they were seeking or, better yet, were to browse the site to discover something they didn't know they wanted. A usable site was one that was inviting, approachable, and even familiar. The Web, its technology, and the online experience of shopping were, however, unfamiliar territory for everyone when Amazon.com opened for business. The engineers of Amazon.com's Web site, therefore, needed to invent ways to make the technology seem less forbidding and at the same time convince visitors of the benefits of online shopping. They turned to the technology to accomplish both of these goals.

One of their first, and perhaps their most effective, Web technology creations was their patented one-click shopping. Once you have made a purchase at Amazon.com you can elect to turn on this feature, which enables the site to remember your credit card, shipping, and other personal information. Your next purchase can then be completed in a single mouseclick, distilling the process of making a purchase down to the simplest, quickest step. This seemingly simple feature addresses two key Web shopping issues at once. First, it greatly reduces the burden of online shopping by completely eliminating the tediously repeating task of entering all the typical information required for purchasing and shipping a product. Second, it provides an added incentive for a customer to return and do more shopping.

Product reviews are another inventive Web site feature that Amazon.com created to attract buyers and to differentiate the online Web-based shopping from traditional store-based shopping. Customer reviews and, in the case of books, editorial reviews, provide additional information that a customer can use in deciding whether or not to make a particular purchase. Additionally, they give customers the opportunity to voice their opinions, enabling those who feel strongly about an item to recount their experience in using a product (or reading a book) and encourage or discourage others with respect to making a purchase. Product reviews apply a fundamental feature of the Internet and the Web — the free and open sharing of information — to the practice of selling merchandise through the Web.

Other ways in which Amazon.com employs the technology of the Web and Internet to attract customers and boost sales include the following. It dispatches email alerts to notify customers when products or books similar to those they have purchased in the past become available. The Web site provides online recommendations of other products that may interest customers, based on the products each customer has previously selected to examine or buy. Tools on the site allow a customer to create wish lists that friends and family can examine and use when they need to purchase a present. The site even keeps track of recently viewed items to remind a customer of products that were examined but not purchased. Finally, like information Web portals, Amazon.com enables an individual to express preferences to personalize his or her experience with the Web site; a customer can identify the types of products and stores that are of particular interest and in so doing customize the storefront and products that Amazon.com presents.

Amazon.com did not just create a new type of store; it changed the way we seek out products to buy and how we make purchases. It accomplished this through a masterfully designed Web interface, rich in features that simplify the tedium of shopping, and through enhancing our ability to find what we really want, whether or not we know what we really want when we first arrive at the site. Essential to the success of Amazon.com was their creation of a sophisticated back-end system of databases and data warehouses that store information on the products, on us, and on our selections, as well as reviews of the products. The Web site interconnects and uses this vast and ever-growing stockpile of information to further personalize our shopping experience, thereby increasing the likelihood that we will continue to shop at Amazon.com. Ignoring the issue of whether or not the business will ultimately be considered a financial success, Amazon.com pioneered and continues to represent the leading edge in the Web's technology as applied to the business of product merchandising and virtual storefronts.

Ebay

Ebay, like Amazon.com, is a business constructed exclusively for the Web and from the Web. Described as the world's online marketplace, Ebay was founded in 1995 by Pierre Omidyar and Jeff Skoll and is also one of the most frequented online shopping sites. But, while Amazon.com principally employs a business-to-consumer (B2C) sales model, with customers purchasing products from manufacturers or distributors, Ebay built itself on the consumer-to-consumer (C2C) sales model popularized by yard sales, swap meets, flea markets, and auctions. Simply stated, Ebay is in the business of facilitating the selling and trading of goods, no matter where the buyer and seller are located or the type of goods being sold. To accomplish this, Ebay provides a virtual meeting ground, in addition to a virtual community, where consumers buy and sell goods amongst themselves.

Ebay is first and foremost a network. Its network consists largely of individuals, who are categorized either as buyers or sellers, although companies are also joining Ebay in order, for instance, to sell surplus merchandise. Its product database consists of whatever the sellers enter into the system. So, while Amazon.com opened its virtual doors with the largest selection of books available from a single merchant, Ebay's store of goods started with nothing and built itself slowly over time. Ebay very effectively simplified the process of putting items up for sale and provided search and browsing mechanisms that enabled buyers to find items quickly and easily. Consequently, Ebay's network of people and its revolving store of goods has grown exponentially. Ebay pioneered this type of Web-based auction/resale business and it commands the largest share of this market, with more products and more buyers and sellers than any of its competitors. Given the nature of the business, one that relies on a large number of registered users and a wide variety of changing merchandise, Ebay enjoys a dominant position that will be difficult to compete with, although Yahoo!, Amazon.com, and others are trying.

You can buy just about anything on Ebay, from computers, to autographed baseball cards, to one-of-a-kind oddities that defy any simple categorization. Conversely, you can sell just about anything, too, and do it right from your home or business, simply by entering the information into Ebay's Web forms. Meanwhile, Ebay offers the necessary services that help to ensure that business is transacted safely, securely, and honestly. These services include insurance for purchases, mediation for resolving issues, and payment processors like PayPal.

Most items for sale on Ebay are put up for auction for a specified amount of time, such as a week or ten days. You enter bids on what you want to purchase; if your bid is the highest when the auction ends, you make arrangements directly with the seller regarding payment and shipping. Once the transaction is concluded and you have the item, both you and the seller enter feedback on each other. This information is collected by Ebay and constitutes an essential aspect of the Ebay network. Sellers and buyers accrue histories from these transaction reviews that enable others to assess the reliability of the individual and the likely condition of the merchandise. Each review is made available to everyone; Ebay categorizes the reviews according to whether they are positive, neutral, or negative in nature, and provides summary information to better distinguish the relative merits of each member in the network.

Ebay's business model of an online trader's marketplace has nicely dovetailed with the business dynamics of pawn shops. When someone comes into a pawn shop with an item that they hope will secure them a short term loan, the pawn shop owner must somehow put a value on the item that balances the customer's need for cash with his or her risk in taking the merchandise. Many pawn shop owners use Ebay to help them better determine such valuations by locating the same or similar items from among the millions of items listed for sale on Ebay every day and using that information to set a price for any particular item. They also use Ebay as another means to sell the items that they have acquired through foreclosure, effectively adding yet another dimension to Ebay's marketplace.

In terms of their technology and even of their basic Web-related business principles, Ebay and Amazon.com are more similar than different. Both rely on a growing database of returning customers; and the more information they can extract from their customers, the better they can personalize the customers' experiences on their Web site and the more they can induce them to make transactions. Both rely on a growing database of products in order to increase their customer base and the number of transactions. Both have engineered their Web sites to be as simple, friendly, and intuitive as possible in order to appeal to novice as well as experienced Web users. Most importantly, both are completely dependent on the World Wide Web and the Internet in order to conduct their business.

Yahoo!

Yahoo! is first and foremost the behemoth of Web portals; it wants nothing more (or less) than to satisfy all of your Web and Internet needs. Even the other types of Web businesses discussed in this chapter are present on Yahoo! For example, Yahoo!'s shopping mall competes directly with Amazon.com and its auction area competes directly with Ebay. Millions of people have chosen Yahoo! to provide for their repeating online information needs, such as breaking news stories, sporting event scores, weather reports, financial information, and television listings. For many people, Yahoo! is the online equivalent of a favorite daily newspaper. But this is a far cry from Yahoo!'s simpler and much more humble beginnings.

Yahoo! was founded in 1994 by Stanford graduate students David Filo and Jerry Yang. Their Web site, initially named "Jerry's Guide to the World Wide Web," consisted of lists of their favorite hyperlinks, which were nothing more than a pooling together of their bookmarks. Over time, these lists were organized into categories, and the categories were further divided into subcategories. Eventually, Yahoo! evolved into a deceptively simple, but highly effective, human-engineered (as opposed to computer-generated) hierarchical listing of information resources.

The site became an early favorite on the Web because of Filo's and Yang's skill at organizing information. It was easier and faster to start a search at Yahoo!, navigate through the category listings and locate a particular Web site or resource, than it was to use the existing search engines or any other site's Web resource listings. The reason for this was the application of human intelligence. Computers excel at storing vast quantities of information, performing calculations at ever-increasing speeds, and transferring data quickly and efficiently. Their capacity to comprehend and evaluate the information they store, however, is limited. Yahoo!'s hierarchical information listings were created and maintained by individuals who followed URLs to their destination, evaluated the information they contained, and then categorized that information so that it could be indexed correctly and located for others to easily find. No computer program or search engine could compete with this approach in overall effectiveness.

In June, 1994, after the site had developed a following but while it was still more hobby than business venture, Filo and Yang renamed the site Yahoo (the exclamation came later). The name was a descriptive acronym for Yet Another Hierarchical Officious Oracle. The definition of a yahoo as someone "rude, unsophisticated, and uncouth" (derived from its use in Jonathan Swift's "Gulliver's Travels") also appealed to Filo and Yang when choosing their new name for the site. Neither the definition nor the acronym, however, fits the site any longer. Like the exclamation at the end of Yahoo!, the name now has more sound than meaning;

and the sound it makes is that of a highly successful market branding, one that echoes across the Internet and that most people quickly recognize.

To the individual, Yahoo! offers an enormous array of free as well as fee-based services. It is impossible to describe all of these services here, but Yahoo! strives to be a sort of cradle-to-grave Internet and Web companion. Yahoo! is an Internet service provider (ISP), offering both standard dialup access and higher bandwidth access through DSL. It sells a Web site hosting service that can be combined with services for creating and maintaining a Web site. It offers free email accounts for those who want basic email access (and who do not mind advertising tag lines added to their outgoing messages), and it offers fee-based email for those who want additional features (e.g., greater controls over spam and larger storage capacity). It has its own chat network called Yahoo!Messenger that integrates broadcast radio, gaming, and avatars (i.e., created characters for role playing) with the traditional text messaging features of Internet chat. It provides tools to help with managing personal information, such as a notepad, calendar, and address book. It even includes services for paying bills, finding a job, and finding a date.

Yahoo! created a Web portal site named My Yahoo! to collect and consolidate access to the many different types of tools, services, and information that it offers. My Yahoo!, like the Web portals run by Netscape, Microsoft, and others, enables individuals to create an account and customize a type of home page on the portal's Web site. The purpose behind the site and these home pages is to deliver and manage various types of public and personal information according to the needs of each individual. Each individual chooses the content, colors, and layout of their home page; they can further customize their use of the site and its information resources by supplying personal information (e.g., birthday reminders for the calendar program, stock portfolio information for the financial information area) that will be retained on the portal site and will be integrated with the other information displayed on the individual's home page.

The effect (and intent) of My Yahoo! is to bring together many of the different types and sources of information that are available on the Internet and package them in a way that simplifies their use for frequent users of the Internet. Individuals visit My Yahoo! to check their calendar, read the latest news headlines, examine how the stock market is doing, and see what movies are playing at the neighborhood cinema or on television; they do this in place of using the calendar tool installed on their computer and visiting a series of different Web sites to retrieve all the different types of information they routinely want to know. Individuals benefit by this type of information consolidation and easy customization; and Yahoo! benefits by using this free information access to bring millions of people to their site every day, to show them advertisements, to sell them products and services, and to collect information about them to resell to other companies. (Note that when you have all or most of the information you need presented neatly on one page by one provider, you are no longer surfing the Web.)

To a business, Yahoo! offers everything a small or medium-sized company needs in order to set up shop on the Web, whether it is selling donuts or a weight loss program. Yahoo! also builds portal sites tailored to a company's needs, complete with tools that enable employees to communicate with each other and with customers, provide streaming audio and video for meetings, corporate functions, and product launches, and supply information channels to distribute different types of information throughout the company. In other words, Yahoo! wants your business as part of its business.

Yahoo! is in the business of serving Web pages and charging for Web services. For Yahoo!, more information channels and tools mean more subscribers viewing more pages. More viewed pages mean more advertising revenue. More registered users mean a larger and wider demographic to sell to advertisers. More fee-based subscription services like email and Web site hosting mean reduced overall cost for providing such services. Yahoo!'s success, like that of the other Web portal providers, depends on a large base of users who frequent their Web portal and their other sites and who make its portal site their home on the Web.

Ironically, Yahoo! grew to early popularity as an advertising-free, highly organized, and information-rich Web resource that helped individuals navigate the Web's expanding information space and locate information and resources. Over the years, Yahoo! has transformed itself into an advertising-rich, customizable Web portal with its own array of content channels, search mechanisms, productivity and communication tools, and even games, that serve to induce individuals to remain on the Yahoo! domain for as long as possible. In a way, Yahoo! represents the Web and the Internet in miniature, but controlled by one commercial entity.

Google

Google is a variation of the word googol, the mathematical term for a 1 followed by 100 zeros that was coined by Milton Sirotta, the nephew of a mathematician. Since nothing exists in this quantity, not sheep to count at night, not the dollars in the U.S. federal budget deficit, not stars in the sky, a google represents a measurement bordering on infinity. Not a bad name to choose for a company in the Web search engine business that faces the challenge of indexing the ever-growing, already unquantifiable number of pages on the Web.

Google's history, like that of Yahoo!, begins with two graduate students at Stanford University in California. Larry Page and Sergey Brin began work on their search engine in 1996. They originally called it BackRub, in reference to how their program analyzed Web pages, retrieved links in those pages that pointed *back* to other pages, and then repeated the process. In 1998, after refining their technology and securing private funding, Page and Brin incorporated their company as Google Inc. It did not take long for Google to become one of the most popular search engines on the Web.

Shortly after winning awards for their search engine at the end of 1998, Google was handling more than half a million search requests a day. Between the media attention and the attention of users, the company started to develop what they needed most to build Google's economic viability: partnerships with existing technology companies. These partnerships were responsible for bringing in revenue from licensing and usage fees for Google's technology, directing more traffic to its Web site, and increasing its branding, or name recognition, as a leader in search engine technology for the Web. Google's first partnership was with a company named RedHat, one of the largest and best known providers of a computer operating system called Linux. Linux was a popular choice of many Web technology companies, including

Google, because it was an inexpensive, open source (as opposed to proprietary) operating system that ran on personal computers (in direct competition with Microsoft's operating systems) and on other more sophisticated computers, such as workstations and mainframes. Following RedHat, AOL/Netscape and Yahoo!, two of the Web's largest portal sites, and onetime search engine developers themselves, selected Google as their sites' search engine. Due to these and other partnerships, search queries executed on Google soon numbered in the millions per day and the number of pages indexed by Google exceeded one billion.

More than a few search engines and search engine technologies have come and gone since the Web started serving up pages. Google has succeeded in the competitive Web business of search engines because it provides speed, coverage, intelligence, and ease of use. Its speed is a product of the proprietary technology it developed to index its database of pages, which is a critical component of the search engine given that the size of this database is only going to increase over time. Its coverage of the Web and the number of Web pages it catalogs equals or exceeds that of any other search engine. Its intelligence is a factor of the algorithms that its engineers created to index the contents of Web pages and to refine and rank the Web page listings returned by a search. Its ease of use is apparent in the simplicity of its site; performing a search is as straight forward as entering a few keywords and clicking a button. Also contributing to Google's success are the advanced features it provides to further refine search results, including the ability to restrict pages to those written in a specific language, stored in a specific file format or on a specific Internet domain, and updated in a specific time frame, and the ability to control how much or how little filtering is automatically performed to remove potentially objectionable material.

Google is no longer just a Web search engine, although all of the services it offers make use of its core search technology. In general, the company has succeeded in diversifying its operation by providing specialized interfaces to the vast wealth of information it has located and cataloged. For example, a service named Froogle searches exclusively for online stores and merchandise while a related service limits shopping-related searches to online mail-order catalogs. A service called Answers enables users to ask a question, set a price they are willing to pay for the answer, and expect to be sent a reply within twenty-four hours. A searchable hierarchical information listing called Directory functions like the same service pioneered by Yahoo! and described earlier. A service called Groups offers an interface to browse information found in the discussion forums managed by USENET, and it includes a function to search the forums' questions and answers. Google even provides a service engineered specifically for the rapidly growing community of wireless Web users who are connecting to the Web via mobile phones, personal digital assistants (PDAs), and other devices. This service includes features that simplify the task of entering criteria on devices that have limited keypads and translate Web pages on-the-fly into a format designed specifically for the limited displays of these small devices.

Google's success as a Web business is a testament to its technology and to its understanding of the changing needs of users on the Web. Unlike Yahoo!, Amazon.com, Ebay, and Netscape, Google cannot rely on a large and established database of users returning tomorrow or the next day to buy another book or check the value of their stock portfolio. Individuals do not have the same kind of incentive to return to Google that they have elsewhere, other than knowing that Google's search engine works, and works well. But if someone invents a better technology — and new types of search engines are being launched all the time — Google may find itself in the same position as some of the companies described in the following section.

Web Business Failures

The companies described above illustrate that there is no single path or strategy for creating a successful Web business. The founders range from students to seasoned technology executives. A few knew something about business, but nothing about the Web or the Internet, while others knew the technology, but nothing about the business world. But they all knew what people wanted; and through smart engineering, sound, sometimes innovative technology, and persistence, they met those needs and developed leading enterprises on the Web. Many others tried and failed. Some of the reasons for failure were relatively common, like grossly over-anticipating revenues and a basic inability to control spending. But, ultimately, every Web business that failed did so due to its own unique set of overlooked, unseen, or unresolved problems and errors of judgment.

Webvan

Webvan brought your grocery store to the Web. The company survived for about two years, starting operation in 1999 and filing for bankruptcy in 2001. The general business model was sound, from an Internet and e-commerce perspective. Invest in trucks and large, high-tech food distribution centers. Provide a friendly Web site through which customers could select their groceries and arrange for delivery. Become the Amazon.com of grocery stores.

Webvan's business plan argued that the consumer would prefer its services over that of a traditional local grocery store because it stocked a greater selection of products, offered the convenience of ordering online from one's computer at home or at work, and removed the burdens of pushing a cart and hauling heavy packages. Equally important, the plan also argued that the food suppliers would benefit by finally being able to establish a direct connection to the consumer. They could, for instance, more effectively test market new products because they would be able to offer samples to and gather responses from individuals who, based on information about the products they already purchased, would be more inclined to like what they were being offered. The food suppliers would also no longer be restricted by a grocery store's limited shelving or the dictates of large-scale regional preferences that result in some products being commonly available in one part of the country and hard-to-find or unavailable elsewhere. Webvan would provide the e-business system to seamlessly combine all the disparate parts, offering an exciting new service to consumers and establishing an innovative way for food suppliers to market their goods and better test and target new products.

What the technology can offer, however, is not always what people want. Buying books online is one thing. Buying groceries online, apparently, is something entirely different. Only about 20% of those who tried Webvan returned to use the service again; and only about 20% of those individuals, or 4% of those who sampled the service, became regular customers. Nevertheless, Webvan operated under the popularized Internet investment premise of the time, which called for growing the business as fast as possible even when faced with considerable short-term business losses. Branding the company name and achieving early market dominance were the battle cry of venture capitalists and technology leaders alike. In pursuing such a strategy, Webvan spent over $800 million to expand its service into 26 cities at the same time. But, with time and money running out, not enough people used Webvan's services and the enterprise failed.

Kozmo

Kozmo was a one-hour delivery service that combined the instant access and instant gratification services of the Web with an e-business solution composed of bicycle-riding couriers in bright orange jackets. The concept was simple enough. If a person could go online and order a product, like a book from Barnes and Noble, and select a next-day delivery option, why not offer a same-day or one-hour delivery option in locations where the consumer, the store, and the product were all in close proximity.

The company began its operation in New York City in 1997 as a free service for the delivery of video rentals selected online. Over time, it expanded its operation to other cities, such as Boston, San Francisco, Los Angeles, and Seattle, and delivered a variety of other products, such as books, ice cream, and candy. It acquired venture capital backing amounting to hundreds of millions of dollars, including $60 million from Amazon.com. Amazon.com used Kozmo to provide a one-hour delivery option for some of its products. Kozmo also developed a partnership with Starbucks and installed drop boxes in their locations for the return of videos that had been delivered by Kozmo.

Kozmo never brought in the revenue it needed to survive. The expense of delivering such low cost items, like a video rental or a pint of ice cream, could not be offset by more people using the service. When it costs a company $10 to deliver a $5 item, it cannot expect to stay in business very long. When Kozmo tried to apply the same business model to higher priced items, like electronics, a one-hour delivery option did not prove as marketable. Kozmo took to the extreme the overnight delivery services offered by established and traditional delivery companies like Federal Express and Airborne Express. But its Web business model, even with an outrageous amount of capital and promising strategic partnerships, was better on paper than it was on two wheels.

Pets.com and eToys

Pets.com and eToys brought high demand, high volume retail merchandising to the Web. Pets.com, founded in 1998, took the big business of pet supplies and products onto the Web. The company was well financed (Amazon.com was one of its backers) and aggressively marketed (it was promoted through television and print advertising, and it created a sock-puppet dog that helped it achieve some brand name recognition). Similarly, eToys took the large, competitive toy business market onto the Web and also sold video games, software, music, and baby-related products. It was founded in 1997 by a former Walt Disney Company executive, was well funded, and was strongly marketed in an attempt to achieve name recognition quickly. It achieved an amazing market valuation of $7.7 billion the day it went public in 1999, which was 35% higher in value than the long established Toys-R-Us; and it was run by business professionals with Harvard and Stanford MBAs.

Both businesses offered all the conveniences of the Web: competitive prices, various delivery options, and an easy-to-use interface with a search mechanism and shopping cart. Both had short, memorable, highly descriptive domain names, making them easy to find, remember, and return to. (Note that, while the original business enterprises failed, their names live on in one form or another on the Web. Names alone represent a commodity on the Web, and ones as simple and direct as these are quite valuable.)

Pets.com and eToys suffered from low margins and fierce competition with other startup e-businesses and with larger, more established companies. Neither company succeeded in using the Web to provide something unique and compelling to customers that earned their loyalty and repeat business. Nor were they able to supply better service, products, or prices than their brick-and-mortar rivals, which were also creating virtual storefronts on the Web to supplement the sales from their street front stores. In the end, old fashioned business economics took hold and caused their demise, as losses mounted, capital was depleted, and projections of profitability became increasingly remote.

govWorks

Unlike the companies profiled above, govWorks was not interested in e-commerce or in selling products. Instead, govWorks brought government forms and payment processing to the Web. Founded in 1998 by two high school friends, Kaleil Isaza Tuzman and Thomas Herman, govWorks set out to transform the way individuals interacted with the local, city, state, and federal government. More specifically, govWorks tried to apply the efficiencies and economies of e-business to how government agencies processed information and collected fees and taxes. Its business model focused on the highly profitable area of transaction processing, which meant charging fees to help others conduct business.

Online shopping was changing the way business was conducted and online information access was changing the way people found answers to their questions and stayed informed. People could pay their phone bills and view their banking transactions online. But something as basic as property taxes was still paper bound: printed, mailed to each home owner, and payable by check. Many people were already starting to demand the same type of online bill paying and information access from the government as was being offered by the business community when the govWorks Web site was created and promised to offer these services and solve the long-standing complaint regarding government red tape. Through the site, individuals could access government information and news, secure permits, locate and print forms, and submit various types of applications. Most importantly, individuals and businesses would be able to use govWorks to pay taxes, fines (e.g., a parking ticket), and bills (e.g., sewer and garbage collection) online.

While the govWorks Web site provided information access and greater convenience for individuals, the business model depended on the savings govWork's services promised to the government agencies that signed up. One example they used of the savings govWorks could provide was that, while it cost up to 7 dollars for the state government to process a tax payment offline, the same transaction would cost it only 35 cents through govWorks. Even though government agencies were among the first institutions to employ and profit from the use of computers, they were notoriously slow to integrate Web and e-business solutions into how they performed work. Therefore, govWorks, as well as other companies, found an excellent opportunity to market their services to government agencies by asserting how they could reduce costs, paperwork, and red tape. For govWorks to fulfill its aggressively optimistic earnings projections, however, it first had to secure enough government contracts and process enough transactions to cover its costs of doing business, which it never did.

It took govWorks about two years to transform its promising business venture into another dot com failure. The company filed for bankruptcy early in 2001. Like many similar ventures, it over-anticipated revenue, expanded too quickly, spent all of its venture capital, and failed to account for the expense of its operations and the effect of competing services. The rise and fall of govWorks became the subject of a documentary called "Startup.com."

Businesses that Build and Support the Web

A big part of the business Web is the business of supplying the technology and infrastructure for the Web itself. Sales of software for building and hosting Web sites constitutes a significant percentage of this business, as does the sales of the various types of computers that operate as Web servers and of the adjunct devices, such as firewalls and proxy servers, that help to control traffic, filter information, and manage information resources. Additionally, a huge service industry has emerged that assists individuals and businesses in creating, managing, maintaining, and hosting their Web sites. This industry consists of a wide range of new business ventures, some of which are briefly described in the following sections.

One of the things that sets the Web apart as a place (or space) for conducting business, however, is that no one owns the Web or controls its technology. Moreover, a lot of software used for accessing the Web, running Web servers, and building and managing the content of the Web is free for the taking; and, more often than not, this free software is as good or better than software that must be purchased or licensed. Free Web software includes browsers, like Netscape's Communicator and Microsoft's Internet Explorer, as well as what has been the most popular and widely used Web server software for nearly all the years that the Web has been in operation, the Apache HTTP Server from the Apache Software Foundation. Some of this free software is created by individuals and is generously donated for others to use, following a tradition championed by the Free Software Foundation and exemplified by Tim Berners-Lee, who released into the public domain all of the software he wrote in creating the Web. Software is also developed and given away by organizations and corporations in order to do such things as promote a new software development language or jump start a new business model.

The ability of individuals and businesses to access and use the Web without being required to buy software or pay some type of licensing or royalty fee helped to accelerate the Web's early acceptance and contributed to its exponential growth. Each of the Web businesses described earlier in this chapter benefited from the existence of this free software and the open source technology of the Web. The many businesses that were started to assist others in building a presence on the Web and, in so doing, build and support the Web itself, also benefited. It made it easier and far less costly to start such businesses as well as to succeed alongside competition from larger companies and major corporations. The types of services provided by businesses to help others build a presence on the Web — content creation and management services, design services, and hosting services — are described below.

Content Creation and Management Services

The creation of content for distribution on the Web ranges from the very simple to the very complex. The simplest Web content is stored as static HTML pages. Many products are available that allow individuals to create and interconnect simple HTML pages; they work very like other electronic publishing tools, with features for doing such things as identifying text as part of a heading, a paragraph, or a list, highlighting text using different typefaces and point sizes, and importing and positioning graphics files that contain photos or artwork. For those not interested in doing this work themself, agencies in the business of developing Web content will create a small number of basic HTML pages for a very modest fee. For most individuals and small businesses, a half dozen or so HTML pages is all that they will need to store the information they wish to publish on the Web; and, frequently, the same business that created the HTML pages will also provide services for designing the site and hosting it on the Internet.

Content creation and management, however, becomes more difficult, time consuming, and expensive when a site needs to include dozens of pages, when dynamically created content needs to be incorporated, or when more advanced Web page technologies are used to increase the functionality, usability, or impact of a site. Many of the tools and applications required to develop and manage the content for these larger, more complex Web sites are free, but learning how to use them and, more importantly, how to use them effectively, demands some degree of technical proficiency and experience. Professional assistance is normally required to create and maintain such sites. Most small companies outsource this work to service organizations, while larger companies typically hire staff to perform this work.

Advanced Web page content can be created using a wide assortment of applications, languages, and technologies, each of which requires extensive training and experience before they can be mastered. For example, Flash, Java, and Javascript can be used for such things as animations, mouse-over effects (e.g., text popups or swapping images), tutorials, and interactive Web forms, games, and tools. Languages such as PHP and Perl can be used to build Web pages dynamically based on user input and to include common page elements (e.g., the current date and time, a navigation bar, or a footer with a copyright notice). Specialized CGI programs can be written in all sorts of languages in order to validate and process Web page forms (e.g., a login authentication or a sweepstakes entry). An industry has emerged to create these applications, languages, and technologies for the Web; another has emerged to train people in their use, which includes the publishing of books and the creation of tutorials and training programs; and another has emerged that offers the services of people trained in creating this content for the Web. Creating and managing content for the Web, whether for a simple site or a not-so-simple site, is big business.

Design and Graphics Services

It did not take long for the content of Web pages to expand from the presentation of plain text, to text intermixed with images, to sophisticated, magazine-like page layouts, to animated, interactive pages embedded with all sorts of multimedia objects. The problem with the vast majority of Web pages is that they do not match form with function; they do not demonstrate an understanding of how people read and react to Web pages. The technology and tools of the Web have succeeded in reducing the effort and experience needed to create complex and dynamic Web pages. But what many individuals and businesses have failed to recognize is that there are reasons why some Web pages look and function better than others; there is both art and science applied in the design and layout of an attractive and effective Web site. Services in the business of site design and the creation of graphics specialize in this area.

Large corporations employ graphic design teams to come up with a unique presentation and layout for their Web sites. The work performed by graphic designers includes such things as high-end photography, artwork that sets a specific tone or conveys a consistent theme, and icons and background images that define the look and feel of a site. Frequently, corporations also employ design specialists who specialize in something called usability analysis. Usability engineers or analysts study how we interact with computers and with different types of page layouts and information structures. They use specially designed laboratories to survey, record, and analyze how test subjects respond to and comprehend different presentations of information. They apply this knowledge — of what works and does not work with respect to such things as the amount of information on a typical page, the use of typefaces and colors, and the size and positioning of graphics — to engineer how we navigate a Web site. The work they do helps to ensure that the form and function of a page work together and that the overall interconnection of information allows us to find what we are looking for and not become lost in a maze of flashing images and boxes of text.

The Web is filled with a remarkable diversity of sites, and this diversity is a function of both content and design. Many people may not recognize why one site seems to work or flow better than another; they will, however, notice the difference between a site that is easy to read and navigate and one that is more of a challenge to understand and use. Notably, there are also a number of now familiar site designs that are commonly used on the Web, especially on e-commerce sites, such as storefronts, and on portal sites. This is because it is easy to copy the overall design of any Web site, and when a design works well for one business, like the one Amazon.com designed for its storefront, it can often work equally well for another.

As with the business of creating and managing Web site content, the business of creating and designing Web site graphics and layouts and analyzing the usability of Web sites is big business. Countless companies, small and large, provide these services; a search for such businesses on the Web will quickly confirm this. Dozens of books have been written on the subject of Web site design and others explain how to use the various applications for creating illustrations, working with digital photographs, and creating animations, advertisements, and other types of multimedia content. Also, many online courses and tutorials have been created to teach this information, and classroom-based courses are now offered at local high schools, colleges, and community centers.

Hosting Services

Once a Web site's content has been created and its design has been finalized, the site needs to be hosted; its files and any dependent applications (e.g., a database) must be installed on a computer that is connected to the Internet. For most individuals and the majority of small to moderate sized businesses, this means buying space and service from one of the many thousands of businesses providing Web site hosting. Before a Web site can be hosted, however, a domain name (e.g., netscape.com, moveon.org, vassar.edu) must first be purchased from one of the accredited domain name registrars on the Internet.

A domain name registrar is an organization that has been approved by the Internet Corporation for Assigned Names and Numbers (ICANN) to handle the registration of a new domain name, a process that includes handling the fees for this service and making sure that the name and the owner's information is recorded and processed. Registering a domain name ensures that the Internet address of a site is unique, which also ensures that the Web site address and all URLs that reference files or resources on the site are unique in the Web's information space. Many businesses that provide Web hosting services are also domain name registrars and, if they are not, they typically offer a service to register a domain through one of the registrars on behalf of a customer.

It is possible, although far less common, for individuals and small businesses to host their own Web site on the Internet. The requirements for doing so are a networked computer connected through a high bandwidth Internet service (e.g., a T1 line, which is expensive, cable, or satellite) and some type of Web server software (e.g., the free Apache HTTP server). Larger businesses and organizations, government agencies, libraries, research facilities, and educational institutions can host their own Web sites, if they wish, because most already have high bandwidth Internet connections and any number of computers connected on one or more local area networks. The most common way to get a Web site hosted, however, is to pay a Web hosting company to provide space for the site's files, an IP address for the site's domain (as described in *The Internet Revolution*, the domain name system stores domain names and associated IP addresses to enable any Internet-connected computer to locate any other Internet-connected computer), and a Web server configuration to handle serving the files. The cost of a basic Web hosting service can be as little as a few dollars a month. This modest cost typically includes a maximum amount of space for the files, a maximum amount of data transfer (i.e., measured traffic) per month, and some number of email accounts, including email forwarding from one address to another and automated replies.

Web hosting companies run the gamut from mom-and-pop organizations that provide basic services at inexpensive rates to large corporations, like Yahoo!, that provide full e-commerce services with database access, assorted programming models and languages, dedicated servers, very high bandwidth, 99.9% guaranteed up time (i.e., they have redundancies in their operation that ensure a site remains online and accessible at virtually all times, even in the event of a hardware failure or a loss of power), file backups, and much more. So many companies are now in this business that prices and services vary tremendously; and care should be taken to ensure that the provider selected offers the right services for the particular needs and budget of the site.

The People Web

6

The People Web

Do you have a home page? How about your son or daughter, or perhaps your grandmother? The Web was created with you in mind; the great quantity and diversity of personal home pages on the Web bears witness to this fact. Among many other things, the World Wide Web is a web of people, from pre-teens to octogenarians, from auto mechanics to mercenaries to musicians, from the technology-crazed to the technology-impaired, from lonely hearts to lifelong lovers.

The people Web, however, is a lot more diverse and engaging than a distributed collection of personal home pages. All sorts of people have placed themselves on the Web for all sorts of different reasons. Self-promotion, for example, is a common purpose behind the creation of many sites that make up the people Web. For instance, there are the sites of public figures, such as those of entertainers, personalities, and politicians, that serve to further the careers and promote the interests of these individuals. The official Web sites, moreover, created by or, more typically, on behalf of these individuals and approved by them, often inspire the creation of unofficial sites by admirers or detractors that add yet more (and sometimes very different) information onto the Web about the personal and public lives of these individuals.

Another part of the people Web comprises self-promotion of a different sort; it consists of information about people in search of work or in search of companionship or love. These people inhabit a Web in which countless individuals are seeking some sort of personal fulfillment. They use the Web's global information space to put themselves out there, literally, by describing personal, and sometimes very intimate, details of their lives for anyone to read. Newspaper want ads and magazine lonely hearts listings represent the closest equivalent to such self-promotion before the arrival of the Web. These services were effective, if somewhat limited in their scope and appeal. Once again, the Web demonstrated its capacity to adapt existing services such as these to the far larger and more individualized information space that it had established. This very personal part of the people Web was responsible for the creation of new business ventures that cater to people in search of work, romance, or companionship, empowering individuals to reach out to others in a way best suited to their unique needs and desires.

Another significant and growing part of the people Web concerns genealogy: the study and documenting of family histories. The Web might as well have been designed for just such an activity. Its ease of use and many search facilities combined with its global reach and its increasing store of records about us together provide a type and scale of information access that never before existed. Here, also, the Web was responsible for the creation of new business ventures, some that focus exclusively on the collection of genealogical records and others that focus on selling applications that help individuals build, study, and share their family trees. This part of the people Web uses the Internet's network of interconnected computers and the Web's information space to help individuals and families explore and discover their own personal interconnections in pursuit of finding other, living relations or recovering the family's unique roots and history.

The newest component of the people Web may also be its most distinctive. It is something called blogging, and it represents a new type of self-expression designed exclusively for the Web. Blogging consists of the publishing of personal journal entries on the Web, providing yet another way for individuals to put something of themselves out there onto the Web. Blogging is another example of how inventive people are employing the Web for new pursuits, thereby enlarging the Web's overall impact and relevance.

The people Web is all about personal pursuits. It caters to the individual. It is not about technology or big business, although both are certainly well represented. It offers all of us new capabilities to reach out as individuals, share information, and connect with other people. This chapter explores the different areas of the people Web introduced above: personal home pages, the Web sites of public figures, job hunting, dating, genealogy, and blogging.

There Is No Place Like Home: Web Home Pages

The home pages of individuals on the Web comprise the purest and most familiar part of the people Web. Many ISPs provide a place on their Web site for members to publish a limited number of pages, which is perfect for people who simply want to describe themselves or their family and to share some photos and stories. Some companies offer a comparable environment for free, as long as you allow them to include advertisements on your pages. Most of these same companies also offer Web site packages in a range of prices and services that will satisfy the needs of most individuals. All things considered, there are many types of services and many options to choose from should you want a personal presence on the Web, as many people do.

So, why publish on the Web? Why bother to create a personal home page or a personal Web site that millions of strangers and perhaps a few friends and family members can visit? For one, it's easy and it's fun. It's a wonderful way for adults and children alike to express themselves. It's also a good way to learn first-hand about the Web and about how Web pages work. But the most common reason probably relates to the Web as a tool that fosters communication and sharing. Personal Web pages offer a simple, and often free mechanism to take just about anything you can store on your computer and share that information with others: opinions on current events, photos of friends, your family, your pets or your latest vacation, recipes, anecdotes, links to other sites you think are valuable, and so on. The list is endless, as are the possibilities. Another reason for creating a personal presence on the Web has to do with the use of a home page as a jumping-off-point for exploring the Web. Rather than using your browser's bookmarks, for instance, a home page can become your personal portal onto the Web, from which you can easily venture out to your favorite places and on which you can capture information that you want to keep. Such pages serve much the same purpose as Berners-Lee's original Enquire program.

The types of home pages and personal sites people publish vary tremendously, not just in terms of their content, but also with respect to their quality, the sophistication of their presentation, and their purpose. Several general types are common. For example, many are strictly family-oriented. Often, a single family member creates a site and uses it to share information with other members of the family who may be far from home, such as a parent or child on military duty or an aunt or uncle who has moved abroad. The site may recount stories about each member of the family, describe the latest exploits of the dog, and include an anecdote about a home repair gone awry. Snapshots taken during the latest vacation are very common, as are baby photographs. Other family members are told about the site, and suddenly grandparents and uncles and cousins are connecting to see pictures of the latest addition to the family or to get the recipe for Uncle Mike's lobster pie. Some of the family members visiting the site are, in turn, inspired to create their own family site with their own assorted photos, and perhaps even their own version of lobster pie. Over time these family home pages and the links between them form a sort of personal family Web. They develop into a wholly new way for the immediate and extended family to communicate, interact, have fun, and share information.

Other personal Web sites and home pages are used as artistic expressions and function as a way for individuals to self-publish their artwork. The Web offers an immediate and dynamic environment in which budding, as well as established, artists can publish their creations. In particular, given the ever-lowering prices of digital cameras and the ease at which digital photos can be transferred to a computer and uploaded to a Web site, these personal sites are frequently filled with all sorts of photo albums. Some of these sites include more advanced multimedia elements, such as narration, while others present their photos as a type of online slide show. Photo albums on the Web promote the art and impact of photography more than any other event in the history of photography. Poetry, fiction, film, and the graphic arts are no less at home on such sites, as more and more people reach out through the Web to express themselves and become their own publishers.

Some of these personal home page sites are business-oriented. People use them to promote themselves or their business interests in the hopes of securing a new job or as a resource for others to consult in order to learn more about them, their background, and their accomplishments. A resume or curriculum vitae is commonly included on such sites; and often there are links to articles the individual has published or products he or she has created or worked on. Some of these sites include handmade products that are for sale, or other creations that can be purchased directly from the site. Such personal Web sites, therefore, act as an extended advertisement for the individual, and sometimes for that person's business interests, too.

Other personal sites are activity- or group-oriented. Activity-based sites offer a place to display collections, like baseball cards or comics, and to present the stories behind the collections or to provide important links to related sites. Many such sites focus on games, computers, health issues, and music, but they cover just about any subject imaginable. The sites provide a way for people to use the Web to form further associations, to reach out and help develop or interact in extended communities. At the same time, creating the Web site enables people to document, organize, and develop their own information collection on a particular subject. The Web becomes a personal tool used in the pursuit of this area of interest.

Group-oriented sites are similar in scope. One such site, for example, devoted to a particular high school's graduating class, was created to help locate classmates, and it includes an area where class members can post notes and pictures. Another group-oriented site holds individual biographical pages for the residents of a retirement home; it was created by a 12 year old boy who is presumably one of the residents' grandchildren. These sites speak to that fundamental component of the Web that uses the sharing of information to bring people closer together.

To many, these personal home pages on the Web may sound trivial, especially when compared with the giant Web portals, online shopping malls, and other commercial sites that are mistakenly considered the bulk of what the Web has to offer. Nevertheless, these home pages constitute a large part of the Web that often gets overlooked, and the diversity of the information contained in these pages is startling. More importantly, perhaps, they exemplify the egalitarian nature of the Web, in which the home page for IBM and the home page for your Aunt Millie in New Hope, Vermont, are on one level utterly equivalent. They also hearken back to Berners-Lee's original vision of the Web as a place where everyone is a publisher; they illustrate that we all have information to share, whether for fun, education, or any number of other reasons.

One thing to keep in mind, however, is that you may want to think twice about the type of information you (or your children) plan to publish on the Web. Even if you take the added security step of protecting your site with a password so that only you and your friends and family can view it (this is more the exception than the rule), you should still be especially careful about unwittingly exposing too much personal information about you or your family. This is particularly important when children are involved. Not everyone surfing the Web is going to read your information with the same, benevolent perspective you had in mind when publishing it.

In Search of Publicity: Public People on the Web

If you have a name or a face people might recognize, chances are you have a Web site devoted exclusively to you. It does not have to be of your making, however. A great many professional people in the business of promoting themselves, such as entertainers and politicians, have what are usually referred to as unofficial sites dedicated to them. These unofficial sites can be complimentary, or not. But they are commonplace on the Web, and the better known you are, the more such sites are likely to exist.

Pick your favorite celebrity, go to a search engine such as Google, and enter his or her name. Unless you have chosen someone relatively obscure, you will be amazed at the number of sites that are found. What is truly impressive, however, is the quality of many of these sites. An unofficial site may contain a greater quantity and variety of information and be better designed than the official site published by the celebrity or the celebrity's agency. Most interesting, perhaps, is that many of these unofficial sites — typically created by a fan or a fan club — are not only comprehensive in their coverage, but they deliberately exclude advertising or any sort of self-promotional element; they represent time and effort donated by individuals solely for the purpose of sharing information about and demonstrating their collective interest in and appreciation for the celebrity. Such sites are pure Web tributes. They are also another way in which the Web facilitates the creation of virtual communities on the Internet. They establish a location where people with common interests can gather, interact, and express themselves. In this instance, that common interest just happens to be a celebrity.

Official celebrity sites, on the other hand, are, by their very nature, self-promotional. They are designed to sell a celebrity by presenting a positive and informative history of his or her life and accomplishments. Many, if not most, of these sites also either sell products directly or they provide links to sites that offer an assortment of collectible merchandise or memorabilia. For such sites, the people Web is first and foremost about commerce rather than community. The dichotomy represented by these two very different types of Web sites that deal with the same subject matter mirrors in miniature the larger dichotomy of the Web, which consists, on the one side of business interests and the commercial Web and on the other side of individual and community interests and the personal Web that each of us can contribute to should we choose to do so.

Politicians are a particular, and peculiar, type of celebrity. As such they engender their own particular types of Web sites. The problem is that few politicians or political groups use the Web for anything more or different than disseminating the same kind of partisan views and propaganda that these same types of individuals and groups distributed through broadcast and print media before the Web, even though the Web is capable of doing so much more. If, for instance, you do a search for Web sites devoted to the current president of the United States, the resulting list will contain the official government site of the president, www.whitehouse.gov, along with any number of highly popular, unofficial sites. The White House site, stately and refined, presents images of the president along with links to biographical accounts, his cabinet, his speeches, and so on. But the majority of the site is, as you might expect, carefully tailored to push the political agenda of the president and his supporters. It is an extension of his political persona and serves to advance his particular goals and interests. This applies equally well to the Web sites of other politicians. The unofficial sites promote a somewhat different view of the president and his politics. They run the gamut from less than flattering, even disparaging depictions to highly supportive sites bordering on hero worship. Each site includes its own pictures, biographical links, and other associated information, in support of its particular interests, opinions, and agenda.

Together all of these sites provide a valuable, perhaps even necessary balance of information. This sort of balance was impossible to achieve before the advent of the Web. The difference rests with us and with the basic facility of the Web that can turn each of us into publishers. This part of the people Web may be dominated by rhetoric, but this rhetoric and the sites on which it exists represents a new type of equal opportunity forum. These personal, often one-sided sites constitute today's global equivalent of Speaker's Corner in Hyde Park, London, where anyone can get up on a soapbox and speak his or her mind on any subject. The Web gives everyone a voice; and, as at Speaker's Corner, you can choose to listen or to walk away.

In Search of Work: Web Job Hunting

The Web is full of people in search of a job, corporate Web sites that post their job openings, and many highly competitive Web businesses trying to make money by acting as online job brokers. There are Web sites that contain job banks, others, run by state agencies, that offer employment services, and some that provide career counseling and assistance with developing a resume. The Web has transformed the way many people find out about and apply for jobs, just as it has transformed the way many organizations — commercial, non-profit, and governmental — advertise and fill their openings. The Web has become a people-rich resource (i.e., filled with personal information about people seeking employment) that includes many individuals and services focused on the search for better employment opportunities.

The information space of the Web is ideally suited to job hunting. Both resumes and job postings consist largely of quantifiable pieces of information that can be easily categorized, such as salary history and salary requirements, years and type of education and education requirements, previous jobs and experience and job/skill requirements. Accordingly, the Web has become a two-way information highway, equally suited to job hunting and job advertising, and ideal for performing well-defined, machine-executed searches.

You have many choices if you are searching for a job on the Web. You can visit companies directly and review their list of openings. This has the benefit of saving your prospective employer money, since it will enable the company to avoid any type of agency fee for your referral. You can use one of many services that, like an online extension of traditional head hunting agencies, post your resume to the companies they serve. You can also join one or more of the job searching sites that effectively function as Web portals onto the online job market.

These job hunting Web portals demonstrate the full power of the Web with respect to the increasingly diverse and demanding job market. While all the sites are different, and some sites only cater to certain types of jobs or to specific geographic areas, most include the same basic services. Browsing for jobs in a specific location and/or in a particular field is a common way to start. But it is through the search facilities offered on these sites that you can best take advantage of the information resources that these sites provide. One of the more advanced features offered at some sites allows you to program a type of automated search bot (short for robot) with your search criteria for the perfect job. The bot periodically searches new job listings for matches with your criteria and then saves the results for you to review when you next return or emails the results directly to you. This type of service effectively combines the information space of the Web with the communication functions of the Internet.

For many individuals, the Web offers a smarter and more efficient way to search for a new job. For companies seeking to fill positions, the Web greatly increases the chances of finding the best person for each job. As a consequence of providing these services, the Web with its growing wealth of job-related information has also made available several new types of information resources.

Information about people seeking jobs can now be used, for instance, to establish demographic data about the localization of certain types of skills, trends in unemployment, regional wage information, and other types of information related to employment. Such data remains a largely untapped resource. Nevertheless, it constitutes a sizable portion of the people Web waiting to be exploited by any number of organizations, including the government.

The Web has transformed what was a highly personal, private, and time-consuming labor into a far more public, information-driven, and expedient pursuit. It is difficult to determine which side of the equation, the employers or the individuals seeking employment, has the upper hand. But it stands to reason that both sides have profited from the open and free availability of so much job-related information. This part of the people Web may eventually transform not just how we find and fill job openings, but also how we manage our careers. It was not that long ago that the development first of the automobile and then of our highway system altered forever a long-standing interdependence between where we worked and where we lived. The Web and its job-related information and employment resources may end up having an even greater impact. What that impact will be remains to be seen.

In Search of Love: Web Dating

Members of another area of the people Web are sharing information about themselves and conducting searches with a very different objective in mind. Instead of a job, they are seeking that certain someone, or perhaps just a date or even a new friend; or they are in search of an encounter of a more intimate nature. Instead of a resume, these people are posting personal biographies on the Web, complete with some highly specific details about their physical characteristics, interests, and lifestyle. These are the members of the people Web who make up the new community of online dating.

Online dating has become one of the fastest-growing areas on the Web, because demand is high and the business model of the companies providing this service is profitable. Competition among these services is fierce, and yet it is not cheap to become a member at one of these sites. A typical monthly charge is \$20 to \$25. Nevertheless, millions of people across the globe have joined online dating services and more are joining every day. These individuals range in age from teenagers to men and women in their 80s and 90s, and their desires and expectations are as diverse as their age range is wide.

The practice of using a dating or match-making service is nothing new. Its online implementation, on the other hand, has transformed the experience, expanding an individual's choices and opportunities while introducing some new risks. These risks are a consequence of the vast quantity of highly personal information that online dating has introduced onto the Web. This personal and private information constitutes a growing part of the impersonal and public people Web; it contains the names, faces, detailed physical attributes, individual likes and dislikes, and often quite intimate desires of many thousands, if not millions, of people distributed across the globe.

No matter who you are, where you live, or the type of relationship you are after, there is a service out there designed to meet your particular needs. That is largely because these sites have already demonstrated a history of being profitable, which is not common for many Web businesses, and the forecast for the foreseeable future is bright. A continuous and growing revenue stream from ever-rising membership is one reason for their success. Another is Web page advertising and promotional partnerships with any number of associated services and product manufacturers. Romantic movie tie-ins are one simple example; singles' cruises are another.

Most dating sites will allow you to join for free. But this option will limit you to a predominantly passive role, which is not all that helpful if you are serious about reaching out across the Internet to connect with someone new. But attracting new members is essential for the success of these sites, especially given how many of these dating services are competing for people to add to their databases, and free memberships go a long way toward increasing the size of these databases. A free membership will allow your personals advertisement to be viewed by others, but you will not be able to start up any sort of communication with another member or, typically, even answer another member's email or chat request. Until that initial contact is made, you and your prospective friend, date, or soul mate are simply aliases with no tangible means of contacting each other outside of the service.

There are some striking similarities between searching for a job and searching for a date on the Web. Both employment and dating services provide search engines with extensive drop-down selections to help with refining the parameters for a search. Common search criteria, for instance, from which you can select on a dating service include geographic area, shared traits or interests, an age range, certain physical characteristics like height or hair color, and education. Both types of services allow you to browse through their databases to find a match. Both also allow you to choose whether you want to be passive and wait for someone to respond to your posted information, or you want to take the first step and make contact yourself. These search mechanisms clearly demonstrate, whether used for pursuing employment or companionship, the power and versatility of collecting and categorizing so much highly specific information. What (if anything) does it signify, however, that we can use the Web to search for a person as easily, quickly, and effectively as we can use it to search for a job or a book?

A few of the Web's dating services go one step further in their efforts to help you find your ideal match. They use (sometimes patented) algorithms to compare your search criteria and the information you have entered about yourself against their database to seek out individuals who best share your interests, meet your criteria, and whose search criteria is also met by your traits and characteristics. The process is straightforward enough, from a computerized, information-matching perspective. Computers excel at storing, evaluating, and matching information that has been identified and categorized (e.g., sex, height, hair color, body type, hobbies, location); finding a prospective mate, just like finding a product or a job, is simply a matter of comparing selections in like categories and identifying those that match. But there are a lot of things about who we are and the type of relationship we may want that do not easily fit into a category that can be represented in a database or match a quality that can be selected for performing an automated search. To a lesser extent, this applies to job hunting, too. The Web, and by extension the Internet, can only do so much.

So, why do so many people subscribe to online dating services on the Web? The simplest answer is: there are more singles today, and their numbers are increasing. Most people also have less free time. Work weeks have grown longer, as has the time it takes to commute back and forth to work. Meanwhile, computers and Internet access have become commonplace at work and at home; and their use for communicating and socializing is greatest with the younger segment of the population. Accordingly, using the Web to search for someone with similar interests is a lot more convenient and fits better into more lifestyles than relying on random encounters at a party, a group outing, or a singles' bar. Another factor is that the changing job market means that many people are switching jobs and job locations more frequently, which adds to the difficulty of establishing relationships. Add in the fact that workplace dating has been steadily declining, due in large part to the growing attention paid to sexual harassment issues, and online dating starts to look more and more like the right solution at the right time.

Whether it is the convenience, the confidentiality, or the greater effectiveness offered by Web dating, there is no denying that the use of online dating will increase over time. Suitable safeguards exist to protect an individual's privacy, and with a service's blind email system or chat environment you can withhold your identity until you feel comfortable sharing it. Sites that provide dating services also offer advice and guidelines for conducting yourself on the Web when going to start up a relationship online, and suggest how best to pursue such a relationship. Given the newness of the technology, the costs involved, and the associated issues behind privacy and security in willingly making known and available so much personal information, it is worthwhile educating yourself on the process and potential pitfalls before diving in head first. The greatest potential danger rests with people who misrepresent themselves. This is clearly much easier to do with online dating, at least up to a point; but it is nothing new to the dating experience, nor is it something that the Web is likely to resolve.

In Search of Family: Web Genealogy

As you can now better appreciate, there is no shortage of 'people' data on the Web. Between self-published home pages, sites devoted to people in the public eye, online resumes, and dating personals, there is a wealth of information that depicts who we are, the work we do, what we like and do not like, where we went to school, and so on. If you could locate all this data, collect it, categorize it, and analyze it, you would probably be able to form a fairly accurate picture of today's Web denizens. While this type of information analysis has yet to happen in any large-scale way, there is nevertheless a far greater amount of data about us and our families collected and available on the Web than has ever before been amassed; and, because of the Web, this information is easier than ever to access and explore.

One positive and popular use for this collected data can be found in the pursuit of genealogy on the Web. Census data, along with immigration records, constitute a considerable percentage of the source information used in these explorations of family ancestry and history. Herman Hollerith and his tabulating machines of the late 19th and early 20th centuries first transformed the basic census data into usable and explorable information about the growing and changing population of the U.S. His machines did the same for many other countries, too. He accomplished this by storing individual and family data on cards and by designing programmable machines to check the cards to determine whether or not certain conditions were met. His technology provided governments with access to information about their citizens and the property of each citizen that went beyond simple counts of males and females, children, farm animals, and the like. Through this technology and the advances that followed, the census takers were able to accumulate data about more people, continually expand the types of information they collected, and use this data to better understand how the population was changing.

One hundred plus years after Hollerith's first tabulating machines, the World Wide Web was born. It established an environment ideally suited to collecting and presenting all the recorded census data, and many other types of public records; and it made it possible for anyone to examine this information from the warmth and quiet of a home office, living room, or public library. What could be better suited to the global information space of the Web than decades upon decades of government recorded data with names and dates, addresses, family relationships, and lists of possessions. All that was needed was to take the raw data, transfer it into a digital representation for computer storage, and then insert it into a database or some comparable storage device in order for the data to be easily accessed, searched, collated, and displayed.

Much of the difficult and labor-intensive work of transforming this raw data into something accessible from the Web has already been done for us. This work, however, will continue for many years to come as more and more paper documents get converted into digital records. A simple search for census records or genealogy will return a large listing of service-oriented Web businesses ready to trade information access for a membership or usage fee. Many of these sites were developed in response to the widely growing interest of individuals in researching their family ancestry. The types of information databases available vary from site to site, but typical sources of data include: census records, immigration and emigration data, newspaper files, military records, birth and marriage records, and draft registration cards.

Many people begin exploring and documenting their family history by using the resources at one of the Web sites devoted to genealogy to start recording the family information they already know. Alternatively, many commercial and free products that can be used for recording a family history are available for downloading onto a personal computer. Genealogical records are fairly standardized in their composition. They typically include such basic information as a person's name, date and place of birth, date and place of marriage, date and place of death, and the names of a spouse and children. Individual records are then linked through their association, parent to child, brother to sister, and so on.

Once the records are created and the associations are formed, any number of family trees can be drawn based on the selected point of origin (e.g., your father, your mother, or your mother's father).

The Web has both facilitated your ability to research your family history and provided you the tools with which to document and share this information. Through easy-to-use forms you can build your own database of records. You can then start searching for more information and more family connections through any number of powerful search engines and databases. Some services will even conduct additional searches for you, sending you the results in email as new information is discovered. Finally, you can make your genealogical information easily available to other family members by publishing this information yourself on the Web; and if other family members do the same, you will effectively create a personal family web on the encompassing people Web that will grow larger and richer over time.

Consider for a moment what has happened with Ellis Island. Roughly forty percent of Americans have one or more ancestors who arrived through Ellis Island, which served as an entrance point to the U.S. for twenty-two million people from 1892 through 1924. In 2001, the records from Ellis Island, which started out as a giant handwritten archive and were later put onto microfilm, became available over the Internet, thanks to the efforts of some 12,000 church members who worked 5.6 million hours to transcribe the information. You can visit the site, www.ellisisland.org, check passenger records for one of your relatives by name, date of arrival, departure point, and ship, examine the original passenger manifests, and find out information on the ship that delivered them. You can even use the site to create your own family scrapbook, complete with stories, photographs, and audio recordings. The immense popularity of this Web site devoted to the rich information resources produced from the records from Ellis Island stands in sharp contrast to the common view that the Web has become largely a place to buy and sell products and services.

Few things illustrate the power and usefulness of the Web as much as its application for researching and sharing genealogical information. You can reach out across the globe and back through time in search of your family's past. You can then proudly display your family history for any and all to view. This part of the people

Web exemplifies how the Web connects people through its interconnection of information.

The Quest for Self Expression: Blogs and Blogging

Blogs are the Web equivalent of frequent, even daily, diary or journal entries. Blogging is the act of self-publishing these entries on the Web, creating a type of personal, chronological publication of one's thoughts and feelings on any subject imaginable. The terms, blog and blogging, seem to have originated as a contraction of web log. In addition to describing the logging of one's thoughts about the Web or on the Web, the terms are now also used in conjunction with the products and services designed to assist in the creation and publication of these journal entries.

Blogs represent yet another way that people are choosing to take themselves onto the Web, adding yet another growing and unique dimension to the people Web. Blogs are a Web-specific and Web-engendered form of social commentary and social interaction through which individuals can both discover and deliver their personal voice. Like the Web itself, blogging is something entirely new and empowering, and it is responsible for a significant change in the type and diversity of first-person information that can be readily and freely accessed by the public.

Prior to the Web, only a very small number of people, such as professional newspaper columnists, were capable of publishing material that resembles the first-person accounts found in countless blogs on the Web; moreover, the topics that were written about and the opinions expressed in these publications were largely controlled by the media giants that published them. Blogs signify a nascent, but important, shift in publishing control from the media giants to individuals. For the first time in history, individuals can document the trials and tribulations of their daily life, explain their philosophy, describe the events taking place in their local community, and write about how they feel about those events, and, through a single mouseclick, publish all of this material on the Web. If they have produced something worth reading, something of interest to others, their writing may reach hundreds, thousands, or millions of other people.

Some blogs take the form of instant messages posted to the Web. Others are more diary-like in style. There are even collaborative blogging efforts, providing yet another way for people to share ideas and work together across the Internet. A few individuals have become well known bloggers with large followings, due either, it seems, to the event-filled nature of their lives, their writing style, their particular perspective on life, the subject matter they have chosen to comment on, or any number of other factors. You will find blogs spread out across the Web. Some are collected onto blogging sites; others are on personal Web sites; and some can now be found on commercial sites, where they exist as a new form of editorial, or running commentary, and provide a personal perspective related to the site's service, merchandise, or information.

Ironically, blogging made it to the attention of the media when the media was not providing coverage of news-worthy events that bloggers were actively expressing their views about. One incident, in May 2002, involved activists with pro-Palestinian views attacking a group of Hillel students at San Francisco State University. The national press provided no coverage, and the local press barely mentioned the attack. But after a few days of growing blogger entries related to the event, newspapers articles about the event finally appeared in *The New York Times*, *The Lost Angeles Times*, and *The Washington Post*. Stories like this are becoming more and more common, as the commercial news media look to blogging as a new source of breaking news and emerging issues. Meanwhile, news organizations must also contend with the information published by bloggers, especially when that information contradicts what is being presented by the news organizations or when it accuses them of some type of bias in their coverage of events.

Blogs are inherently personal in nature. The vast majority of blogs represent the best and simplest form of free expression. They do not necessarily have to amuse or interest anyone other than the person writing them. The simple fact that anyone can download free blogging software and easily write and publish his or her own blog exemplifies that blogging, like the Web itself, is first and foremost about the free and open sharing of information. But as blogging catches on, you can expect to see it become a more common feature on commercial sites, too, as corporations hire bloggers to apply a personal touch to selling the company's products or services. For instance, a site that provides television listings as part of its service might accompany those listings with one or more blogs that describes the bloggers' viewing habits and recommendations.

Blogging is another area of the Web with largely untapped potential. Its power and significance, however, derive from its grassroots approach to publishing personal information in a way that anyone can access. Blogs provide the people Web with its most compelling and unique perspective, on the Web itself and on that big world outside the Web.

The Shadow Web

The Shadow Web

The shadow Web is a part of the Web we do not see; but it sees and watches us as we browse the Web, make purchases, and read our mail. The information that constitutes the shadow Web is our information, supplied willingly and innocently by us, derived from our actions, and taken from the computers and applications we use as we navigate the Web. Few people are aware of its existence, but its size, impact, and value expands each and every day. The main reason for its existence and for its continued growth is money. There is a lot of money to be made in knowing about us and about our behavior and movements on the Web.

The shadow Web captures and tracks our movements as we browse and click our way across the Web. It knows which browser we use, which operating system is on our computer, and roughly, if not exactly, where we and our computer are located. It knows which products we buy and the kind of window shopping we do. It knows about the types of entertainment, news, and sports we routinely read about. It may even know such things as our age, height, weight, medical condition, and marital status. The covert collection of this information is one half of the story behind the shadow Web; and it raises the issue of our right to privacy while browsing the Web, or, more exactly, what is currently the right of Web businesses to deny us that right. The other half of the story involves how this information is being used, for what purposes, and by whom.

The shadow Web is a product of exploiting the Web's basic technology as an information management system to collect, combine, and analyze information for the benefit of Web site owners, merchants, and other commercial enterprises. Commerce is the driving force behind the shadow Web and the technological innovations — some quite sophisticated — that are used for collecting so much information about our behavior on the Web. One of the fundamental issues resulting from the creation of any new technology, however, is how that technology gets employed and how it inevitably gets exploited. The technology of the Internet and that of the World Wide Web are unfortunately no exception to this. But exploitation is a highly subjective term, perhaps even more so when applied to technology. Exploiting a technology, as opposed to employing it, may simply involve using it for a purpose unrelated to what the technology was specifically designed to accomplish or what generally its designers originally conceived of with respect to how it might be used. There is, therefore, nothing necessarily wrong in creatively adapting a technology to perform a function or provide a service that is outside the scope of what was anticipated or engineered for that technology. The introduction of email on the early Internet is an example of just such unexpected and benign exploitation. Unlike email, however, the exploitation of the Web's technology to create the shadow Web was motivated purely by profit and we unwittingly pay the price through the loss of our privacy and the relinquishing of control over our personal information.

Cookies are a simple example of how a small and basic capability of the Web has been exploited for use in the shadow Web. The original purpose of cookies was innocuous enough. They were created to hold small pieces of data on our computers so that commercial Web sites could later read and use that information when we next visited the site. Their earliest use was with shopping cart applications. As you add items to a site's shopping cart, information about each item is stored in one or more cookies on your computer. If you leave the site without purchasing the items and return at a later date, the site will read the cookie information it stored on your computer during your prior visit and recreate your shopping cart. Another common use of cookies is to store your login and password for a particular Web site, enabling you to gain access to your account without entering this information each time you visit. When you create an account or login you may see a checkbox on the page alongside a question asking you if the site should remember your login and password; if you indicate yes, the site will record this information in cookies on your computer.

The purpose behind creating cookies, as exemplified by the uses just described, was to enhance and simplify our use of the Web. But because cookies can store virtually any type of information (provided it is relatively short) and because the process of storing and later reading this information was made purposefully transparent (so as not to interfere with our interaction with the Web), cookies are now routinely used by all sorts of sites for all sorts of purposes, many of which are not for our benefit. As is explained in detail below, this includes using cookies to track our movements on the Web.

A more extreme example of the shadow Web's exploitation of a basic Web technology component involves the creation of something called Web bugs or beacons. Web bugs are, in effect, listening devices secretly implanted in Web pages and in email messages. They are cleverly disguised as simple HTML code, using the markup created to identify the location of an image file, like a photo. They do not, however, identify an image or cause any information to be displayed to us. We do not know they are there, but when we load a page or read an email message, they are activated and collect information about us that becomes part of the shadow Web.

The shadow Web first came into existence when commercial Web sites started to appear on the Web. These sites introduced the first advertisements, called banners, on the Web, which, in addition to displaying information about a product, service, or company, quickly became a principal mechanism for capturing information about us. Banners, unlike Web bugs, are at least something discernible; we know they are there. But, very like Web bugs, the operations carried out by a banner when we click on one typically include collecting and recording information about us in the process of directing us to the advertiser's Web site; these operations occur without our knowledge or consent. Web banners remain a principal part of the shadow Web.

Increasing use of Web banners brought about the creation of a new type of Web business venture called affiliate management organizations. These organizations specialize in managing marketing efforts across the Web by providing a service that enables Web site owners to form relationships with companies that want to advertise their products and services on the Web. The services provided by these organizations, however, are not confined to establishing relationships. A central part of their business involves information tracking and management. They provide the underlying technology, for example, that records when banners are shown and that tracks such information as who clicked on a banner and whether or not that click resulted in the purchase of a product. These organizations push the limits of the type and amount of information that can be collected about us as we navigate the Web. They have in their possession a vast amount of personal information that has been acquired through the shadow Web on a daily basis, over several years, from millions of people across the globe. If you are not in the business of Web advertising, it is unlikely you know the names of any of these organizations. But it is very likely they know your name, as well as a great deal of other information about you.

The information that makes up the shadow Web is derived from many sources; these sources include Web bugs and banners, affiliate management organizations, and the log files produced by Web servers. The following sections describe each of these sources in detail. A final section describes the latest type of business venture to be created out of the vast amount of information that has accumulated on the shadow Web. It is called data mining and its goal is to use our personal information to discover patterns and evaluate trends in our browsing and buying habits on the Web. This chapter will explain how, where, and why our personal information is being collected, recorded, tracked, and used. Once you understand what the shadow Web consists of and how it works, you may not like its implications with respect to the privacy of your information or the expectation of anonymity that comes with using the Web.

Web Banners: Advertisements that Track Our Movements

Advertising was first introduced on the Web in the form of banners, those rectangular images or animations that appear on the vast majority of commercial Web pages. Banners differ significantly from earlier forms of advertisements. Their appearance and purpose may be familiar to us, especially since they often copy or mimic the same advertising used in the print media or on television. But their ability to collect information when they are displayed, and again when they are clicked on, makes them different. This ability is directly responsible for their immense popularity with advertisers because it enables each banner's effectiveness to be measured quickly, inexpensively, and, best of all, accurately. Not only do banners provide product or service information, like traditional advertisements; they also function as a direct gateway, leading us straight (or sometimes not so straight, as explained below) to the advertiser's Web site, which is just a mouseclick away.

But every time a banner is shown to you, it is not only recording information about when and where it was displayed, it is also recording information about you. The type of information that is recorded varies from site to site, but it generally includes the IP address of your computer, the browser you are using, and the computer's operating system. When you click on a banner, a lot more of your personal information is recorded. That's because the advertiser, or the advertiser's agent (e.g., an affiliate management organization), needs to track information related to your click in order to compensate the Web site owner. The site owner will be paid some amount simply for directing you to the advertiser's Web site. But that payment will typically be significantly higher when that click leads to your making a purchase or performing some other activity, like taking part in a survey or entering a sweepstakes, on the advertiser's site.

Consider the following simple, and representative, scenario. You click on a banner to learn more about the product it advertises: a new cell phone, in this instance. You decide, however, not to buy the product. The following day, or perhaps even a month or more later, you return directly to the Web site where you saw the cell phone for sale and you make the purchase. There has been no further interaction between you and the Web site where you first saw and clicked on the banner advertisement for the phone. Nevertheless, there is a strong likelihood that the owner of the Web site where you saw the banner will be compensated for your purchase, even if days, weeks, or months have elapsed between when you saw the advertisement and when you purchased the product. This is due entirely to the information collected and stored related to the showing of that banner advertisement. There is a lasting trail of information that connects your initial visit to the Web site containing the advertisement, your click on that banner, and the advertiser's Web site. This type of information tracking, storage, and use represents a fundamental and integral part of the shadow Web.

What makes this information tracking possible is neither complicated nor innovative. It is simple Web mechanics, some specialized programming, and databases to store the information. What is critical, however, is that all this information gets stored and tracked in the shadows, so to speak (i.e., behind the scenes), and that the process of collecting the information happens very quickly. Speed is especially important when third-party organizations, like affiliate management companies, are involved in tracking this information. That's because, when you click on certain banners, you may actually visit one of these third-party sites before you are redirected to the advertiser's site. But because this happens so quickly, you remain unaware of visiting any site other than the advertiser's and you also remain unaware of any information about your click being recorded. It is, however, through this process that many such organizations secretly track our movements, interests, and purchases on the Web; and this type of information collection is growing.

Advertisements first appeared on the Web in October, 1994, on the Web site for the online magazine HotWired. HotWired named these advertisements banners and pioneered their general look and page placement. The purpose of the banners on HotWired and the technology used in creating them was simple, especially by today's standards: gain revenue for the site by displaying banners for each of the magazine's advertisers and use the banners as hyperlinks to direct readers to the advertiser's site. That was it, pure and simple; no information about us was being collected and no third-party sites were involved. Today, most people believe that this is all banners are used for, despite the presence of privacy policies on most Web sites that state in no uncertain terms how and why our personal information is being collected and used. Of course, when the first banners were created by HotWired, the Web was still in its infancy and many of its clients needed Web sites built in order to capture the attention of this new audience. No one was thinking yet about any hidden relationship between banners and browsing the Web, but the seeds had been planted.

It did not take long for banners to spread across the Web. Their presence contributed to the exponential growth of the Web by providing the means for many sites to fund — at least in part — their creation and continued operating costs. Over time, common ways evolved to charge for the display of banners and measure their effectiveness. The process of displaying banners came to be referred to as generating impressions; and costs for generating impressions were calculated at some dollar amount per thousand shown, known commonly as cost per mille (CPM). Another common and important measurement was called the click-through rate. This figure represented the number of people who clicked on a banner to visit the advertised site for every 100 banner impressions. So if, on average, two people clicked on a banner for every hundred impressions, that banner was said to have a 2% click-through rate.

All of these elements combined to form the early and lasting foundation for marketing practices on the Web. Banners provided a way to direct individual traffic to specific merchant sites. They also supported the more traditional marketing goals, which were regularly pursued through radio, television, and print advertising, of promoting products and services and branding product and company names. The use of banners provided a continuous, and often substantial, revenue stream for informational Web sites, such as Web portals. This, in turn, established a growing interdependency between two types of Web enterprises: the merchants, or purveyors of goods and services, and the affiliates, or Web site owners. The only thing missing from this picture was the means to use all of the ever-growing and disparate personal information generated by Web browsing and apply it to the practices of product marketing. The solution to this endeavor was not long in coming, as explained later in this chapter.

Banners that Play and Record

As we have seen, people trying to capitalize on the new technology introduced by the Internet and the Web typically fell into one of two camps. There were those who failed to recognize what the technology offered and saw only its effect, its surface. For them, the Web in particular was simply another medium through which to advertise and sell, another means to increase market share and extend profitability using traditional, tried and true methods. The more technically savvy and astute individuals, however, recognized that the technology could achieve that end, and far more. For them, the Web offered the means to know their customers as individuals and to reach out to them accordingly; building better, and smarter, banners was the place to start.

The desire to better understand the customer drove banners to evolve from a simple combination of advertisement and doorway into a primary tool of the shadow Web used in the collection and tracking of information about our movements on the Web. The specific, technical changes to the banners themselves are described later in this chapter. For now, all you need to understand is that the code created for displaying a banner on a Web page was modified to enhance its capacity to capture more and more specific information. Tracking codes embedded in each banner identified the Web site and particular Web page on which the banner was displayed, how you were directed to that page (i.e., which page you were on before), and sometimes even information about you (e.g., your login on the site, age, sex). Moreover, the way in which all of this information was recorded was also modified to enhance how it could be analyzed, used, and reused. All of this tracked data added value to the one-time display of a single banner. But that data became even more meaningful when it was combined with a lot of other banner-generated data and was viewed in an aggregate form. While the code used for displaying the banners and embedded within them became more and more complex, the banners themselves appeared unchanged.

The development of the technology surrounding banners, which was quickly integrated into associated online advertising techniques like popup windows, electronic coupons, and sweepstakes tickets, resulted in the creation of a growth industry that would transform Web advertising and marketing. What had begun as a simple, static, and benign broadcast marketing model, indiscriminately pushing advertising information down to us, quickly developed into a far more dynamic model that collected as much or more information about us as it directed at us. The information highway of the Internet was designed from the start to be a two-way communication system, and the Web, as the Internet's information space, was engineered with this in mind. The new banner technology took full advantage of this engineering.

The data generated through these banners, therefore, told two important stories to the Web marketers. One was about us as individuals: what we liked and didn't like, what we responded to and what we ignored. The other was about us en masse, as part of one or more groups, and as part of a single, general audience. Consider how many thousands of times individual banners are being displayed throughout the Web, twenty-four hours a day, seven days a week. The amount of data generated by these banners is enormous; it is all about us and our use of the Web; and it is accumulating at an exponential rate. One of the simplest and earliest benefits to marketers of this accumulating information was how quickly and effectively they could compare one marketing approach to another; as a result, they could modify a particular advertising campaign while it was still running by replacing less effective banners with those that were achieving a higher click-through rate. Marketers also soon discovered that they could test marketing theories by developing a wide assortment of banners, accumulating information about their effectiveness, and analyzing the results. Early testing, for example, revealed that adding the word 'free' somewhere in a banner dramatically increased click-through rates; and many companies adapted their banners accordingly to reap the benefits.

The ability to collect information about our browsing habits and the types of merchandise we purchased and to gauge the effectiveness of individual banners to generate click-throughs promised to provide advertisers, marketing firms, and merchants with what amounted to a far more expedient and cost-effective way to target products and services towards audiences already predisposed to their use. A plain banner by itself was able to capture only so much information. But even plain banner impression and click-through data, when collected over time and from different sites, can together tell a compelling and highly valuable story. Meanwhile, better, more advanced banners, like those described in the next section, were already being developed to capture not only more information, but more specific and personal types of information. But the only thing most of us were aware of was that banners were becoming more and more commonplace, and that advertisers were finding new ways to include more information in each banner and to present that information more forcibly. How many people realized what was occurring behind the scenes?

Rich Media Banners

In the late 1990s, banners evolved from static displays of graphics and text to more complex and dynamic Web page elements that became known as rich media advertisements. Not only were these banners capable of collecting and tracking more information about us, they were the first banners to dramatically advance the look, functionality, and impact of advertisements on a Web page. Rich media banners attracted attention through animations as well as through audio and video clips. More importantly, they were capable of including an interactive component that was designed to induce us to enter information directly into the banner. Common techniques used to create interactive banners included Java applets that started up a game and Web forms that prompted you to enter your zip code or select from a product listing. Some rich media banners even allowed you to complete a transaction through the banner itself by, for instance, filling out a registration form or entering a contest, effectively turning the advertisement into a small, independent Web page. Other rich media banners allowed you to click or mouse-over the banner in order to expand its contents. This feature had two significant effects. One, it enabled the advertiser to convey considerably more information than it was possible to fit in the few square inches allotted for most banners. Two, it allowed us to learn more information about a particular product or service without changing our location (i.e., leaving the current Web site), something that testing revealed was preferred by many people and, at the same time, was an attractive feature to Web site owners who displayed these banners.

The enhancements that were part of rich media banners meant that our clickstream — which is how marketers designate our navigation of the Web — would for the first time not necessarily be interrupted by our interaction with a banner. We stayed longer on each Web site we visited, which helped in the accrual of more information on each site and led to more meaningful results from an analysis of that information by Web site owners and marketers. The enhancements also meant that far more specific types of information could be collected from us, some of which we would be prompted to enter and we would willingly provide. All of this quickly accumulating information — from rich media banners and others — had to be stored somewhere. Most of it was stored in Web site log files, as is described in the next section.

Web Logs: Files that Record Our Movements

Just as phone companies keep detailed records of every call we make, Web servers record all of our transactions on the Web sites we visit. For instance, when we load a typical Web page, more than likely that page is composed of several separate elements or files: an HTML file, a few image files containing icons, buttons, or photographs, one or more files that make up the Web banner, and so on. The Web server must locate, retrieve, and transfer all the separate elements that compose the page, and each of these separate transactions is recorded by a Web server in one of several log files. So every time you load a Web page, at least one Web server, and often more than one, adds a series of lines to its log files with information about you, the date and time, and the requested information. The raw data stored in these log files is used in part to facilitate some of the tracking and behavioral analysis conducted for the banner advertisements described above. But it is invaluable in other areas, too.

Logs files have been a standard part of Web server software since the earliest days of the Web. Their initial purpose was to produce an audit trail for a Web site, and this remains their primary purpose today. In essence, these logs files contain a sequential record of individual Web server transactions — one record or line per transaction — that is created by the Web server as it answers requests for files and resources from connecting clients. When we examined the details of an HTTP conversation in an earlier chapter, we saw how the information stored in these log file records is communicated between the client's browser and the Web server. A typical log file record includes:

- The client computer's identification (i.e., hostname or IP address).

- The date and time, known as a timestamp.

- The type of action: typically either a GET (i.e., getting information from the server) or a POST (i.e., posting information to it, as from a form).

- The specific request being made by the client: the full name and location (i.e., URL) of the file or resource that the Web server is being asked to retrieve (e.g., an HTML file, a GIF file, a CGI program).

- The three-digit status code resulting from the transaction and indicating the success or failure of the request (e.g., 200 means OK, 404 means Not Found).

- The size in bytes of the data being transferred.

Because each and every Web page loaded by each and every Web site visitor can easily generate four, or six, or a dozen log file records, Web log files grow rapidly and soon become very large. Moreover, because HTTP is a stateless protocol (i.e., each transaction is a separate and complete event), the log files themselves cannot make any connections between transactions, that is, they cannot connect event A with event B with event C. The independence of each transaction contributes to the size of log files because each record must contain a full accounting of the information, as opposed to omitting repeated information (e.g., the client's identification) that might be the same in the previous or following record. This independence also makes log files unsuitable for humans to analyze without the aid of a computer. But since the composition of the data is so basic and since it is recorded in a well documented and uniform manner, log files are perfectly suited to be read, interpreted, and analyzed by computer programs. Accordingly, many such programs have been written to analyze the content of Web server log files.

The data recorded in a Web server's log files is used for a wide variety of purposes. The earliest programs were created to evaluate the data in order to analyze how a Web site was performing. Later programs focused more on the experiences of individual users in order to discern how a site was being navigated. Today one of the most common purposes is to enable Web site operators to understand how their site is being used. The log files record how many times each page on the site was loaded (i.e., the number of hits) in any given period of time, how much data was transferred, what the peak hours or days of usage were, how many unique visitors came to the site and how many returned again. This data can be used to produce pie charts and bar charts representing Web site usage by hour or day or month, by types of browsers being used, or by types of files being viewed. It can also be used to examine averages and reveal how many pages were typically viewed during one visit or how long visitors typically remained on the site. Data from the log files might indicate, for instance, that most people were spending very little time on the site, and that for some reason they were never venturing beyond the home page to view specific information about the products or services being sold. Or the data might reveal that visitors were reviewing the products, but right after they brought up the pricing and/or licensing page, they left and never returned. The review and analysis of such fundamental information is critical to the success of any Web site. Log files make this work possible.

Another use for log files is in the performance of Web site maintenance and administration. Because log file records capture information about every file and resource requested by a connecting client, they can be used to identify which files, if any, are taking too long a time to load and might therefore be having a detrimental impact on the overall performance of the site. The records can also be used to identify problems on the site, such as a file not being found because it has been deleted or because the URL specifying its location is incorrect, programs not executing because of file permission issues, or files being requested that do not exist or should not be available because people are trying to break into the site or disrupt service. Log files hold all the raw data about a Web site's interactions and, when subjected to even the most rudimentary analysis, they enable site administrators, developers, managers, and marketers to understand all the events occurring on any Web site.

More advanced analytical tools are able to take this same data, either on its own or combined with other data, such as clickstream information, to develop profiles regarding our navigation through a Web site. These profiles can be created on an individual basis, revealing the exact navigation of a site as one person clicked from one link to the next. Generalized profiles can also be created that are developed from the aggregate data of multiple users, revealing trends in the navigation of a site.

Consider the case of a single visitor. The log entries make it possible to reconstruct the visitor's movements, starting with where the visitor came from before he or she loaded that first page, which pages the visitor viewed while on the site, roughly how long the visitor stayed on each page, and in which order the visitor viewed them. This study of a single visitor may not mean all that much on its own. But when a higher and broader view is taken and thousands of individuals are studied over a period of days, weeks, or months, patterns start to emerge and conclusions about how the site is being used, what may be working and what may be failing, can be drawn. To many people, studying the data of log files to discern exactly how a site is being navigated is considered necessary to ensuring the success of the site.

Log file records are also analyzed to provide insight into the composition of a Web site's audience. Tools designed for this purpose are used to develop profiles that describe and categorize the types of people visiting a site. When these profiles are collected together for analysis, they can be used to categorize the audience for a site according to such criteria as age, gender, location, and interests. This information is critical to marketing a site to potential advertisers and sponsors. When these profiles are examined individually, they can be used to identify individual visitors when they return, which makes it possible to customize the site information for a particular visitor as he or she navigates the site. Customization may take the form of sending New York Giants and Jets football scores and stories across an information ticker to a visitor connecting from New York and known to be a sports enthusiast or displaying a banner for an ongoing book sale to a visitor known to buy a lot of books. Log files capture much of the raw data that make possible developing audience profiles and directing customized information to specific visitors.

Web server log files may continuously record our use of the Web, but their records are far from complete. Firewalls, for instance, help to mask the information of desktop computers and their operators behind a single IP address, while proxy servers cache pages, resulting in uncounted page views. Nevertheless, our journeys through the Web, no matter how frequent or infrequent, are being captured and represented in log files scattered across the Internet's Web servers. Consequently, our presence on the Internet as we visit Web sites, gather information, and make purchases is neither anonymous nor fleeting.

As more of these log files are collected and merged, more analysis will be performed and more conclusions will be drawn about the overall patterns of our behavior on the Web. This may not concern you. But what may bring "Big Brother" to mind is the possibility of one organization or government agency examining massive amounts of merged data in order to track and analyze the behavior of specific individuals. This has recently become a hotly debated subject on the Web and it represents a key concern among the Web's growing number of privacy advocates. One particularly unnerving example of the arrival of "Big Brother" is described briefly at the end of this chapter.

Web Bugs: Code that Captures Our Actions

Good programmers are typically clever people. Often they convert simple, innocuous features into something that their creators never anticipated. Such is the case with the invention and large-scale adoption of Web bugs, more innocuously or politely called Web beacons, 1 by 1 pixel GIFs, or clear GIFs. These Web bugs exploit the very simple functionality in HTML that is used to tell browsers where to find the source file for an image by instead using this functionality to store and transmit data about us. Web bugs are often mistakenly categorized alongside cookies, since both are used to transmit data about our actions on the Web without our knowledge. But Web bugs are not connected to cookies, nor do they have much in common with cookies with respect to how they work or what they are used for. Moreover, Web bugs are actually far more devious than cookies in both form and function.

Like Web bugs, cookies are an integral part of the shadow Web. They are employed by Web sites to remember who you are, any preferences you may have specified, purchases you made or were interested in making, and many other small pieces of information. As explained in an earlier chapter, cookies are used to write information directly to your computer so it can be recalled by a Web server at a later date. Unlike Web bugs, the code that was created to implement cookies was designed specifically and exclusively for this purpose of writing and reading small pieces of information to and from your computer. Your browser, therefore, knows when a cookie is being written to your computer because it contains program code to handle this functionality; this, at least, affords you some control. You can, for example, configure your browser to accept all cookies and not bother you about them (the default behavior). Or, you can set your browser to automatically deny all cookies and thereby turn off their use entirely; as a result, many Web site features that rely on cookies (e.g., shopping carts) will also be disabled. You also have the option to set your browser to warn you when a site wants to write out a cookie, allowing you to review each one and individually accept or deny it (a compromise that sounds reasonable, but one that quickly reveals itself to be highly impractical due to the sheer number of cookies being used). With cookies, you at least have some options and some control.

Web bugs, on the other hand, remain entirely hidden from both you and your browser. Moreover, they record and transmit data whether you want them to or not. As far as your browser is concerned, the code (or markup) for a Web bug is indistinguishable from the code used in specifying the location of a graphics file for display on the page; the browser interprets the code, requests the file from the Web server, and waits on the server's response. The server returns data to satisfy the browser's request, but nothing appears on the page. Consequently, Web bugs appear innocuous to your browser and are invisible to you.

Consider the following two samples of code:

```
<img width=24 height=48
  src="http://www.mylobster.com/images/claw.gif">
```

```
<img width=1 height=1
  src="http://www.mylobster.com/HP/
  hp.cgi?tag=6&si=138&id=898&js=no">
```

The first sample causes your browser to retrieve and load the image of a lobster claw contained in the file named claw.gif. The code identifies where to find the source file for the image and defines its width and height in pixels. The second sample is identical in terms of its syntax, but its function is unrelated to displaying an image. First, note the width and height specification; the size of the image is 1 pixel by 1 pixel. That is the smallest possible size for an image (i.e., the size of a single pixel), and renders the image effectively invisible; even if the data returned by the server in response to the file request contained an image (most are empty or contain white space), it would be far too small to be recognized as anything other than a dot. This explains why neither we nor our browsers can identify the presence of Web bugs on a Web page.

The second difference to note between the two code samples relates to the source or target location of what should be a graphics file (i.e., the information following the src= tags). The first sample identifies the location of a graphics file. The second sample, however, identifies the location of a CGI program named hp.cgi (the file name extension, .cgi, identifies the target as a CGI program, just as the file name extension in the target of the first code sample, .gif, identifies its target as a GIF graphics file). Note the series of four separate pieces of information in the form of name/value pairs that immediately follow the CGI program's file name (e.g., tag=6 and si=138) That information — whatever it may mean — is also being transmitted back to the Web site named in the target's URL, www.mylobster.com. The CGI program could be performing any operation; we have no way of knowing what it is doing. It could simply be recording that the particular Web page that included this code was loaded and viewed, effectively performing the function of a counter. Or it could just as easily be recording that *you* loaded the page and it could be sending any number of other types of information back to the Web server. What it is definitely *not* doing is retrieving a graphics file or providing any information to load onto the page for you to view.

Whenever you load a page containing a Web bug, your behavior is being tracked, and the type and amount of information that can be tracked this way is remarkably broad. But the use of Web bugs is not limited to Web pages. It is important to realize that HTML-based email can, and frequently does, contain Web bugs. Their earliest use was in email, and their continued use in email represents a popular and valuable choice for covertly gathering information about our online behavior and preferences. That is because Web bugs can easily, effectively, and transparently report back to the sender of an email not only *if* you viewed the sender's message, but precisely when, on what type of browser, and so on.

Consider a business that is sending out 10,000 emails in order to promote interest in a new product. By including a Web bug in the message that incorporates each recipient's email address or unique customer identification code, the merchant can, without any further effort, collect data on the effectiveness of the email; it will know, for example, which customers actually opened the email and how soon the email was opened after it was sent. If the merchant includes a Javascript program with the email that allows the reader to display additional information about the product or it includes a hyperlink for the reader to click on that directs the reader to the merchant's site, it can also record which of its customers read the email and expressed interest in the product. Collecting this type of information is vitally important to a merchant and to people in the business of promotional emails. For them, Web bugs are an inexpensive and highly effective tool. The problem is that their use of Web bugs is entirely at our expense and without our consent.

What type of information can these Web bugs record and transmit? Since they use HTTP, they have at their disposal all the various pieces of information tracked automatically by the protocol, such as your IP address and possibly your host name, your browser information, the languages and character sets you have loaded, and the date and time. They can also transmit the URL of the page you are loading and any parameters that have been passed along, such as information from filling out a Web form. They can also transmit previously stored cookie values, provided the domain names match (Web sites can only read cookies that were created by computers from their own domain). Finally, they can transmit any other type of information that the Web server has under its control. This might be the URL of the site that referred you to the current page after you clicked on a banner, for instance. Or it might be your local user name or other personal information that is part of your account on the site.

What is done with the information collected by Web bugs? It is used to increment Web page counters that record the number of times a page was loaded and to track Web site usage by recording how individuals navigate from page to page on a particular site or between one site and another. It is used to measure how many times a banner advertisement is shown, as well as the banner's overall effectiveness in directing individuals to the advertiser's site and leading these individuals to make a purchase. It is used to facilitate the logging of information by third parties, such as affiliate management organizations. It is also used to track the effectiveness of email campaigns, as described above. The only limiting factors on the type of information transmitted by Web bugs (or what that information might be used for) are the information made available through the Web site itself and the programmer's imagination.

Web bugs have generated a considerable amount of controversy, much as cookies did soon after they came into widespread use. At the heart of the controversy is the issue of privacy and the existing imbalance between how much information the technology is capable of collecting about us and how little control and say we have in determining who collects this information, when, how, and for what purposes. Commerce sites on the Web proclaim the effectiveness of Web bugs in helping to provide faster and better customized shopping experiences on the Web. The owners of such sites argue that Web bugs not only help promote better targeted browsing and shopping for individuals, but by aggregating the data they produce, site owners can better understand which practices generally work well and which need to be changed or dropped. Some sites that use Web bugs declare in their privacy policy statements that they only use the data collected through this and other methods in an aggregated form, which eliminates its infringement on an individual's right to privacy. Other sites, through acknowledging use of Web bugs in their privacy statement, declare that all personal information they collect is kept strictly confidential. How many privacy policies have you read from beginning to end (and understood)? How many sites do you think give you a choice about whether or not Web bugs will be used to track your information?

Privacy advocates, however, tell a different story. They see the potential for misuse of the personal information collected by Web bugs and they argue that the collection of such information without our explicit consent is, at the very least, questionable, and perhaps unethical. The fact that Web bugs collect, track, and transmit all sorts of information about us, our computers, and our behavior on the Web, not simply without our consent but without our knowledge, is considered by many people to be a serious violation of our right to privacy. Web bugs are just one glaring example of information use or abuse (depending on your perspective) in the larger, heated debate over how much, or little, of our information on the Web we truly can, or should be able to, control. Privacy issues on the Web, and on the Internet in general, are discussed at greater length in *The Technology Revolution*.

Affiliate Management: Organizations that Live Off Our Movements

Many aspects of the shadow Web converge under the business heading of affiliate management. Generally speaking, affiliate management is a Web-centric view of product marketing and sales. More specifically, organizations in the business of affiliate management enable merchants to create and monitor their own personal network of Web site owners, their affiliates, to help them promote their business interests across the Web, regardless of whether the merchant is selling products, services, ideology, or something else.

Consider the marketing of a product through television advertising. A merchant needs to examine the program offerings and audience demographics of any number of television channels to find the most suitable program content and the most appropriate audience composition for the particular marketing campaign it plans to promote. But what if instead of a dozen or a hundred television channels to choose from, there were hundreds of thousands of channels? How would a merchant contact so many potential advertisers? How would it gather and analyze sufficient information to choose the right channels with the right audience composition for the product being marketed? How would it manage and monitor the relationship it creates with each channel? How would it measure the effectiveness of its promotional campaigns on each channel? The services provided by affiliate management organizations were created to meet these needs, with Web sites providing the countless channels of information and banners supplying the principal advertising/data collection mechanism.

Affiliate management organizations provide the means for merchants to establish contractual relationships with Web site owners in order to distribute the merchant's advertising throughout the Web and direct more traffic to the merchant's own Web site. The goal for the merchants, which sell the products or services, is to broaden their exposure across the Web in a highly controlled manner. The goal for the affiliates, which sell the advertising space, is to join as many merchant programs as possible to maximize their ability to generate advertising revenue.

The principal commodity of an affiliate management organization is its network of affiliates. The greater the number and variety of Web site owners that have joined an affiliate management organization (becoming an affiliate is typically free), the more choices a merchant will have in building their own network of affiliates. Merchants choose the individual sites, or types of sites, with which to form a relationship. The criteria they can use to make this decision includes such things as a site's services, information content, and audience demographics. Sites chosen by a merchant are accepted into one or more of their marketing programs and become the merchant's affiliate; these affiliates can then copy the merchant's banners for display on their Web sites. The code that composes the banners is unique to each affiliate. It contains all the hidden information that must be tracked to connect the specific affiliate with the merchant and with the particular marketing program that the banner is part of. When the affiliate shows one of the merchant's banners and, more importantly, when someone clicks on a banner, the affiliate management organization records this information on behalf of both the affiliate and merchant in order for the merchant to compensate the affiliate at some later date according to the terms of their contract.

The types of compensation an affiliate may receive vary from merchant to merchant and may also vary from marketing program to marketing program. Depending on the terms of the agreement between the merchant and an affiliate, the affiliate can get paid for showing banners (i.e., impressions) and for directing an individual to the merchant's site (i.e., click-throughs); the affiliate can also receive a flat fee or a percentage of a sale as compensation when a click-through results in the individual making a purchase on the merchant's Web site. Meanwhile, the affiliate management organization makes money through some combination of fees paid by the merchants, transaction charges, and assorted other types of commissions. They also typically provide software for the merchants that is used in tracking transactions; and they provide the reporting tools necessary for merchants to analyze the effectiveness of their programs and for affiliates to track their commissions.

The relationships in affiliate management programs always start with the merchant. Consider a merchant that manufactures computers. The merchant joins an affiliate management organization (there are a great many to choose from) and creates a program to promote a new model of laptops. The program defines how the merchant will compensate affiliates; and it includes half a dozen banners designed to sell the new laptops. In this example, the merchant will pay a flat fee of $5 for every click-through generated by the affiliate and 1% commission from sales for any click-through that results in a sale. The next step involves accepting affiliates into the merchant's program.

Affiliate members of the affiliate management organization apply to enter the merchant's program. The merchant reviews each application, examines the type of information or service that the affiliate provides, and perhaps even visits the affiliate's Web site, in order to decide whether to accept or reject the affiliate's application. Once accepted, an affiliate copies one or more of the merchant's banners created specifically for the program and installs them on its Web site. It then includes the unique HTML code — which it also copies from the affiliate management organization's Web site — in its Web pages that will display the banner; the code includes the URL of the banner (e.g., the location of a GIF graphics file that contains the advertisement of the new laptops) and the tracking codes that identify the affiliate, the merchant, and the program. Alternatively, the affiliate may only need to copy the HTML code; in this case, the banners remain on the Web site of the affiliate management organization and are served (i.e., transmitted) from there. This is another way that these organizations generate revenue (e.g., by serving banners). This option is typically chosen when it is more expedient (faster and/or cheaper) for the affiliate management organization's Web site to serve the banners. But either way, once the code is in place, the program is active.

So, what does all this mean to you as you browse the Web? Probably not a lot. But affiliate management is really all about tracking information: the display of banners, the click-throughs generated by these banners, and purchases made as a consequence of one of these click-throughs. This information, therefore, is actually all about your behavior on the Web: which banners you are viewing, how you are responding to them, and which purchases you are making. The tracking of all of this information is entirely hidden from your view. Plus, the use of this information may go beyond its original intention of tracking advertising and purchases and be reused or resold by the affiliate management organizations that control most of it for other purposes entirely.

All the players in affiliate management have distinctly different interests and needs. The merchants want to use the system not just to market themselves and their products, but also to more directly measure the relative success or failure of their marketing and to connect more directly with us, their customer base. The affiliates want to generate revenues through their Web sites; accordingly, they want to be a part of the best paying, most effective programs. The affiliate management organizations want more transactions, because more transactions mean higher revenues; and they want more information about those transactions and about us, either to sell back to the merchants or to collect in an aggregate form for data mining purposes or resale to other businesses. Like most other enterprises on the Web, affiliate management is dependent on the collection, management, and distribution of information. But this information is about us, and it is generating a lot of revenue at our expense.

So where is all this information? How is it being transmitted? It all starts with the banner being displayed on the affiliate's Web site. Most banners are simply hyperlinks that define the destination of the link (i.e., the page or resource that gets called when you click on the banner) and the source of the graphics file or program that holds the image you are shown. First, look at the code for a simple banner that is not connected to any affiliate management organization.

```
<a href="http://lobsterusa.org/bluelobsters.html">
  <img src="/images/bluelob.gif"
  width=640 height=60></a>
```

Nothing much to it: the destination is an HTML page, bluelobsters.html, which is the page that will be loaded when someone clicks on the banner. The image that comprises the banner's advertisement, which will be displayed on the page, is contained in the local graphics file, bluelob.gif. Now look at the following code that might be used with an affiliate management organization. It contains the same two basic parts, `href` for the hyperlink destination and `img src` for the graphics file, but that is where the similarity ends.

```
<a href="http://click.affmgmt.com/af-bin/record?
    id=3&program=4&type=89&ssid=8">
  <img src="http://ad.affmgmt.com/af-bin/display?
    id=3&bids=4&type=89&ssid=8"
    width=640 height=60></a>
```

The most important difference is that no HTML page or graphics file is referenced in the code. Here is what actually happens when you load the HTML page containing this code. The source for the banner's advertisement is forwarded by a program (named display) that gets executed on the affiliate management site, ad.affmgmt.com. The overall process is similar to what happens with a Web bug. First, the program reads all the associated information (i.e., ids, bids, type, and ssid) in order to recognize which merchant's program and which of its banners is needed. It records the event, along with information about you and about the affiliate. Finally, it transmits the appropriate banner graphics file back to your computer for display with the rest of the page. As far as your browser is concerned, all that happened was that it received a graphics file to display. From its perspective, and yours, the two code samples both performed exactly the same operation.

Moreover, this code does not take you directly to the merchant's site when you click on the banner, as would happen with the reference to the HTML file in the other code sample. Instead, it calls a program (named record) on the affiliate management site which records information about the event, you, and the affiliate. The final action that program performs is redirecting you to the merchant's site. The entire operation happens so quickly you never realize that you are clicking through this third-party organization. Again, from the perspective of your browser, nothing different or additional transpired; both code samples are effectively equivalent.

Many different methods are used by affiliate management organizations to achieve the same result. They must track a lot of disparate information about the banners we are shown and which ones we click on. They must also retrieve additional point-of-sale information from the merchant when a sale occurs, in order to connect all the parts of the process: from banner, to click, to purchase, to compensation back to the affiliate. Some of this collected information is made available to the merchants; and through it they learn about the varying effectiveness of their programs, which banners generate more click-throughs, which geographic regions or demographics produce the best results, which types of Web sites generate the most interest, and so on. To a lesser extent, the affiliates can use the information made available to them in order to determine which banners work better or, more generally, which programs are generating more revenue for them.

Finally, the affiliate management organization itself may have its own uses for all this collected information, aside from what they share with their merchants and affiliates. They retain far more information about the advertising efforts of the merchants, the transactions initiated by this advertising, and our associated behavior on the Web than the affiliates and merchants combined. The greater the number of merchants and affiliates in their network, the greater the quantity and diversity of this information. This information, in and of itself, has value. But first you need to find a way to extract that value. Data mining has become the way to do just this.

Data Mining: Operations that Turn Our Data into Gold

Once you understand that there is a considerable amount of information about you being tracked, stored, and examined in the shadows of all those flashy, and not so flashy, Web sites, you may realize that the shadow Web is a more significant and more personal issue than you first imagined. Nothing in the Web's design was engineered to track our movements. Tim Berners-Lee was not interested in recording and later examining how people browsed the Web. He just happened to innocently facilitate the process, providing any number of organizations, corporations, and governments the capability of using Web-generated records to determine the interests, purchasing habits, and informational pursuits of individuals and groups.

It all started innocently enough with the creation of banner advertisements. It did not take long, however, for simple advertisements, beckoning us to visit a merchant's Web site, to become part of an effort to record information about our behavior on the Web. Banners combine the information stored on our computers in cookies with the information stored on one or more Web servers with yet more information that the banners themselves prompt us to enter. This combination of information is more than the sum of its parts and, accordingly, it is responsible for an increasing number of efforts directed at learning about the lives we lead on and off the Internet. Factor in the vast amount of raw data contained in Web server log files, the information collected by Web bugs, and the additional information tracked and stored by affiliate management organizations, and the result is an incredibly rich resource of personal and private information just waiting to be exploited.

Where all this seemingly innocuous information is brought together, an operation called data mining will be found. Data mining is pretty much what it sounds like. It constitutes a secondary and future use of information collected to fulfill other, more immediate and specific purposes (e.g., compensation to affiliates for banner impressions and click-throughs). Data is a valuable resource, a natural byproduct of our use of the Web, just waiting for the right tools, organization, and purpose to turn it into a commodity for sale and resale. There exists a burgeoning data mining industry that includes specialists with Ph.D.s and very expensive applications and equipment. Their sole purpose is to take all this data generated on and by the Web, shape it, discover patterns in it, and evaluate trends. The information they extract may be used to send you an advertisement for a toaster just when you are in the market for a new toaster or to invite you to visit a car dealer's Web site before your existing car decides it's been of service to you long enough. But there are also endless other, less commercially obvious uses for this information.

We have little to no control over the information being collected about us and from us or how it is being used. More importantly, the vast majority of people navigating the Web are totally oblivious to all this accumulating information that constitutes the shadow Web. Even people with the best intentions, using this information to customize and personalize our Web site visits, may not recognize the potential for harm if others choose to use this same information for less than benevolent purposes. Consider the following mission statement from the U.S. government's Information Awareness Office, an office formed under President Bush in 2002:

> The DARPA Information Awareness Office (IAO) will imagine, develop, apply, integrate, demonstrate, and transition information technologies, components, and prototype closed-loop information systems that will counter asymmetric threats by achieving total information awareness that is useful for preemption, national security warning, and national security decision making.[1]

It is impossible for anyone to know exactly how this statement will be realized; that may very well be intentional. But its focus is on information; and that information is about us. The objective is to mine existing data sources that include financial and transactional data, such as those of the shadow Web, and combine this information with other information sources such as health records, communication records, and housing information in an effort to preempt terrorist acts. This means looking at everyone's data relating to such things as the purchases we have made, the information we have accessed, the courses we have enrolled in, the books we have borrowed, and the flights we have taken — no matter the purpose — and applying specially designed algorithms and analytical tools to this information in order to distinguish (theoretically) the good guys from the bad guys. The technology exists to make this possible, and the raw data necessary to conduct such analysis is ready and waiting. The legal system, unfortunately, is lagging far behind, putting at risk our right to privacy and leaving unanswered the question regarding the amount and type of personal information we should be able to control in our use of the Web (and elsewhere in our lives).

Read all the privacy statements you want. The one thing they all have in common is an acknowledgment that information about us and our use of the Web is being routinely recorded. What is done with this information varies considerably, as do the statements and promises regarding its treatment. This does not, however, negate the fact that the information is being collected, stored, and examined (and very often sold and resold for any number of purposes). The technology, how it is being used, our rights regarding our privacy and the information being collected, and the legal system, are all in a state of flux. For the time being at least, the most we can do is be aware of what is possible with the technology; that knowledge is our best defense against any potential abuse.

The Semantic Web

The Semantic Web

While today's World Wide Web is an information space, tomorrow's Web may be a knowledge space. This is what is promised by the Semantic Web, the name used by the Web's creator, Tim Berners-Lee, and many others to refer to a vision for the Web of tomorrow — an extension of today's World Wide Web — in which information is represented in a way that machines and programs, not just people, can easily understand, follow, and interconnect.

For the vision of the Semantic Web to be realized, it requires returning to what made the Web successful in the first place and examining what has worked, and why, discovering what is lacking, and determining what new features and capabilities need to be added to overcome these deficiencies. But tampering with success is no small challenge, and this is particularly true in the world of computers. Most people are very unforgiving when a system or application they have become familiar with and rely on works fine one day and behaves differently, or appears broken, the next. The World Wide Web, moreover, is no ordinary system; it operates on more computers and is used by more people than any other program, application, or system ever created.

Berners-Lee built the World Wide Web by engineering a simple and fast information management system that would operate over the Internet and that would locate, transfer, and interconnect pages of information and, more generally, information objects. He created the URL to identify and locate information objects (e.g., Web pages). He created HTTP to transfer the data content of information objects. He created HTML to encode (mark up) the content of information objects and included a hypertext component, the hyperlink, to interconnect those objects, giving the Web a form that matched its name. What Berners-Lee omitted from the Web, however, was the capability to describe, define, or categorize the content contained in an information object.

With respect to content, the Web makes no distinctions or demands. Moreover, the Web offers no means whatsoever to take the content of an information object — any information object — into account. As far as the Web and HTML are concerned, one page is roughly equivalent to another. That's because the markup that constitutes a page is generic in its design; it is incapable of conveying any information that is specific to the contents of the page. A heading in one page is equivalent to a heading in any other page. The same holds true for a list of items, an image, even a hyperlink. There is no intelligence at work in this area of the Web. The author of a Web document cannot categorize and describe different distinct elements in her document. She cannot, for example, distinguish (i.e., through markup) an image file containing the photograph of a siamese cat from an image file of an abstract painting of a Maine coon cat; nor can she distinguish a hyperlink to the homepage of the artist who created the abstract painting from a hyperlink to an art gallery in Greenwich Village with an exhibit of cat photographs. The Web's simple, common markup language of HTML focuses on the form and presentation of information, entirely at the expense of this information's function, meaning, type, and purpose.

Consider the following situation. A friend tells you about her new cell phone. You want to use the Web to learn more about it, and perhaps even buy one. You know the manufacturer's name and even the model number, so you can easily search for and locate Web pages that contain information about the product. But there is no automated or programmatic way to identify and separate the resulting pages from the search that contain objective reviews of the phone from those distributed by the manufacturer, from other pages that allow you to buy the product new or purchase a refurbished model or bid on one that is being auctioned. It may or may not take long to sift through the resulting pages to find the right type of information, but it is still a tedious and manual process. Better search engines with more advanced heuristic mechanisms might improve the process, but they cannot solve the inherent problem: the way the information is currently represented on the Web makes no such distinctions. Instead, you must read and sift through all this assorted information in the hope of coming upon the desired information.

But what if the Web allowed for such distinctions? What if you could create a Web page that clearly identified the categories and types of information it contained? Such a page might categorize its contents as describing the sale of a product, and it might refine this information by describing the type of product as a particular model of cell phone, the condition of the product as used, but in good working order, the type of sale as an auction, and the auction expiration as forty-eight hours. Another such page might categorize its contents as a comparative review of cell phones, and it might refine this information by listing the model numbers of the phones it reviews, the criteria used in its comparison, the scale used in its ranking, and so on. What if such descriptive information could be read and interpreted by search engines and other types of programmable agents?

When a Web page can categorize and describe its contents, instead of simply presenting its information for display and relying on outside agents (e.g., search engines) to index its contents through keywords that lack context and meaning, the information in that page becomes knowable and, for the first time, it becomes an integral and far-reaching part of that page. That page is no longer one Web page among countless million other Web pages, distinguished only by the inclusion or exclusion of certain words or phrases. Rather, it is a very specific type of page with specific categories of information, and specific values of information stored for each of those categories, sharing its particular features with some number of other similarly categorized pages spread out across the Web. It is part of the Semantic Web, a Web composed of meaning, knowledge, and intelligence, not just pages and pages of unqualified data.

What if this same sort of descriptive information existed for hyperlinks, too? The Web's deficiency in not allowing us to categorize and describe the content of a Web pages is compounded by our inability to categorize and describe the links we make from one Web page to another. Ironically, this second, missing element in today's Web was an integral part of Berners-Lee's original pre-

Web Enquire program; it was never implemented in his second version of Enquire and was omitted from his engineering of the Web. When you added a hyperlink in the original Enquire, the program required you to describe the nature of the link, that is, to explain the relationship between the reference (i.e., the hyperlink) and the destination it was pointing to. For instance, if you created a page describing the C programming language and included a hyperlink to Brian Kernighan, one of the creators of the language, you could classify the link as pointing to the creator of the subject matter being described. This classification or metadata (i.e., information about information) provided an additional and significant layer of information that added meaning to the link, facilitating your navigation through Enquire's store of data while refining your ability to locate the information you were searching for.

In the Semantic Web, an information space that includes the classification and description of hyperlinks, we may be able to discover a richness of information and a finely mapped Web of interconnections that would make the composition of today's Web look surprisingly empty and chaotic by contrast. In today's Web, the interconnection of information is vague. We click on a link and load a new document with at best some inkling of its contents. Worse yet, we can only derive this notion or expectation regarding the content of a link's destination from the highlighted text that composes the link and its context on the page; in other words, we must read and comprehend the information on a page to acquire any sense of the relationship between one of its links and that link's destination. We must, more often than not, click on a link in order to make any determination as to whether or not the information it points to is at all useful or pertinent. In the future, however, hyperlinks may not just point to a destination; they may also contain information to help us determine if we want to go there before we click. Moreover, if hyperlinks evolve from simple, one-directional pointers into objects that describe and categorize both the information source and the destination, these new and enhanced hyperlink objects will enable automated programs and machines to travel and map the Web on our behalf.

In the Semantic Web envisioned by Berners-Lee and others, all information is described, categorized, and identified in a form that can be processed by machines and automated programs; and through facilitating this type of machine-to-machine, program-to-program, interpretation and exchange of information, they hope to transform the Web from an information space into a knowledge space. While the scope of this undertaking may seem daunting, the purpose and benefits of such a systematic approach to the storage and representation of information have long been understood. Databases provide a simple example of a systematic representation of information. For instance, when you define a table in a database to store information (e.g., customer account information), you must first determine how to separate that information according to its constituent parts; this means identifying the individual elements that constitute the data and categorizing each of those elements. Each information category becomes a separate column in the table's definition. A customer account table might, therefore, contain the following columns of data: the customer's unique identification (e.g., a username or numeric code), first name, last name, city, state, gender, and age. Representing information in this manner takes time and effort to do and, to do it well, demands some recognition of how the particular information being divided and categorized will or may be used. Information stored in a database or represented in a similarly systematic way is ill suited to how we read and interpret information. It is, however, ideally suited to how machines and computer programs read, recognize, and process information.

Once information is represented in this manner, the information itself is transformed; it takes on new meaning and value. It can be used as it was before, as content on a Web page, for instance. But because this newly described and categorized information can also be located, extracted, and combined with other information, it can be used and reused for any number of purposes. For example, it can be used to answer questions, to produce reports, and to conduct statistical analyses.

Consider the database table of customer accounts. The table's storage and representation of information make it possible to easily and quickly locate all accounts in Maine, or all accounts with a first name of Marvin, or all the Marvins who live in Maine. The table's categorization of information also makes it possible to sort the information by last name, state, age, or some other criteria. Moreover, the information in the accounts table can be joined with information stored in one or more other tables, thereby extending how the information might be used. Joining the customer account table information with another table that contains sales figures would make it possible to show which accounts and regions were responsible for the greatest revenue; combining this information with the information stored in other tables might even explain why certain accounts and certain regions were responsible for more sales than other accounts and other regions.

A database of information is a base of knowledge. Every database contains all sorts of metadata describing and categorizing the information it stores, thereby enabling machines and programs to understand and interact with that information and process it on their own. Imagine the Web as such a database. But its database is global and it is capable of encompassing all stored information. This is the Semantic Web, a Web in which individual elements of information — and the information objects that contain them — are identified, described, and categorized, allowing the information objects and their content to be recognized, comprehended, explored, and analyzed. The knowledge space created from this newly categorized and described information will contain more than Web pages and it will be navigable by smarter and more sophisticated applications than today's simple Web browsers, search engines, and the like. It will be capable of being used for an endless variety of purposes, a few of which are described in the following sections.

The remainder of this chapter explores some of the work under way to realize this vision of the Semantic Web. It presents an overview of the most fundamental — and perhaps most challenging — aspect of the work: how to represent the information of the Semantic Web. Sample files are included to show what this information may look like and how it contrasts with the representation of information on today's Web. It also examines how we will navigate the Semantic Web and what our new capabilities of navigation will mean with respect to asking questions and discovering information. It then takes a broader view of the Semantic Web and explores the ramifications that may result in our realizing the vision of this knowledge space. One such ramification concerns how we will find a way to trust the information we discover and the information sources we encounter.

Representing Information: Metadata, RDF, and XML

So, how do we get from today's World Wide Web to tomorrow's more intelligent, knowledge-based Semantic Web? Equally important, what does this Semantic Web look like? Where and how do we create all this metadata describing and categorizing our information? How do we represent and store the information itself — the text, images, audio and video content — that constitutes the Semantic Web? Will HTML go the way of 8-track tapes and vinyl records? The answers to all of these questions have one thing in common, which is the creation and use of new types of information objects.

The latest computer engineering methodologies, programming languages, and development efforts are object oriented. That is, they focus on the use and reuse of objects with respect to how they conceptualize, control, and process information, and they are used to create entire object-oriented technologies. Object-oriented programming, for instance, uses a library of code objects — independent building blocks of program code — to reuse and build on earlier work. The programmer references and/or adapts these objects as needed for the task at hand, greatly reducing the amount of new code that needs to be written and the time required to complete the work while utilizing the reliability and functionality of the existing objects.

Within this new environment of object-oriented technologies and object-oriented programming, the ideal information space would consist entirely of information objects. Think of information objects as small but independent building blocks of information. An information object can consist of a word, a phrase, a sentence, a paragraph, or an entire chapter of a book; it can also consist of a hyperlink, a photograph, or an audio clip. Any identifiable and independent piece of information that the author (or editor, or someone else) can describe and categorize is an information object. These objects can be easily combined with other objects, they can be used and reused for any number of suitable purposes, and they can be built upon, in small or large increments, to create bigger and more powerful information objects.

Consider language from an object-oriented perspective. Letters make up the most basic objects; they can be combined to form an unlimited number of words. In turn, words compose larger and more complex objects; they can be combined to form an endless number of phrases, sentences, paragraphs, documents, books, and libraries. The letters and words that make up any language are documented, described, and categorized; this is what enables us to learn a language and communicate, but it is also what enables automated programs to perform such work as sorting information alphabetically and indexing a document.

Now consider the Web from this perspective. The most basic object of today's Web is an HTML page. HTML proved itself very successful in establishing a fast and simple way to represent information that would satisfy Berners-Lee's requirement of interoperability (i.e., enabling different types of computer architectures, devices, and applications to create, share, and display one common information file format). As we have seen, each HTML page conforms to certain basic rules regarding its overall structure — it has a well-defined beginning (a header area), middle (a body area), and end — and regarding the type of markup it can use to identify page elements (e.g., a heading, a paragraph, a list). These rules are sufficiently general to make HTML pages capable of containing any type and quantity of information.

But the rules that define and implement the interoperability of HTML pages across the Web — that make one HTML page equivalent to any other HTML page — are the same rules that limit the usefulness of HTML pages as information objects. The limitations of HTML require us to read HTML pages to understand the information they contain. Moreover, they preclude the use of automated tools for searching, sorting, and cataloging the contents of the Web in an intelligent manner. These limitations, for example, make it impossible for any automated tool or search engine to distinguish with any degree of certainty an HTML page that describes a child's response to receiving a Siamese cat for her birthday from one that describes an artisan's new collection of ceramic Siamese cats from one that describes a museum exhibit of Egyptian Siamese cat ceramics from one that describes the prominence of Siamese cats in several ancient cultures.

The road to the Semantic Web requires transforming the information of the Web from generic HTML page objects into an endless array of highly specific and distinctive information objects. These information objects will contain features and qualities that can be described, categorized, and represented in some consistent and well documented manner. Unlike today's HTML pages, these information objects will stand apart; they will be unique in terms of their specific content and recognizable in terms of the type of information they contain, the purpose of that information, and any number of other defining characteristics. For instance, information objects on the Semantic Web will be identified as a book review, a product description, an editorial, a weather report, and so on. Consequently, we will know far more about the type and nature of the information we will be retrieving from the Semantic Web before we start to read it, and the automated tools at our disposal will be able to differentiate one information object referencing a Siamese cat from another, enabling us to retrieve only those pages describing museum exhibits or only those pages describing items that are for sale.

If it sounds like this road will take us from one extreme to the other — from today's situation, in which information is represented in predominantly general and simple terms, with few rules or restrictions and with little consistency, to a future in which representing information is highly specific and regimented and is predominantly engineered to meet the requirements of machine processing — that is because there is no middle ground. The Semantic Web is necessarily a Web of precise rules, strict conformance, and exacting specifications. Transforming today's Web into the Semantic Web will, therefore, require considerable time, effort, and expense. In the simplest terms, the work will entail adding the information that is currently missing on today's Web in order to define, describe, and categorize the information objects that will become part of the Semantic Web. But this work will also entail defining one or more systems to store this additional information and creating the technology to read, write, and evaluate this information.

The Semantic Web will ultimately succeed or fail based on the engineering of these systems and the ease of use of its technology in helping individuals create content and describe and categorize that content. Most people today know little or nothing about the language specification that is HTML and the few, but necessary, rules and restrictions it imposes on the creation of HTML files. Web page creation and management tools transparently handle all the details of the language that define how a HTML file must be coded and the precise requirements regarding where to locate and how to interconnect files. Smarter, more advanced tools will need to perform similar and additional functions for the Semantic Web for it to meet the more stringent demands of its information objects.

There are many possible ways to create the information objects that may one day constitute the object-oriented, knowledge-based Semantic Web. The most promising and most widely discussed approach involves using XML — the Extensible Markup Language discussed in a previous chapter — to identify information in combination with something called the Resource Description Framework (RDF) to describe information characteristics. Both XML and RDF are described below using HTML as a point of comparison.

One of the strengths of XML is that it can be as simple or as complex as it needs to be. Small specifications can accommodate smaller objects; a set of XML markup can be created to represent the contents of recipe files and another set can be created to represent the various types of information stored for a company's customer accounts or for the products it sells. Larger specifications can accommodate larger objects, such as the contents of a book with its assorted chapters, sections, subsections, paragraphs, lists, references, and so on. XML can effectively replace HTML, allowing us to represent any and all types of information in a way that is best suited to the particular type of information being represented.

XML enables an information object to stand alone; its constituent parts (objects themselves) are arranged in some required order, with each of those parts separately identified and defined. When information content is categorized in this manner, it becomes possible, for example, to clearly identify and distinguish a product name from its description, from the sizes it comes in, from its price. This new capability is built into the information object using the language constructs (i.e., the markup) of XML, and it means that no longer does the information have to be read and its context understood for knowledge of its content to be grasped. The markup can describe as well as delineate the information object and its parts because it can be adapted to meet the particular needs of the information itself, as is shown in the sample code below.

At the same time, XML separates information content from information presentation, eliminating the need to embed presentation-related information into an information object. Decisions regarding which typefaces will be used, which text will appear in a larger size or in an italic font, and which type of information will be formatted into a bullet list or a numeric list can be handled separately, apart from the information object. This separation of content and presentation allows one person or group to focus entirely on creating, describing, and categorizing the information content and another person or group to focus on how that content should be presented. This separation also enables presentation to become a matter of filtering; the same information object can, if desired, be processed and presented for different purposes and/or different audiences. One filter, for instance, might produce an HTML file for display by one of today's browsers. Another filter might create data for a spreadsheet. Yet another filter might handle the more demanding presentation requirements of high-resolution printing for a magazine article, a company prospectus, or a book. In other words, one information object can be created for any number of purposes and its content can be presented in any number of views or formats.

Compare the following HTML and XML representations of the same recipe for scrambled eggs. Note that the elements enclosed in angle brackets (< >) in both sample files constitute the markup (e.g., <h1>, <ul>, <ingredient>, and <direction>). The markup identifies its associated content by delineating its beginning and end. For example, in the following line of HTML code the markup to identify a list item surrounds the text that will be displayed as one item in the list of ingredients.

```
<li>2 large eggs</li>
```

The following shows the HTML version of the recipe file:

```
<!doctype html public "-//w3c//dtd html 4.0 transitional//en">
<html>
  <head>
    <meta name="Author" content="James Beard">
    <meta name="Description" content="Recipe for scrambled eggs">
    <link rel="stylesheet" href="recipe.css" type="text/css">
    <title>Scrambled Eggs</title>
  </head>
  <body>
    <h1>Description</h1>
      Simple recipe for making creamy,
      large-curd scrambled eggs.
    <h1>Ingredients</h1>
      <ul>
        <li>2 large eggs</li>
        <li>1 tbsp. milk</li>
        <li>1 tbsp. butter</li>
        <li>1/4 tsp. salt</li>
      </ul>
    <h1>Directions</h1>
      <ol>
        <li>Heat non-stick skillet over low heat.</li>
        <li>Beat eggs lightly with fork or whisk.</li>
        <li>Melt butter, then add eggs to pan.</li>
        <li>As eggs begin to set, push into
          ribbons with wooden spoon.</li>
        <li>Push fully set eggs onto warmed
          plate and serve immediately.</li>
      </ol>
    <h1>Notes</h1>
      Serves one person.
      Add a dash or two of Tabasco and beat with eggs for some heat.
  </body>
</html>
```

Figure 1.   HTML Recipe File

The HTML file captures all the recipe information and divides the content into four sections using the <h1> heading markup: the 'Description' section, the 'Ingredients' section, the 'Directions' section, and the 'Notes' section. The specific ingredients are contained in a simple bullet, or unordered, list, which is identified by the <ul> markup, and each individual ingredient within the list is identified by the <li> list item markup. The specific directions for the recipe are handled much the same way. The only difference is that they are part of an ordered, or numbered, list, as indicated by the <ol> markup.

The code in this file illustrates how the markup imposes its order and functionality on the content, as opposed to the content determining what the markup should consist of. The recipe information has been adapted to fit the narrow constraints of HTML. Moreover, the coding of the file is utterly disconnected from its contents; the decisions regarding which markup to use for which pieces of information were based on issues of format and presentation. Heading markup divides the recipe into sections, but without reading what is printed in each heading you have no means of distinguishing the section on ingredients from the section on directions, and so on. The ingredients themselves are identified by markup for producing a bullet list, while the directions are identified by markup for producing a numbered list. Here again, the markup in the HTML file does nothing to categorize the type of information in the file. Instead of identifying a segment of text as one of the recipe's ingredients or directions, the markup only serves to identify its associated text as a generic list item; its purpose is a function of presentation. The bullet list of ingredients in this file uses the same markup as a bullet list of the types of cats indigenous to North America, a bullet list of job skills, or a bullet list of weather reports. All are coded identically in HTML because HTML cannot distinguish between different types of content; it can only distinguish between different elements on a page by identifying such things as the text of a heading, the start and end of a paragraph, or the start and end of a list item. You must read the information and understand its context in order to comprehend what the recipe consists of, which items are ingredients, which are directions, and so on.

Now consider what XML can do. The XML file below contains exactly the same information content as the HTML file above, but it does so without sacrificing the identification of its content to issues of presentation. Its coding has been built explicitly for the representation and categorization of the recipe information.

```xml
<?xml version="1.0"?>
<cookbook xmlns="http://www.beardrecipes.org/cbookspace/">
  <recipe>
    <author>James Beard</author>
    <title>Scrambled Eggs</title>
    <description>
      Simple recipe for making creamy,
      large-curd scrambled eggs.
    </description>>
    <ingredients>
      <ingredient>2 large eggs</ingredient>
      <ingredient>1 tbsp. milk</ingredient>
      <ingredient>1 tbsp. butter</ingredient>
      <ingredient>1/4 tsp. salt</ingredient>
    </ingredients>
    <directions>
      <direction>Heat non-stick skillet over low heat.</direction>
      <direction>Beat eggs lightly with fork or whisk.</direction>
      <direction>Melt butter, then add eggs to pan.</direction>
      <direction>As eggs begin to set, push into
        ribbons with wooden spoon.</direction>
      <direction>Push fully set eggs onto warmed
        plate and serve immediately.</direction>
    </directions>
    <notes>
      Serves one person.
      Add a dash or two of Tabasco and beat with eggs for some heat.
    </notes>
  </recipe>
</cookbook>
```

Figure 2. XML Recipe File

Instead of generic <h1> heading markup to divide the recipe into sections, the XML file uses specific, descriptive markup (<description>, <ingredients>, <directions>, and <notes>) to identify each distinct area of information. Consequently, the content and its markup are closely and meaningfully related to each other in the XML file. Instead of unordered or ordered lists with generic list items, the XML file contains specific elements of type <ingredient> and of type <direction>. Both you and a program can now easily distinguish one of the recipe's ingredients from one of its directions or a note relating to its preparation. XML makes this possible by allowing you to define the markup that will describe and categorize the specific content of any information object. You can create markup named <ingredient> to identify the individual ingredients in a recipe just as you can create markup named `<ComputerSkill>` to identify the individual computer skills in a resume. Only when such specific and precise identifiers are used to mark up a file's contents can that file become suitable for machines to process in any type of meaningful way. For instance, a search program on today's Web looking for recipes that include eggs as an ingredient would use one or more keywords (e.g., recipe and egg) to conduct the search, and it would return all the files that simply included those keywords. A similar search on the Semantic Web would be able to distinguish between files that contained recipes and included eggs as an ingredient and other types of files that simply made reference to the word recipe and the word egg, such as the review of a cookbook or the description of a cooking show on television.

Consider how the recipe information contained in the files above might interact with other applications, like a database. If the recipe information were stored in a database, a program could easily be written to create both the HTML and XML files from that stored information. That's because the necessary work of identifying and isolating each individual type of information and storing that information accordingly (i.e., in separate tables and columns) was done when the recipe information was put into the database. The reverse process, however, of populating one or more database tables from the information contained in these files, would be relatively simple with the XML file, due to the specificity of its markup, and impossible with the HTML file, due to the generic nature of its markup.

XML provides the framework for creating structured documents on the Semantic Web. It is already being used on today's Web to replace pages of data that demand human interpretation, which are represented in HTML, with information objects that can be interpreted and processed by machines. The Resource Description Framework (RDF), on the other hand, while expressed in the syntax of XML, provides the framework that supports the exchange of knowledge on the Semantic Web.

RDF content is metadata, that is, information used to describe and define the information content of the Web. For instance, RDF can be used to capture information about the XML recipe file, such as who wrote the file, when it was last updated, copyright information, and access information specifying who should be able to view it and who should be denied access. This type of information, just like formatting instructions that specify that ingredient elements should display as bullet list items and direction elements should display as numbered list items, is best kept separate and distinct from the recipe content. Not only does this separation greatly extend the flexibility of all these different types of information, but it simplifies the representation of the content and it enables applications to exchange information about the content, creating a Web filled with related objects of knowledge instead of linked pages of unqualified information.

The purpose of RDF is to provide a general framework that machines can use to interpret descriptive information. Consider the following plain-language statement about the scrambled eggs recipe:

> The recipe for scrambled eggs was written by James Beard on July 14, 1958 and can be found in his book, "American Cookery," published by Little, Brown and Company, copyright 1972, in the chapter entitled "Eggs."

This simple, declarative statement is easy enough for us to comprehend. It contains metadata regarding the recipe, that is, it describes and categorizes the recipe's content, but exists outside and distinct from the contents and purpose of the recipe. Any existing search engine could scan and index the statement, recording all the keywords. But none is capable of extracting the meaning contained in the statement as we do when reading it. RDF can be used to capture and convey that meaning so that a search engine, or some other type of program, would be capable of extracting the purpose and meaning of the statement. Here is one possible representation of the statement using RDF:

```
<?xml version="1.0"?>
<rdf:RDF xmlns:rdf="http://www.w3.org/rdf-syntax-ns#"
    xmlns:rterms="http://www.beardrecipes.org/terms/"
    xml:base="http://www.beardrecipes.org/cbookspace/recipes">

  <rterms:Recipe rdf:ID="recipe08984">
    <rterms:title>scrambled eggs</rterms:title>
    <rterms:author>James Beard</rterms:author>
    <rterms:createdate>07/14/1958</rterms:createdate>
    <rterms:cookbook>American Cookery</rterms:cookbook>
    <rterms:publisher>Little, Brown and Company</rterms:publisher>
    <rterms:copyright>1972</rterms:copyright>
    <rterms:chapter>Eggs</rterms:chapter>

  </rterms:Recipe>

</rdf:RDF>
```

Figure 3. RDF Recipe File

The RDF file bears little resemblance to the simple, declarative statement above. It does, however, capture and convey the exact same information and, while it may seem otherwise to our eyes, it does so in a way that is clearer and more succinct. The file's markup incorporates property names to identify each individual piece of information, such as the recipe's title and author. The creation of these property names to capture all the information that needs to be stored, whether for a recipe, a resume, a book on American feminist history, or any other information object, is the single most difficult and important task in using RDF. While a computer program could not be expected to create this file from the sentence above, a program could be written to do the reverse. That's because the RDF file documents and describes the recipe in terms of highly specific properties and values. It can even be used to build declarative sentences for us to read, like:

> The <title> recipe written by <author> was published in <copyright> by <publisher>.

The sentence above uses several of the RDF file's property names as tokens in order to illustrate how the program might build the sentence. In the sentence below, the property tokens have been replaced with their values from the RDF file.

> The scrambled eggs recipe written by James Beard was published in 1972 by Little, Brown and Company.

The metadata stored in an RDF file can be used for any number of purposes. Using this information, for example, to build descriptions for inclusion in dynamically generated HTML pages represents one of its simplest and most trivial applications. Its greatest potential can be found in providing machine-readable information and in facilitating the exchange of that information between programs and computers without any loss of meaning. Moreover, since RDF files can just as easily describe the relationship between objects as the objects themselves, they can also be used to capture and relay information about how and why one object is linked to another. Not unlike the signposts on our roads and highways that establish and enforce rules of conduct, direct traffic, identify locations, and aid our navigation, RDF can add meaning to the Web, meaning that will be discernible by both our information agents (i.e., the programs navigating the Web on our behalf) and by us.

As shown above, the combined use of XML and RDF can transform simple data into different types of information objects. These objects serve to describe, categorize, and make accessible and understandable the information they contain, to us, to other objects, to search engines, to databases, or to any other type of application. These objects will, therefore, be able to fulfill the information demands of the Semantic Web; they will help to turn today's information space into tomorrow's knowledge space. However, in order to realize the benefits of the Semantic Web, we will also need to establish rules regarding conduct (i.e., how we and our information agents will navigate the information of the Semantic Web) and some capacity for reasoning. These elements are described below.

Discovering Information:
Navigating the Semantic Web

In the world of the Semantic Web, where information is *known* rather than simply stored, it is possible to employ agents to discover and correlate information on our behalf. For instance, the Semantic Web will be able to accept, interpret, and reply to the following questions:

> What wines go with steamed lobster, are available at a store within 20 miles of my home, and cost under $15?

> Find me the flights between New York City and Austin that will get me to Austin in time for my Monday meeting with IBM and back to New York City in time to attend my son's birthday party, and sort by cheapest fare.

In order for such queries to produce results, two basic conditions must be met. First, the requested information must be stored and accessible. The agent must have access to a database of information about wine that includes information about which foods go with which wines. After it has produced a list of acceptable wines, it must shorten the list by taking price into consideration and then correlate that shorter list with a list of wines sold at the stores that sell wine within the specified distance. A similar process of discovery must occur to return the list of possible flights. But, in this case, the agent must correlate flight schedule information with information stored in a local calendar program that contains entries for the IBM meeting and the birthday party.

XML and RDF facilitate such a process of discovery by categorizing and describing information resources about wines and the foods they are best suited to accompany, stores and their locations and inventory, commercial flights and their schedules, available seats and costs, and calendars and the date, time, and nature of their recorded entries. But the second condition, the one that makes possible the sort of machine-based discovery of information required to answer the questions posed above, goes beyond the storage and accessibility of information. Its focus is on the interrelationship of this information and the need for an additional layer of information to describe and define how information objects relate to one another and what constitutes the encompassing environment in which they exist. This additional layer of information is composed of something called the ontologies of the Semantic Web.

Ontology has traditionally been defined as the branch of metaphysics that deals with the nature and relations of being; it attempts to define the basic characteristics and entities that comprise the world and how these entities are related in order to provide a framework for studying and discussing reality. The definition of ontology has been amended to include the study of what constitutes knowledge and the ways in which knowledge can be represented. In the context of the Semantic Web, an ontology is a collection of definitions of information objects and their properties, and the rules or constraints regarding how these objects and properties can be used. It is through these ontologies that the various machines, applications, and information stores on the Semantic Web will be able to exchange information. Ontologies will, for instance, incorporate the necessary semantics for a program to understand that the wine object for sale down the street at the supermarket is the same sort of wine object found in the database linking it to an entree of lobster and the same wine object expressed in the question.

In addition to setting up these sorts of equivalencies for the exchange of information, ontologies add another dimension of intelligence through something called inference rules. Such rules help to refine relationships and establish a factor of logic and reasoning on the Semantic Web. For instance, if a store records that it carries all the wine produced by a specific vintner, and you want to purchase that vintner's chardonnay, an agent can infer that the chardonnay you want is sold at that store. The same sort of inference rules and applied reasoning pertain to the distance factor in the first question. The agent knows your street address and zip code and it can discover the names and locations of stores within the same zip code and adjoining zip codes. It can then use this information in association with accessible maps to determine which stores fall within the 20 mile radius.

When these ontologies are combined with stores of data, the result is something called a reasoning system. Such a system bridges the gap between all of the information objects that make up the Semantic Web. A reasoning system will allow us to locate information with a speed and precision that is impossible on today's Web, and it will enable reasoning agents to seek out information on our behalf by interpreting and answering questions like those presented above. This is the objective of the Semantic Web: to create a Web of knowledge. Such a Web implies the existence of reason as well as the ability to interconnect information in a way that's not all that different from how the Internet seamlessly interconnects countless computers and networks of computers.

Now go one small step further. Today's Web already extends beyond its information space into the physical space that we inhabit. Applications have been around for quite some time that provide for the remote viewing and operation of physical objects and their controls, allowing us to do such things as change the settings on a distant computer and tell it to restart, or turn on lights and adjust the thermostat in a vacation home from our desk at work before we set out on that long drive to the country. When the Web came along, it simplified and extended access to many of the tasks performed by these applications. It allowed us to monitor conditions and interact with controls locally or across the Internet. The Semantic Web promises to take these same physical objects and controls and interconnect them in much the same way that it will interconnect information objects.

Physical objects like phones, televisions, radios, and thermostats can also be described — like the recipe presented above — in terms of their properties and values. For instance, televisions and radios have volume controls, while thermostats have temperature scales. A house agent that contains such information can easily monitor and control these physical objects in a unified or integrated fashion. So when the phone rings, the objects that have volume properties are muted or turned down by the agent. When the doorbell rings, a video camera sends the arriving guest's image onto the television screen, after pausing the movie that was playing. When the temperature outside drops below a certain set value, the thermostat is adjusted accordingly. By establishing a context in which information can be contained in objects and such objects can be described in a way that promotes self-discovery and information exchange, all sorts of new and powerful paradigms come into play. Many things that had been considered impossible — like being able to ask complex questions of a reasoning agent — become feasible.

Trusting Information: The Web of Trust

When we connect the information objects of the Semantic Web with a means to verify the source and authenticity of that information, something that has been named the Web of Trust is created. Another name commonly used in this work to bring some measure of trust onto the Web is Trust Management. Questions regarding who and what we can trust on today's Web — which people, computers, and organizations — remain unanswered as the debate over how to introduce the characteristics and measurement of trust onto the Web continues. But the existence of trust is a requirement of the Semantic Web, because the agents it will have working on our behalf to discover information will need some means to verify the source and authenticity of the information they find.

Few people bother to consider who is responsible for the information presented on a Web page. Even fewer people question — or think to question — whether the person or organization listed as the author or provider of a Web page really is who they say they are. But the Web is unlike other information providers that push data down to us and, in so doing, identify themselves through their information channel. The newspaper or magazine that gets delivered to us through the mail, the radio or television channel that we tune to, these sources are impractical, if not impossible, to mimic and replace. But the Web, where one page is equivalent to another, where we go to the source and pull the information we want, is a breeding ground for fraud, deception, and impersonation.

We cannot take the information on today's Web at face value; we put at risk our money, security, and privacy, and we risk being misled or otherwise being taken advantage of every time we do. We will not be able to take the information on the Semantic Web at face value either. We will need some means to ascertain that the person representing himself or herself is that person, and that the information we are collecting is from a valid and trusted source. But what will constitute a valid and trusted source? What can be built into the Web to help us gauge the integrity and authenticity of a source of information and, conversely, enable us to securely and unequivocally identify ourselves? How do we transform today's Web into the Web of Trust?

One proposed solution to verifying the authenticity of an information source on the Web is through something called digital signatures. Digital signatures are a form of encrypted data that can be used to uniquely and securely identify any individual person or entity on the Internet. The operating principle behind digital signatures is similar to that of the private and public encrypted keys exchanged by browsers and Web servers for secure Web transactions, such as those typically used in the process of making a purchase in which sensitive information, like a credit card number, must be communicated. Digital signatures are roughly equivalent to digital fingerprints; they are unique and can be traced back to the one identity for whom (or which) they are valid. Just as the introduction of encrypted keys and the creation of a secure version of HTTP (e.g., HTTPS) to securely exchange encrypted information were prerequisites to the Web being transformed into a thriving marketplace, the widespread use of digital signatures (or some other technology designed to satisfy the same basic requirement) and a mechanism for their exchange and validation will be needed on the Semantic Web to help build the Web of Trust.

But digital signatures alone cannot establish or build trust on the Web. They can be used to verify an identity, but they cannot help us determine whether the individual, computer, or organization they have identified should be trusted. Trust on the Web, like trust outside the Web, is a personal matter; it is affected by our individual experiences and it changes in response to new experiences and new information. Therefore, the Semantic Web will need a system that will accommodate our individual needs and values with respect to who and how much to trust. Moreover, this system will need to scale in accordance with our growing interaction with the Web and with the perpetual growth of the Web itself. But the vast size and distributed nature of the Web limit the practicality of each of us making a determination about how much or little we should trust all of the people, computers, and organizations we encounter.

The Web of Trust must, therefore, be just that — a web of interconnected, trusted relationships. It will need to extend outwards through our individual trusted relationships to encompass the trusted relationships of our friends, family members, business associates, and others. For example, if you trust your friend Fred and Fred trusts his friend Sue, you can by inference trust Sue; and if you trust an organization that evaluates the trustworthiness of businesses on the Web, you can by inference trust in their conclusions about which businesses to use. The same holds true for conditions of distrust. Over time, as these relationships grow, and as the number of sources through which to acquire information about trustworthiness also grows, it will become progressively easier for us and our information agents on the Semantic Web to determine how much we can trust any one source of information or individual information object.

The Big (Semantic Web) Picture

When all the elements of the Semantic Web are brought together — XML files that represent information in a form that also specifically identifies and categorizes its content, RDF files that describe XML files and other types of information objects and describe the relationships that connect these information objects, ontologies that define the behavior, rules, and constraints regarding how these objects can be used and how information can be exchanged, and authenticity methodologies such as those presented in the Web of Trust — the information management system that emerges is very different than the system of today's Web. Comparing the Semantic Web and its promised knowledge space with today's Web makes today's Web seem strikingly and surprisingly simple and its information space seem chaotic and obscure.

Despite the considerable differences between the infrastructures of the two systems, the Semantic Web does not have to look or feel different than today's Web. Nor should it be any more difficult to use. Moreover, the Semantic Web will not require us to become information experts in order to publish information, any more than we need to know how to code HTML today in order to build our own, or a business's, presence on the Web.

What the Semantic Web will require is smarter tools with which to build and maintain all of its information objects and their interconnections. Information consistency and strict validation tools will be key to the success of the Semantic Web. Tolerance for mistakes and the capacity to overlook and move beyond incorrect or misleading information are human virtues. The information agents navigating the Semantic Web on our behalf, and the machines processing and exchanging information, will need to operate according to more stringent demands and will necessarily be far less forgiving.

But if the Semantic Web comes to pass, its effects will likely be as transforming, if not more so, as those of the World Wide Web. The Web has proven itself a cornerstone of our Information Age. Nothing comes close to its utterly egalitarian and universal approach to information access and sharing. But information is one thing and knowledge is another. If the Semantic Web can establish a global knowledge space out of today's information space, a great many changes in our world and in ourselves will surely follow.

Milestones, Netiquette, and Jargon

World Wide Web Milestones

The following milestone information focuses on the Web and Web-related applications and information services.

1945   Vannevar Bush publishes, "As We May Think" in the *Atlantic Monthly*.

1965   Ted Nelson coins terms Hypertext and Hypermedia.

1967   HES hypertext system developed at Brown University.

1968   FRESS hypertext system developed at Brown University.

1980   Tim Berners-Lee creates Enquire program at CERN.

        The SGML standard is published.

1984   CERNDOC created at CERN.

1985   Intermedia hypertext system developed at Brown University.

1987   First Hypertext Conference, held in Chapel Hill, North Carolina.

        Apple releases Hypercard.

1989   Berners-Lee submits "Information Management: A Proposal."

1990   Berners-Lee and Cailliau submit "WorldWideWeb: Proposal for a Hypertext Project."

First Web server at http://info.cern.ch.

Archie created at McGill University.

1991   San Antonio Hypertext Conference.

World Wide Web software first published at CERN.

Line mode, Viola and Erwise browsers created.

First U.S. Web server at SLAC.

WAIS created at Thinking Machines Corporation.

1992   Web is assigned port 80 for Internet traffic, establishing it as a recognized Internet service.

MidasWWW and Lynx browsers created.

Veronica created at University of Nevada.

1993   First Web developers' meeting, held in Boston.

CERN puts Web software into the public domain.

Cello and Mosaic browsers created.

White House launches Web site.

1994   First CERN Web conference.

Netscape formed and releases Navigator 1.0.

W3C founded.

Web becomes 2nd most popular service on the Internet (FTP is first, TELNET is now third).

Pizza Hut Web site accepts orders over the Internet.

Shopping mall Web sites appear.

First Virtual becomes first cyberbank.

First banner ads appear (for Zima and AT&T).

1995   CERN transfers European W3C to INRIA.

Web becomes most popular service on Internet.

Sun launches JAVA.

Netscape goes public.

Vatican launches Web site.

1996   Netscape Navigator and Microsoft Internet Explorer browser wars heat up.

2000   Number of Web servers exceeds 10 million.

Number of Web pages estimated to exceed 1 billion.

Growth Table of World Wide Web					
Date	Sites	Date	Sites	Date	Sites
06/93	130	09/97	1,364,714	11/99	8,844,573
09/93	204	10/97	1,466,906	12/99	9,560,866
10/93	228	11/97	1,553,998	01/00	9,950,491
12/93	623	12/97	1,681,868	02/00	11,161,811
06/94	2,738	01/98	1,834,710	03/00	13,106,190
12/94	10,022	02/98	1,920,933	04/00	14,322,950
06/95	23,500	03/98	2,084,473	05/00	15,049,382
01/96	100,000	04/98	2,215,195	06/00	17,119,262
03/96	135,396	05/98	2,308,502	07/00	18,169,498
04/96	150,295	06/98	2,410,067	08/00	19,823,296
05/96	193,150	07/98	2,594,622	09/00	21,166,912
06/96	252,000	08/98	2,807,588	10/00	22,282,727
07/96	299,403	09/98	3,156,324	11/00	23,777,446
08/96	342,081	10/98	3,358,969	12/00	25,675,581
09/96	397,281	11/98	3,518,158	01/01	27,585,719
10/96	462,047	12/98	3,689,227	02/01	28,125,284
11/96	525,906	01/99	4,062,280	03/01	28,611,177
12/96	603,367	02/99	4,301,512	04/01	28,669,939
01/97	646,162	03/99	4,349,131	05/01	29,031,745
02/97	739,688	04/99	5,040,663	06/01	29,302,656
03/97	883,149	05/99	5,414,325	07/01	31,299,592
04/97	1,002,612	06/99	6,177,453	08/01	30,775,624
05/97	1,044,163	07/99	6,598,697	09/01	32,398,046
06/97	1,117,259	08/99	7,078,194	10/01	33,135,768
07/97	1,203,096	09/99	7,370,929	11/01	36,458,394
08/97	1,269,800	10/99	8,115,828	12/01	36,276,252
				01/02	36,689,008
				02/02	38,444,856
				03/02	38,118,962

Sites = # of web servers (one host may have multiple sites by using different domains or port numbers)

Netiquette

Communicating over the Internet, whether by email, chat, or some other means, is not likely to be well regarded by people who have high standards when it comes to spelling and grammar, or by those who fondly recall learning in school all about salutations and the various and sundry parts that compose a well formed paragraph. You can blame the keyboard or bad typing skills, or both. Or you can blame the innate sense of informality in the medium. Or you can attribute it to the immediacy of the environment and that feeling of urgency to send out a quick email or to keep pace in a fast moving, chat room conversation.

Netiquette, short for network etiquette, is a loose collection of rules and conventions applied to online behavior, particularly to communicating over the Internet. Most of what is commonly understood as netiquette — specific perspectives and formal descriptions vary considerably — represents common sense behavioral considerations, things we try to apply in our general interactions with others but adapted to the new and unique communication environment of the Internet. In general, these conventions focus on respecting other people's time and privacy, sharing knowledge rather than withholding it or lauding it above others, not abusing one's power (e.g., when acting as moderator in a chat room or newsgroup), and forgiving mistakes, especially with respect to new Internet denizens, also known as newbies. Netiquette also tries to cover some operational basics, like knowing when and how to ask for help, understanding that all uppercase letters make you appear as if you are shouting, thinking twice before responding emotionally (also known as flaming someone), not forwarding unsolicited mail to your friends, and so on.

The simplest and most fundamental netiquette rule is not letting the remoteness imposed by the technology allow you to forget that you are interacting with other people. Typing in your thoughts at a computer keyboard, in the isolation of your room or in the public space of an office or library, makes it easy to forget that someone else will eventually be reading those words; and they won't necessarily know what you were feeling when you wrote them, or precisely what you intended. You can't accompany your words with your facial expressions (well, see below, you can try). You can't easily or exactly communicate your tone of voice. You can't clearly identify when you're being serious, and when sarcastic. So, don't be surprised when you are misunderstood, and try to use whatever conventions you can, including those in the tables below, to assist you in communicating both your thoughts *and* the sentiments behind them. Equally important, apply the same conventions when reading what others have written. Do not presume you know exactly what your friend, business associate, or even your favorite in-law meant to convey when reading his or her words in an email message or in a chat window. Give them the benefit of the doubt, because the technology only goes so far.

If you want to communicate over the Internet using some of the language constructs that the Internet has inspired and propagated, or if you just want to better understand the common acronyms and expressions that commonly punctuate much of the Internet's communication traffic, you'll find the following tables of assistance.

Internet Shorthand Acronyms	
Acronym	Meaning
AFAIK	As Far As I Know
AFK	Away From Keyboard
AOLer	America OnLine Member
A/S/L	Age/Sex/Location
BAK	Back At Keyboard
BBIAF	Be Back In A Flash
BBL	Be Back Later
BD	Big Deal
BFD	Big Friggin' Deal
BFN	Bye For Now
BRB	Be Right Back
BTW	By The Way
CUL8R	See You Later
CYA	See Ya
FB	Furrowed Brow
FWIW	For What It's Worth
GDM8	G'day Mate
GMTA	Great Minds Think Alike
GRD	Grinning, Running, Ducking
GR8	Great

Internet Shorthand Acronyms	
Acronym	Meaning
HTH	Hope This Helps
IAE	In Any Event
IANAL	I Am Not A Lawyer
IM	Instant Message
IMHO	In My Humble Opinion
IMNSHO	In My Not So Humble Opinion
IOW	In Other Words
IYSWIM	If You See What I Mean
J/K	Just Kidding
LMAO	Laughing My A-- Off
LOL	Laughing Out Loud
LTNS	Long Time No See
M4M	Men seeking Men
NFW	No Friggin' Way
NP	No Problem
NRN	No Reply Necessary
NW	No Way
OIC	Oh, I See
OTOH	On The Other Hand
PBT	Pay Back Time
ROTFL/ROFL	Rolling On The Floor Laughing
RTFM	Read The Friggin' Manual
SOL	Sooner Or Later
TOS	Terms Of Service
TTFN	Ta-Ta For Now
TTYL	Talk To You Soon
WB	Welcome Back
WTG	Way To Go
YL/YM	Young Lady/Young Man
YMMV	Your Mileage May Vary

Internet Shorthand Expressions	
Expression	Meaning
O:-)	Angel
*^_^*	Big Grin
T_T	Big Tears
@^_^@	Blushing
:'-(	Crying
}:>;	Devil
:-e	Disappointed
:-L~~	Drooling
X=	Fingers Crossed
:-(	Frowning
$-)	Greedy
8:)3)=	Happy Girl
{{{{Whomever}}}}	Hug for Whomever
{}	Hugs
X-)	I See Nothing
:-X	I'll Say Nothing
******	Kisses
:*	Kissing
:=)	Little Hitler
:-D	Laughing
@]'-,-----	Rose
:-@	Screaming
:-O	Shock
:-)	Smiling
:-P	Sticking Out Tongue
^_^;	Sweating
(hmm)Ooo..:-)	Thinking Happy Thoughts
(hmm)Ooo..:-(	Thinking Sad Thoughts
;-)	Winking
\\//	Vulcan Salute

Common Internet Age Jargon

The following list contains a sampling of the jargon inspired by the Web, the Internet, and the ever growing pervasiveness of computers in our lives.

404 — Someone who's clueless. From the Web error message "404, URL Not Found," meaning that the document you've tried to access can't be located. "Don't bother asking him...he's 404, man."

Adminisphere — The rarefied organizational layers beginning just above the rank and file. Decisions that fall from the adminisphere are often profoundly inappropriate or irrelevant to the problems they were designed to solve.

Alpha Geek — The most knowledgeable, technically proficient person in an office or work group. "Ask Larry, he's the alpha geek around here."

Assmosis — The process by which some people seem to absorb success and advancement by kissing up to the boss rather than working hard.

Beepilepsy — The brief seizure people sometimes suffer when their beepers go off, especially in vibrator mode. Characterized by physical spasms, goofy facial expressions, and stopping speech in mid-sentence.

Blamestorming — Sitting around in a group discussing why a deadline was missed or a project failed, and who was responsible.

Bookmark — To take note of a person for future reference (a metaphor borrowed from web browsers). "I bookmarked him after seeing his cool demo at Siggraph."

Blowing Your Buffer — Losing one's train of thought. Occurs when the person you are speaking with won't let you get a word in edgewise or has just said something so astonishing that your train gets derailed. "Damn, I just blew my buffer!"

Career-Limiting Move (CLM) — Used among microserfs to describe an ill-advised activity. Trashing your boss while he or she is within earshot is a serious CLM.

CGI Joe — A hard-core CGI script programmer with all the social skills and charisma of a plastic action figure.

Chainsaw Consultant — An outside expert brought in to reduce the employee headcount, leaving the top brass with clean hands.

Chips and Salsa — Chips hardware, salsa software. "Well, first we gotta figure out if the problem's in your chips or your salsa."

Chip Jewelry — A euphemism for old computers destined to be scrapped or turned into decorative ornaments. "I paid three grand for that Mac SE, and now it's nothing but chip jewelry."

Circling The Drain — Used to describe projects that have no more life in them but refuse to die. "That disk conversion project has been circling the drain for years."

Cobweb Site — A Web site that hasn't been updated for a long time. A dead web page.

Crapplet — A badly written or profoundly useless Java applet. "I just wasted 30 minutes downloading this stinkin' crapplet!"

Crash Test Dummies

Those of us who pay for unstable, not-yet-ready-for-prime-time software foisted on us by computer companies.

Critical Mess

An unstable stage in a software project's life in which any single change or bug fix can result in the creation of two or more new bugs. Continued development at this stage can lead to an exponential increase in the number of bugs.

Cube Farm

An office filled with cubicles.

Dancing Baloney

Little animated GIFs and other Web F/X that are useless and serve simply to impress clients. "This page is kinda dull. Maybe a little dancing baloney will help."

Dawn Patrol

Programmers who are still at their terminals when the day shift returns to work the next morning. Usually found in Trog Mode (see below).

Dead Tree Edition

The paper version of a publication available in both paper and electronic forms, as in: "The dead tree edition of the San Francisco Chronicle..."

Depotphobia

Fear associated with entering a Home Depot because of how much money one might spend. Electronics geeks experience Shackophobia.

Dilberted

To be exploited and oppressed by your boss. Derived from the experiences of Dilbert, the geek-in-hell comic strip character. "I've been dilberted again. The old man revised the specs for the fourth time this week."

Domain Dipping	Typing in random words between www. and .com just to see what's out there.
Dorito Syndrome	Feelings of emptiness and dissatisfaction triggered by addictive substances that lack nutritional content. "I just spent six hours surfing the Web, and now I've got a bad case of Dorito Syndrome."
Dustbuster	A phone call or email message sent to someone after a long while just to "shake the dust off" and see if the connection still works.
Egosurfing	Scanning the net, databases, print media, or research papers looking for the mention of your name.
Elvis Year	The peak year of something's popularity. "Barney the dinosaur's Elvis year was 1993."
Email Tennis	When you email someone who responds while you are still answering mail. You respond again, and so forth, as if you were carrying on a chat via email messages. "Ok, enough of this email tennis, why don't I call you?"
Flight Risk	Planning to leave a company or department soon.
Generica	Features of the American landscape that are exactly the same no matter where one is. "We were so lost in generica, I actually forgot what city we were in."
Future-Proof	Term used to describe a technology that supposedly won't become technologically outdated (at least anytime soon).
Glazing	Corporate-speak for sleeping with your eyes open. A popular pastime at conferences

and early-morning meetings. "Didn't he notice that half the room was glazing by the second session?"

Going Cyrillic
When a graphical display (LED or LCD screen, monitor, etc.) starts to display garbage. "The thing just went cyrillic on me."

GOOD Job
A "Get-Out-Of-Debt" job. A well paying job people take in order to pay off their debts, one that they will quit as soon as they are solvent again.

Gray Matter
Older, experienced business people hired by young entrepreneurial firms looking to appear more reputable and established.

Graybar Land
The place you go while you're staring at a computer that's processing something very slowly (while you watch the gray bar creep across the screen). "I was in graybar land for what seemed like hours, thanks to that CAD rendering."

Hourglass Mode
Waiting in limbo for some expected action to take place. "I was held up at the post office because the clerk was in hourglass mode."

Idea Hamsters
People who always seem to have their idea generators running. "That guy's a real idea hamster. Give him a concept and he'll turn it over 'til he comes up with something useful."

IQueue
The line of interesting email messages waiting to be read after one has deleted all of the junk mail.

Irritainment
Entertainment and media spectacles that are annoying, but you find yourself unable to stop watching them. The O.J. trials were a prime example.

It's a Feature

From the adage "It's not a bug, it's a feature." Used sarcastically to describe an unpleasant experience that you wish to gloss over.

Keyboard Plaque

The disgusting buildup of dirt and crud found on computer keyboards. "Are there any other terminals I can use? This one has a bad case of keyboard plaque."

Link Rot

The process by which links on a web page became as obsolete as the sites they're connected to change location or die.

Martian Mail

An email that arrives months after it was sent (as if it has been routed via Mars).

Meatspace

The physical world (as opposed to the virtual) also carbon community, facetime, F2F, RL.

Midair Passenger Exchange

Grim air-traffic controller-speak for a head-on collision. Midair passenger exchanges are quickly followed by "aluminum rain."

Monkey Bath

A bath so hot that, when lowering yourself in, you go "Oo! Oo! Oo! Ah! Ah! Ah!."

Mouse Potato

The online, wired generation's answer to the couch potato.

Notwork

A network in its non-working state.

Nyetscape

Nickname for AOL's less-than-full-featured Web browser.

Ohnosecond

That miniscule fraction of time in which you realize that you've just made a BIG mistake. Seen in Elizabeth P. Crowe's book, "The Electronic Traveller."

Open-Collar Workers

People who work at home or telecommute.

PEBCAK

Tech support shorthand for "Problem Exists Between Chair and Keyboard." Another variation on the above is ID10T: "This guy has an ID-Ten-T on his system."

Percussive Maintenance

The fine art of whacking the crap out of an electronic device to get it to work again.

Plug-and-Play

A new hire who doesn't need any training. "The new guy, John, is great. He's totally plug-and-play."

Prairie Dogging

When someone yells or drops something loudly in a "cube farm" (an office full of cubicles) and everyone's heads pop up over the walls to see what's going on.

Print Mile

The distance covered between a desk and a printer shared by a group of users in an office. "I think I've traveled enough print miles on this job to qualify for a vacation."

Salmon Day

The experience of spending an entire day swimming upstream only to get screwed in the end.

Seagull Manager

A manager who flies in, makes a lot of noise, craps over everything and then leaves.

Shovelware

A Web document that was shoveled from paper onto the Web, help system, or whatever without much effort to adapt it to the new medium. Betrayed by, among other things, papercentric phrases like "See page so-and-so," "later in this booklet," and so forth.

SITCOMs   What yuppies turn into when they have children and one of them stops working to stay home with the kids. Stands for Single Income, Two Children, Oppressive Mortgage.

Square-headed Girlfriend

Another word for a computer. The victim of a square-headed girlfriend is a "computer widow."

Squirt The Bird   To transmit a signal up to a satellite. "Crew and talent are ready...what time do we squirt the bird?"

Starter Marriage   A short-lived first marriage that ends in a divorce with no kids, no property and no regrets.

Stress Puppy   A person who seems to thrive on being stressed out and whiny.

Swiped Out   An ATM or credit card that has been rendered useless because the magnetic strip is worn away from extensive use.

Telephone Number Salary

A salary (or project budget) that has seven digits.

Thrashing   Clicking helter-skelter around an interactive computer screen or Web site in search of hidden buttons or links that might trigger actions.

Tourists   People who are taking training classes just to get a vacation from their jobs. "We had about three serious students in the class; the rest were tourists."

Treeware   Hacker slang for documentation or other printed material.

Triple-dub	An abbreviated way of saying www when speaking about a URL. "Check out this cool web site at triple-dub dot enlightenment dot co dot uk."
Trog Mode	A round-the-clock computer session in which your eyes get so tired you have to turn off the lights and toggle the monitor into reverse — white letters on a black screen. Often used at Dawn Patrol period (see above).
Umfriend	A sexual relation of dubious standing. "This is Dale, my...um...friend..."
Under Mouse Arrest	Getting busted for violating an online service's rule of conduct. "Sorry I couldn't get back to you. AOL put me under mouse arrest."
Uninstalled	Euphemism for being fired. Heard on the voicemail of a vice president at a downsizing computer firm: "You have reached the number of an uninstalled vice president. Please dial our main number and ask the operator for assistance." Also known as Decruitment.
Voice Jail System	A poorly designed voicemail system that has so many submenus that one gets lost and has to hang up and call back.
Vulcan Nerve Pinch	The taxing hand position required to reach all of the appropriate keys for certain commands. For instance, the warm boot for a Mac II involves simultaneously pressing the Control key, the Command key, the Return key and the Power On key.
World Wide Wait	The real meaning of WWW.

Yuppie Food Stamps   The ubiquitous $20 bills spewed out of ATMs everywhere. Often used when trying to split the bill after a meal: "We all owe $8 each, but all anybody's got is yuppie food stamps."

Notes

Notes

0. The Pre-Web Internet and Information Management

1   Vannevar Bush, "As We May Think", The Atlantic Monthly, July 1945, 1.

2   Ibid, 1.

3   Ibid, 6.

4   Andries van Dam, "Hypertext '87 Keynote Address", http://www.cs.brown.edu/memex/HT_87_Keynote_Address.html, 1987.

5   Ibid.

6   Ibid.

General References
>James Gillies, Robert Cailliau, "How the Web was Born: the Story of the World Wide Web", Oxford University Press, 2000.
>
>Ed Krol, "The Whole Internet Guide and Catalog", O'Reilly and Associates, 1994.
>
>F. Anklesaria, et. al., "The Internet Gopher Protocol", RFC 1436, March 1993.
>
>M. St. Pierre, et. al., "WAIS over Z39.50-1988", RFC 1625, June 1994.

1. The Web is Born

1   Tim Berners-Lee, "Home Page at W3C", http://www.w3.org/People/Berners-Lee/, 2003.

2   Tim Berners-Lee, "Weaving the Web", HarperCollins, 2000, 36.

3   Ibid, 28.

4   Ibid, 33.

General References
James Gillies, Robert Cailliau, "How the Web was Born: the Story of the World Wide Web", Oxford University Press, 2000.

Tim Berners-Lee, "Information Management: A Proposal", CERN, 1989.

Tim Berners-Lee, Robert Cailliau, "WorldWideWeb: Proposal for a HyperText Project", CERN, 1990.

2. The Mechanics of the Web

General References
Tim Berners-Lee, et. al., "Uniform Resource Identifiers (URI): Generic Syntax", RFC 2396, August 1998.

R. Fielding, et. al., "Hypertext Transfer Protocol -- HTTP/1.1", RFC 2616, June 1999.

3. The Business Web

1   Louis V. Gerstner, Jr., "Who Says Elephants Can't Dance?", HarperCollins, 2002, 341.

7. The Shadow Web

1   U.S Federal Government, Information Awareness Office, http://www.darpa.mil/iao.index.htm, April 2003.

8. The Semantic Web

General References
RDF Primer, W3C Working Draft 23 January 2003, http://www.w3.org/TR/rdf-primer/, W3C, 2003.

Tim Berners-Lee, James Hendler, Ora Lassila, "The Semantic Web", Scientific American, May 17 2001.

A. Milestones, Netiquette, and Jargon

General Sources
Milestone information for the Internet and the Web adapted from the following sources:
Robert H. Zakon, "Hobbes' Internet Timeline," http://www.zakon.org/robert/internet/timeline/, 2003; and Lawrence Roberts, "Internet Chronology," 22 March 1997.

Index

1 by 1 pixel GIFS, (see bugs)
404 Not Found message, 121

A

About.com, 149
activity-based pages, 247
Addis, Louise, 90
addressing scheme, 116
Adobe Acrobat, 134
advertisements, 265, 267
advertising, 186
affiliate management, 172, 266,
   282
   compensation, 284
   general operation, 284
   perspectives, 285
affiliates, 283
agents, 174
aggregate information collection,
   271
Alexandria initiative, 67
Alta Vista, 148
Amazon.com, 163, 220
   one-click shopping, 222
   storefront features, 222
America Online (AOL), 96, 99, 219,
   230
Andreessen, Marc, 95, 98
AOL, (see America Online)
Apache HTTP Server, 237, 241
Apache Software Foundation, 237
Apollo space program, 34
Apple Computer, 41, 62, 195
applets
   Java, 203

Archie, 17, 47, 58, 65
   FTP file servers, 47
   indexing FTP sites, 48
   limitations, 49
   server, 48
ARPANET, 37
artificial life bots, 176
artistic pages, 246
As We May Think, 29
Aspen Movie Map, 39
audio files
   compression, 192
   MIDI, 190
audit trail, 273
Augment project, 35
automating information discovery,
   174

B

BackRub, 229
banners, 186, 265, 267, 270, 285,
   288
basic Web components, 291
basic Web mechanics, 107
basic Web requirements, 76
basic Web tasks for servers, 130
beacons, (see bugs)
Berners-Lee, Tim, 21, 59, 68, 170,
   237, 291
Bezos, Jeff, 220
Big Brother, 277
Bina, Eric, 95
birth of Web, 21
blogs and blogging, 188, 259
bookmarks, 169
   as map, 170
bots, 174
bridging information systems, 134
Brin, Sergey, 229

broadcast radio, 189
browsers, 20, 63, 124, 130
  Arena, 94
  Cello, 95
  incompatibilities, 102
  interoperability, 134
  line-mode, 64
  Lynx, 95
  MidasWWW, 94
  Mosaic, 65, 95, 98
  Netscape, 96
  Netscape Navigator, 98
  plug-ins, 94, 195
  Samba, 93
  Spyglass, 99
  ViolaWWW, 93
Bruce, Tom, 95
bugs, 265, 277, 280
Bush, Vannevar, 29, 42
business, 209
  Amazon.com, 220
  authoring services, 238
  benefits, 211
  design and graphics services,
    239
  Ebay, 223
  eToys, 234
  expenses, 212
  failures, 231
  Google, 229
  govWorks, 235
  Internet service providers, 241
  Kozmo, 233
  Netscape, 217
  Pets.com, 234
  successes, 216
  Webvan, 232
  Yahoo!, 225
business and information filtering,
  154
business pages, 247

business-to-consumer (B2C)
  model, 223

C

Cailliau, Robert, 62
cameras, 198
Campus Wide Information Systems
  (CWIS), 50
cataloging information, 164
categorizing information, 293
CD quality music, 189
celebrity sites, 248
census data, 256
CERN, 21, 59, 105, 134
  phone book, 88
CERNDOC, 61, 72
CGI
  environment variables, 137
  programming, 122, 137
  standardization, 138
children and information content,
  153
Clark, Jim, 98
clear GIFS, (see bugs)
clickstream, 273
click-through rate, 269
client application, 124
cognitive associations
  hypertext, 25
collecting personal information,
  166, 263, 267
commerce, 218
commercial hypertext, 80
commercialization
  Internet, 21
Common Gateway Interface, (see
  CGI)
Compaq, 100, 218
Compuserve, 99

computer mouse, 36
confusion with the Internet, 131
Connolly, Dan, 103
Consortium (W3C), 66–67
consumer-to-consumer (C2C)
    model, 223
control of Web, 66–67
controversy over bugs, 281
cookies, 122, 171, 264, 278
    abuse, 172
    affiliate management, 172
    login information, 170
    shopping carts, 171
core Web components, 68, 82, 110
core Web tools, 124
Cost Per Mille (CPM), (see
    measuring banners)
covert tracking, 277
creation of Web, 79
customized information, 128
CWIS, (see Campus Wide
    Information Systems)

D

DARPA Information Awareness
    Office (IAO), 289
data encryption, 123, 313
data mining, 288
databases, 163
DEC, (see Digital Equipment
    Corporation)
decentralized, 100
Dertouzos, Michael, 66, 104
describing hyperlinks, 293
Deutsch, Peter, 48
Digital Equipment Corporation
    (DEC), 104
digital revolution, 185
digital signatures, 313

dinosaur exhibit, 97
document markup samples, 302
document objects
    hypertext, 36
Document Type Definition (DTD),
    103, 167
Domain Name System (DNS), 109
Dougherty, Dale, 65
DTD, (see Document Type
    Definition)
dynamic content, 150
dynamically generated HTML
    pages, 127

E

early multimedia site, 97
early Web engineering, 80
Ebay, 223
    general operation, 224
    network of people, 224
    pawn shops, 225
    virtual community, 223
e-business, 214
e-commerce, 214
e-commerce sites, 128
effect on business operations, 213
Ellis Island, 258
email Web bugs, (see bugs)
Emtage, Alan, 48
Enquire, 60, 69, 170
    functionality, 70
    link descriptions, 71
    sample page, 69
eToys, 234
European authority, 68
European Particle Physics
    Laboratory, (see CERN)
European Union, 67
exploitation of technology, 264

Extensible Markup Language
(XML), 145, 167, 297, 300, 309,
314
    compared to HTML, 302
    sample file, 302

F

family pages, 246
file encoding, 110
file format
    MPEG, 195
File Retrieval and Editing System
(FRESS), 37
File Transfer Protocol (FTP), 65,
125
file type standards, 132
file types
    PostScript, 134
Filo, David, 226
filtering information, 152
firewalls, 178
    application gateways, 179
    circuit level gateway, 179
    packet filtering, 178
first
    Internet book, 96
    shrink-wrapped Internet
        product, 96
    U.S. Web site, 91
    Web advertisements, 268
    Web proposal, 61, 75
    Web server, 63, 84
    World Wide Web conference,
        65
Fish Cam, 199
Flash, (see Macromedia Flash)
forms, 166
free software, 237
Free Software Foundation (FSF),
105, 237

FRESS, (see File Retrieval and
Editing System)
FTP, 65, 131
FTP sites
    indexing with Archie, 48
future navigation, 309

G

Gates, Bill, 99
gateway to CERN phone book, 88
genealogy, 256
General Public License (GPL), 105
generating and tracking sales, 283
geographic independence, 212
Gerstner, Lou, 214
Ghostscript, 94
Global Network Navigator (GNN),
96
goals of W3C, 105
Google, 148, 229
Gopher, 17, 49, 58, 64, 131
    access through Web, 88
    client, 51
    menu-driven interface, 50
    sample screen, 50
    searchable indexes, 52
government transaction
    processing, 235
govWorks, 235
group-oriented pages, 247
groupware, 219
growth statistics, 317

H

helper applications, 133
HES, (see Hypertext Editing
    System)
hidden banner code, 286
hierarchical listings, 149
history details of Web, 68
Hollerith, Herman, 256
home surveillance systems, 198
HotWired, 185
    banners, 268
HTML, (see HyperText Markup
    Language)
HTTP, (see HyperText Transfer
    Protocol)
HTTPS, 123, 218
Hughes, Kevin, 97
HyperCard, 41, 62
hyperlink, 169
hypermedia, 58
    coined, 33
hyperspace, 44
hypertext, 23, 58
    Aspen Movie Map, 39
    change control, 43
    cognitive associations, 25
    coined, 32
    copyright infringement, 44
    document objects, 36
    document versions, 43
    early issues, 42
    FRESS, 37
    HES, 34
    hierarchical information
        storage systems, 25
    history, 24
    HyperCard, 41
    information design, 44
    information objects, 28
    interaction with online
        information, 26

Intermedia, 41
interoperability, 43
micropayments, 44
Movie Manual, 39
navigation, 44
NLS, 35–36
Notecards, 41
paths, 33
standards, 43
Symbolics Document
    Examiner, 40
system size, 43
Web, 23
Xanadu, 32–33
hypertext community, 92
Hypertext conference, 92
Hypertext Editing System (HES),
    34
HyperText Markup Language
    (HTML), 68, 75, 83, 110, 292,
    297
    anchor tag, 114
    compared to XML, 302
    control codes, 111
    directives, 111
    DTD, 103, 167
    embedded tags, 111
    file body portion, 113
    file header portion, 112
    file interpretation, 113
    hyperlinks, 114
    hypertext markup, 114
    image tag, 114
    including graphics files, 114
    incompatibilities, 113
    lacking standardization, 116
    lingua franca of the Web, 111
    mandatory tags, 112
    meta tag information, 112
    sample file, 111
    specification, 66

standardization, 103
tag pairs, 112
use of URLs, 116
working with the language, 115
HyperText Transfer Protocol (HTTP), 68, 83, 110, 120, 125, 274, 292
404 Not Found Message, 121
and TCP/IP, 120
functions, 120
get command, 121
sample conversation, 121
stateless protocol, 122

I

IBM, 34, 214
imagemap, 39
impressions, 269
influences, 22
information
access, 20
caching, 177
categorization, 144
content, 292
controlling access, 144
customization, 160
demands, 143
how to locate, 109
how to represent, 108
leaving a trail, 144
protecting assets, 144
protection, 178
representing, 143
retrieval, 144
revolution, 18
security, 123
services, 131
sharing, 58

storage, 143
synergy, 155
tracking, 286
information management systems, 17, 20, 45
Archie, 17, 47, 58, 65
Aspen Movie Map, 39
before Web, 17
FRESS, 37
GOPHER, 17
Gopher, 49, 58, 64
HES, 34
HyperCard, 41
hypertext, 25
Jughead, 49
memex, 32
NLS, 35
Notecards, 41
Symbolic Document Examiner, 40
Veronica, 49
WAIS, 17, 53, 58, 88
Web, 17, 20
Xanadu, 32
information objects, 297
hypertext, 28
information space, 59, 143, 291
information warehouses
databases, 163
initial public offering (IPO), 216
Netscape, 99
INRIA, 68
interconnecting information, 19
Intermedia, 41
Internet
advertisements, 267
before Web, 17
beginnings, 20
commercialization, 21
confusion with the Web, 131
content filtering, 152

finding files
    Archie, 47
finding resources, 45
information resources
    difficult to locate, 18
interactive video, 196
jargon, (see Jargon)
locating information, 143
locating resources, 116
    Gopher, 49
people Web, 243
representing information, 297
searching information content
    WAIS, 53
shadow Web, 263
television, 199
    ITV, 199
trusting information, 312
video, 195
    standardization, 202
Internet in a Box, 96
Internet navigation, 20
Internet protocols, 22
Internet service, 57
Internet service providers (ISPs),
    198, 227, 241
interoperability, 57

J

jargon, 325
    404, 325
    adminisphere, 325
    alpha geek, 325
    assmosis, 325
    beepilepsy, 325
    blamestorming, 325
    blowing your buffer, 326
    bookmark, 325
    career-limiting move, 326
    CGI Joe, 326
    chainsaw consultant, 326
    chip jewelry, 326
    chips and salsa, 326
    circling the drain, 326
    cobweb site, 326
    crapplet, 326
    crash test dummies, 327
    critical mess, 327
    cube farm, 327
    dancing baloney, 327
    dawn patrol, 327
    dead tree edition, 327
    depotphobia, 327
    dilberted, 327
    domain dipping, 328
    dorito syndrome, 328
    dustbuster, 328
    egosurfing, 328
    Elvis year, 328
    email tennis, 328
    flight risk, 328
    future-proof, 328
    generica, 328
    glazing, 328
    going cyrillic, 329
    GOOD job, 329
    gray matter, 329
    graybar land, 329
    hourglass mode, 329
    idea hamsters, 329
    iqueue, 329
    irritainment, 329
    its a feature, 330
    keyboard plaque, 330
    link rot, 330
    martian mail, 330
    meatspace, 330
    midair passenger exchange,
        330
    monkey bath, 330

mouse potato, 330
notwork, 330
nyetscape, 330
ohnosecond, 330
open-collar workers, 331
PEBCAK, 331
percussive maintenance, 331
plug-and-play, 331
prarie dogging, 331
print mile, 331
salmon day, 331
seagull manager, 331
shovelware, 331
SITCOMs, 332
square-headed girlfriend, 332
squirt the bird, 332
starter marriage, 332
stress puppy, 332
swiped out, 332
telephone number salary, 332
thrashing, 332
tourists, 332
treeware, 332
triple-dub, 333
trog mode, 333
umfriend, 333
under mouse arrest, 333
uninstalled, 333
voice jail system, 333
vulcan nerve pinch, 333
world wide wait, 333
yuppie food stamps, 334
Java, 136
    applets, 195, 203
    applications, 122
    virtual machine, 204
Java applets, 205
Java applications, 122
Jerry's Guide to the World Wide
    Web, 226
job hunting, 250

Jobs, Steve, 62
Johnson, Tony, 94
Jughead, 49, 52

K

Kahle, Brewster, 54
knowledge space, 291
Kozmo, 233
Kunz, Paul, 90

L

lack of intelligence, 292
languages
    Java, 203
    PostScript, 94
libraries, 164
Library of Congress, 165
libwww, 66
Licklider, J. C. R., 35
line-mode browser, 64, 87
Linux, 229
Lippman, Andrew, 39
locating information, 145
locating resources, 116
log file record, 274
log file uses, 275
log files, 273
lost components, 85

M

Macintosh
    hypertext system, 62
Macromedia Flash, 203, 206
mapping information, 174

Massachusetts Institute of
Technology (MIT), 66
Architecture Machine Group,
39
Laboratory for Computer
Science (MIT/LCS), 104
McGill University, 48
measuring banners, 269
memex, 32
Mesh, 79
metadata, 297
Microsoft, 169
embrace and extend, 100
.NET, 136
Network (MSN), 99
position on Web and Internet,
99
strategy, 99
Windows 95, 99
milestones of Web, 317
MIME, 132
Mine of Information (MOI), 79
Montulli, Lou, 95, 98
Mosaic browser, 46, 65, 95, 98,
185
Movie Manual, 39
Moving Picture Experts Group
Audio Layer 3 (MP3), 192
files, 189, 192
Napster, 193
peer-to-peer file sharing,
193
video (MPEG)
files, 195
Mozilla, 98
MP3 files, 189, 192
MPEG file format, 195
MSN, (see Microsoft)
multimedia, 181
audio, 189
MIDI files, 190

MP3 files, 192
streaming audio, 190
data compression, 183
data resampling, 183
documents, 182
Flash, 203
Java applets, 203
Macromedia Flash, 203, 206
network bandwidth, 183
new types, 203
publications, 184
television, 199
three-dimensional (3D)
modeling, 203, 207
video, 195
interactive video, 196
standardization, 202
streaming video, 197
VRML, 207
multimedia objects, 182
Multi-purpose Internet Mail
Extension (MIME), 132
URL usage, 134
music technology revolution, 193

N

Napster, 193
National Center for
Supercomputing Applications
(NCSA), 65
National Digital Library Program,
165
navigation by machines, 291
Navigator browser, 98
NCSA, 65
need for browsers, 93
Nelson, Ted, 32, 34, 44
.NET, 136
netiquette, 321

Netscape, 66, 96, 98–99, 169, 171,
    185, 230
    America Online, 219
    business model, 218
    Communicator, 219
    founding, 98
    groupware, 219
    HTTPS, 218
    IPO, 99, 217
    Navigator, 217
    SSL, 218
network bandwidth
    multimedia, 183
network infrastructure, 22
newer technology, 174
newsgroups, 131
    through Web, 88
NeXT, 62, 81
NLS, (see oN Line System)
not the Internet, 20
Notecards, 41
NSF, 29

O

object oriented technologies, 297
Omidyar, Pierre, 223
oN Line System (NLS), 35
one-click shopping, 222
one-hour delivery service, 233
online dating, 252
online forums, 187
online grocery store, 232
ontologies, 310, 314
O'Reilly and Associates, 65, 96
ownership issues, 105

P

packet filtering, 178
Page, Larry, 229
PDF, (see PostScript Document
    Format)
peer-to-peer file sharing, 193
Pellow, Nicola, 87
people, 243
    Addis, Louise, 90
    Andreessen, Marc, 95, 98
    Berners-Lee, Tim, 21, 59, 68,
        170, 237, 291
    Bezos, Jeff, 220
    Bina, Eric, 95
    Brin, Sergey, 229
    Bruce, Tom, 95
    Bush, Vannevar, 29, 42
    Cailliau, Robert, 62
    Clark, Jim, 98
    Connolly, Dan, 103
    Dertouzos, Michael, 66, 104
    Deutsch, Peter, 48
    Dougherty, Dale, 65
    Emtage, Alan, 48
    Filo, David, 226
    Gates, Bill, 99
    Gerstner, Lou, 214
    Hollerith, Herman, 256
    Hughes, Kevin, 97
    Jobs, Steve, 62
    Johnson, Tony, 94
    Kahle, Brewster, 54
    Kunz, Paul, 90
    Licklider, J. C. R., 35
    Lippman, Andrew, 39
    Montulli, Lou, 95, 98
    Nelson, Ted, 32, 34, 44
    Omidyar, Pierre, 223
    Page, Larry, 229
    Pellow, Nicola, 87

Pesce, Mark, 207
Raggett, Dave, 94
Sendall, Mike, 61
Skoll, Jeff, 223
van Dam, Andries, 34, 37, 42, 80
Wei, Pei, 93
Yang, Jerry, 226
people as operators, 210
personal benefits, 211
personal bots, 175
personal computer, 22
personal home pages, 245
personal information collection, 271
personalizing information, 159
Pesce, Mark, 207
Pets.com, 234
physical space, 311
political sites, 249
portal sites, 128, 160, 226
portals and databases, 164
PostScript, 94, 134
PostScript Document Format (PDF), 134
privacy issues, 263, 281
privacy statements, 290
processing information, 147
profiled information, 128
programming, 124, 134
    advantages of HTML, 136
    CGI, 137
    Java, 136
    library functions, 140
    model, 141
    .NET, 136
    Web, 134
Progressive Networks, 190
protecting information, 174
protocols
    HTTP, 68, 120, 292

proxy servers, 177
public domain software, 66, 105
public personas, 248
public terminals and information filtering, 154
pulling information, 155
pushing information, 155

Q

QuickTime Player, 195
QuickTime Virtual Reality (QTVR), 196

R

Raggett, Dave, 94
RDF, 297, 300, (see Resource Description Framework)
RealAudio, 190
RealNetworks, 190
RealPlayer, 195
reasoning system, 311
Recording Industry Association of America (RIAA), 193
recording locations, 169
RedHat, 229
refining information, 159
Remote Procedure Calls (RPC), 60
rendering HTML with a browser, 132
replacing HTML, 167
Replay TV, 200
representing information, 161, 167, 297
Request For Comments (RFC), 103
Resource Description Framework (RDF), 297, 300, 309, 314
    metadata, 305

purpose, 306
sample file, 306
RIAA, (see Recording Industry
  Association of America)
rich media banners, 272
role of browsers, 131
RPC, (see Remote Procedure Calls)

S

sample CGI program, 139
sample form, 138
sample HTML file, 111
sample HTTP conversation, 121
sample of bug code, 278
sample RDF file, 306
sample URLs, 117
sample XML file, 302
search engines, 148, 229
    Alta Vista, 148
    Google, 148
    usage, 151
searchable databases, 150
searchable listings
    About.com, 149
    Yahoo!, 149
searching, 148
second Web proposal, 63, 78
secure HTTP, 123
Secure Sockets Layer (SSL), 123,
  218
selling toys, 234
Semantic Web, 291, 314
    agents of discovery, 309
    ontologies, 310
    physical objects, 311
    reasoning system, 311
    trust management, 312
    web of trust, 312
Sendall, Mike, 61

server application, 124
server configuration, 130
servers, 124–125
servers and databases, 126
service businesses, 236
SGML, (see Standard Generalized
  Markup Language)
shadow Web, 263
shopping bots, 176
short history of Web, 59
shovelware, 185
Silicon Graphics (SGI), 98
simple files servers, 125, 127
site audience, 276
site usability, 221
Skoll, Jeff, 223
SLAC, (see Stanford Linear
  Accelerator Center)
spiders, 174
SSL, (see Secure Sockets Layer)
Standard Generalized Markup
  Language (SGML), 72–73, 75,
  103, 167
standardization, 102
    document markup
        CERNDOC, 72
        SGML, 72
    HTML, 103
    Internet video, 202
    SGML, 167
    Web, 102
    XML, 167
Stanford Linear Accelerator Center
  (SLAC), 90, 94, 126
stateless protocol, 122, 274
storefronts and databases, 163
storing information, 161
streaming audio, 190
streaming video, 197
subject matter listings, 149
Sun Microsystems, 203

surfing, 147
Symbolics Document Examiner, 40

T

tabulating machines, 256
targeting information, 288
technology
    exploitation, 264
TELNET, 64, 87, 125
The Information Mine (TIM), 79
The Whole Internet User's Guide
    and Catalog, 96
Thinking Machines, 54
Thomas (Library of Congress
    Service), 166
three-dimensional (3D) modeling,
    203, 207
time-sharing, 35
Tivo, 200
toolkit, 64, 66
tracking behavior, 280
tracking emails, 280
tracking information, 285
tracking our movements, 263
Trojan Room, 198
trust management, 312

U

Uniform Resource Locator (URL),
    68, 83, 110, 116, 169, 292
    components, 117
    in hyperlinks, 116
    renaming from URI, 103
    sample types, 117
    syntax, 118
    versatility, 119
University of Cambridge, 198

unraveling of Web, 101
URI, (see Uniform Resource
    Locator)
URL, (see Uniform Resource
    Locator)
use of databases, 163
uses for bugs, 281

V

van Dam, Andries, 34, 37, 42, 80
Veronica, 49, 52
video emails, 195
virtual community, 223
Virtual Reality Modeling Language
    (VRML), 207
virtual storefronts, 220
visitor profiling, 276

W

W3 Organization (W3O), 67–68
W3C, 67–68, 104
    goals, 105
W3O, (see W3 Organization)
WAIS, (see Wide Area Information
    Service)
web of trust, 312
web-cams, 198
Webvan, 232
Wei, Pei, 93
Wide Area Information Service
    (WAIS), 53, 58, 65, 131
    access through Web, 88
    client, 54
    indexed libraries, 54
    resource ranking, 55
Windows 95, 99
Wired, 185

working definition of Web, 57
WorldWideWeb graphical browser,
    84
WorldWideWeb hypertext project,
    62
WorldWideWeb proposal, 78

X

Xanadu, 32–33
XFIND, 64
XML, (see Extensible Markup
    Language)

Y

Yahoo!, 149, 160, 225, 230
    hierarchical contents index,
        226
    services, 227
Yang, Jerry, 226

Ironbound Press
Winter Harbor, Maine

To order copies of this book and other books in The Internet Revolution series:

Visit us on the Internet at:
http://www.IronboundPress.com

Or photocopy the order form on the opposite side of this page and send to:

Book Orders
Ironbound Press
P.O. Box 250
Winter Harbor, ME 04693-0250

Or inquire at your local bookstore.

Ironbound Press books may be purchased for educational, business, or sales promotional use at discounted prices. Discounts also apply when ordering 5 or more books. For information, please write to the address listed above, or send email to:
info@IronboundPress.com

Ironbound Press Book Order Form

Send completed form to:
Book Orders
Ironbound Press, P.O. Box 250, Winter Harbor, ME 04693-0250

Bill To:	Ship To: (if different than Bill To):
Name:	Name:
Address:	Address:
City:	City:
State/Zip:	State/Zip:
Phone:	Phone:
Email:	Email:

Qty.	Item	Description	Item Price	Total
	0-9763857-5-9	The Internet Revolution (paperback)	$22.95	
	0-9763857-6-7	The Internet Revolution (hardback)	$26.95	
	0-9763857-3-2	The Information Revolution (paperback)	$22.95	
	0-9763857-4-0	The Information Revolution (hardback)	$26.95	
			Sub-total:	
			*Shipping and Handling:	
			**Sales Tax:	
			TOTAL:	

* $4.00 for the first book; $2.00 for each additional book.
** Please add 5%, if shipping to a Maine address.

Payment Method:
□ Visa   □ Mastercard   □ AMEX   □ Discover   □ Check
Signature:
Name on card (printed):
Card number:
Card Expiration date (MM/YYYY):